D1610373

Edinburgh
Education and Society
Series

General Editor:
COLIN BELL

Description, Explanation and Understanding

Selected Writings, 1944–1980

TOM BURNS

EDINBURGH UNIVERSITY PRESS

© Tom Burns, 1995

Edinburgh University Press Ltd
22 George Square, Edinburgh

Typeset in Palatino
by Pioneer Associates (Graphic) Ltd, Perthshire, and
printed and bound in Great Britain by
The University Press, Cambridge

A CIP record for this book is available
from the British Library

ISBN 0 7486 0533 9

In none of the papers collected in this book are the discrepancies between the actualities of sex difference and the grammatical conventions of gender at all significant, most of them having been written and published when the use of the masculine for pronouns and the like meant to be of common gender was acceptable. However, the reader is asked to observe that 'he', 'him' and 'his', when they refer to an antecedent noun of common gender, like 'individual' or 'person', should be read as 'he or she', 'him or her' and 'his or her(s)'.

Contents

Introduction

The suggestion that I compile a selection of essays and papers for publication came as something of a surprise. It was, I think, a reasonable reaction. 'Collected papers' on a single specialised topic are often welcome; when they are by a recognised authority they can provide a useful short-cut for fellow specialists and students; for some topics there can be a quite large interested 'lay' public. Firmly at the bottom level of desirability are the miscellanies of bits and pieces based on long-forgotten researches offered by retired professors hoping to memorialise their careers.

I have never thought of myself as particularly modest, but I have to confess that, at first, it struck me that a collection of my own shorter writings clearly belonged at this bottom level. Obviously, any reluctance I had did not last. But it did mean that I felt I should search for something to give the enterprise some extenuating or supportive colouring. What occurred to me was that a series of papers chronologically arranged might serve to demonstrate how much one's working life is a continuous learning process. I know very well that this is true of many people's careers, especially those devoted to some specialised study, but I think the circumstances of my own career have made me more aware of it than most.

Mine is perhaps an extreme case. Not only did I start my academic career late in life, at the age of thirty-six, but I did so with qualifications as a sociologist – which is what I eventually became – as near zero as makes no difference. This meant that for many years thereafter I was frequently and acutely conscious of my ignorance. I was not, I think, much inhibited by it, but I did spend a great deal of time and effort in working out effective, manageable and economical research methods.

Much of this time and effort was undoubtedly misspent. This was certainly true of the attempts to apply P. J. Stone's 'General Enquirer' technique of content analysis to the analysis of recorded discussions, and a protracted testing out of the variety of laboratory techniques inspired by the work of Alex Bavelas and Harold Leavitt produced no concrete results. On the other hand, the development of a self-recording technique derived from Sune Carlson's pioneering study of managing directors in Sweden turned out to be extremely worthwhile, although too expensive for protracted use; and mastering the use of standardised questionnaires was, I suppose, essential, if only to become acquainted with its limitations.

The procedure I settled for eventually approximates to that which social and cultural anthropologists have made their own, although it has certain features which I like to think I have worked out for myself. It is this 'working out' process that provides the main thread running through this introductory essay – hence the title chosen for the book. But it was carried on through the major researches which have taken up most of my time, and these are reported in books rather than in the papers represented here. In tracing the way in which the pursuit of explanation and understanding developed during my research career I have sought to establish some organised background for a collection of essays and occasional papers that would otherwise appear more of a miscellaneous assortment than I would like.

But to begin with, I ought to expand on what I mean by the special circumstances of my career as a sociologist, beginning with the circumstances of the writings included in this collection which pre-date my career as academic sociologist, or, indeed, any thought of one.

I spent the six years of the war – from September 1939 to October 1945, in fact – in the Friends Ambulance Unit. For most of that time I was abroad, in Finland, Norway, Egypt, Greece – and Germany. It was in Greece that the ambulance group I was with were taken prisoner, along with thousands of British and

Australian troops, at the southern end of the Peloponnese in May 1941. Release came in December 1943, when those of the Unit in Stalag VIIIB were included in the medical staff picked out to accompany the thousand or so severely disabled POWs, many of them in the hospital attached to Stalag VIIIB, to be exchanged for the equivalent number of disabled German prisoners to Britain. The next twenty-odd months were spent – after being accepted for the Unit's famine-relief team in Bengal and then failing the medical – as 'press and information officer' at the headquarters of the FAU in Gordon Square.

It cannot now, in the 1990s, be easy to believe, but I had three choices of employment open to me after the end of the war. The first was to return to schoolmastering; I had spent five years before the war at the lower end of the 'private sector' – a cut above Llanabba House, though rather below in terms of salary. This was the least inviting, especially as I was now married. The second was to resume an appointment as 'lektor' in English at Helsinki University, on the invitation of the Professor of English there, then in England for this and other purposes. (I had been appointed to the post in September 1941, but had resigned it immediately when we heard that the British Embassy had finally managed to get transit visas issued to all of us locked up in Sweden after being chased out of Namsos in May.) This option was my wife's preference (she had been 'locked up' in Britain for the duration), but my recollection not just of the Finnish winter but of the two-volume anthology of 'English Literature', a Finnish publication from which I had been expected to teach, were rather too vivid. So I opted for the third possibility. This was in fact two jobs: one as 'press and information' officer for the Bournville Village Trust, the other as research assistant to the West Midland Group on Post-War Reconstruction and Planning.

It turned out to be altogether more worthwhile than I had expected. Bournville was very far from the old-fashioned facto-ry village it was reputed to be (and in fact never had been); it had grown into an agglomeration of housing societies, some of them cooperative, all centrally managed, but separately governed. The Trust had wide interests in housing and housing policy, which had become a major preoccupation in Britain towards the end of the war, interests which had led to its sponsoring a study of housing needs and possibilities by Mark

Abrams and C. B. Parkes, the Trust's chief architect. The book that came out of it, *When We Build Again*, was well-received and influential enough to help stave off the disasters of high-rise housing development for a few years.

But it was the other kind of work which became the major interest and took up most time. The West Midland Group was a consortium of notables in the region, with the Vice-Chancellor of Birmingham University as its chairman. Funded by the Bournville Village Trust, it had made itself responsible for surveys designed to prepare the ground for post-war reconstruction in the West Midlands, using part-time researchers from the University of Birmingham and elsewhere. It had already completed a soil survey of the five counties, a planning survey of Herefordshire, and was in a midst of a large-scale survey of Birmingham and the Black Country.

Working for the West Midland Group was both interesting in itself and valuable as an apprenticeship in social research. By 1948, though, it looked as if the prospect of any practical outcome to the published results of its research activities would be deferred *sine die*. In consequence, the Group decided to end its active life with a study of local government, especially the extent to which it was subject to increasing constraint and positive control by central government. This study became virtually my own responsibility for the last year or so of my time in Birmingham, which was taken up with interviewing local government officials and collecting statistical and other data from all the local authorities in the region. Since it was, though, the last research effort of the West Midland Group, any possibility of going on with that kind of work would have to lie somewhere else.

The 'somewhere else' turned out to be Edinburgh. I applied for and obtained the newly established post of 'research lecturer' in the Department of Social Studies there. There can have been at the time precious little competition, and I could at least claim to have some experience in empirical social research; there were also a couple of articles in established journals.

Sociologist I was certainly not. Nor was I expected to be. There was one already in residence: Werner Stark, who taught a one-year course to postgraduate students preparing for a Diploma in Social Studies. No department of sociology existed in Edinburgh, or in any other Scottish university; there was in fact not much in the way of sociology taught or studied outside the London School of Economics, although it had started up in Liverpool, Leicester and Birmingham. (Not that things improved all that much over the next ten years; in 1960, I discovered there were more academically qualified sociologists in the Centre d'Etudes Sociologiques – one of the three or four state-funded sociological research establishments in Paris, although the biggest – than in all the British universities put together.)

On the other hand it has to be remembered that there was a much stronger tradition of social research in Britain than elsewhere – 'social research' including especially the kind of surveys exposing the extent and depth of poverty which Booth and Rowntree had carried out at the turn of the century, building on techniques developed over the previous generation by the Social Science Research Society. The surveys of unemployment and of the condition of the poor in London, Merseyside, Dundee and elsewhere in the 1930s were a direct extension of this tradition. (They also revealed the extent to which it had become exhausted.) Just before the war, too, 'Mass Observation' had created a sizeable public for the accounts of popular pursuits and popular (rather than 'public') opinion composed by Tom Harrison and Charles Madge out of the hundreds of reports submitted by their small army of volunteer 'observers'. During the war, lastly, the government's Wartime Social Survey had capitalised on the same tradition, developing more rigorous sampling and statistical techniques.

Once settled in Edinburgh, the first researches I undertook were for the Scottish Council (Development and Industry), a voluntary body supported by the Scottish Office, the Scottish TUC, some industrialists and the association of local authorities in Scotland, and devoted to the promotion of the economic welfare of Scotland. Fortunately for me, the researches were subregional and regional surveys not dissimilar, in method at least, to those conducted by the West Midland Group. The first concerned the Scottish (south-east) Border counties; the second was a nation-wide review, under the guidance of a small committee headed by A. K. Cairncross, of the possibilities of economic expansion 'in county towns and in country and mining areas where more industrial employment is necessary and practicable'. The report was published in 1952.[1]

By the time all this was finished I had also completed writing up the local government study I had begun in Birmingham.[2] It was at this point that I began to shift my research interests into industrial organisation. The first attempt was a study of a medium-sized rayon mill, with whose general manager I had become acquainted in the course of the Borders survey; the factory was located in Jedburgh. What I set out to do, as I put it later, was 'to study an industrial concern as a "community at work" in much the same terms, that is, one would use in a study of conduct and relationships in a village or an urban neighbourhood'.[3] I characterised it in this way because, after a couple of months of frequent day visits to Jedburgh spent in interviewing, it did seem that what was called for approximated to a full-scale and lengthy study of the kind James Littlejohn had embarked on in Eskdalemuir.[4]

I had neither the financial nor the departmental backing for anthropological field-work in these terms. So, when another opportunity of studying an industrial organisation presented itself, this time of an engineering concern in Edinburgh with a major interest in electronics, I begun afresh, this time attending more strictly to the organisation structure ('management').

This turned out to be the start of what was, for me, a major enquiry, the results of which were published in *The Management of Innovation*. It also marked a turning-point in my own career.

Up to this time, I had never gone beyond description – description of personal experiences or accounts of material facts, statistical and other, and the commonsense inferences to be drawn from them. As I remark towards the beginning of 'Sociological Explanation', sociology, like all other disciplines, scientific and other, begins with description, is descriptive as well as explanatory, has its fact-finding and taxonomic aspects as well as being a theoretical and model-building endeavour. More than that, it is in their descriptive and taxonomic work that all specialist studies have their historical origin.

The theme could have been developed at greater length. There are several quite different levels – modes, styles, perspectives, degrees of detail – of description. Reduced to four levels or styles, they may serve as a sorting device for the contents of this book – or for most of them, anyway. None of them is to be thought of as more 'sophisticated' than the others. The 'plain, unvarnished' account or narrative, as we all know, is just as much a stylistic device as the most elaborate, persuasive or 'insightful' presentation. The true difference lies in the kind of observing that each records. This may stay at the surface appearance of things and events; or aim at an explanation of what seems strange or unexpected, so as to connect it with what is more familiar and normal; or there is the observation and description of hidden complexities and significance in what ordinarily passes as so familiar, so normal, as not to merit description – or, lastly, of what suddenly becomes conspicuous by its absence from a situation in which it had been so familiar as to pass unnoticed.

The selection of papers in this volume does, I think, contain examples of all four kinds. As I see them now, each level of description serves as the foundation, or vehicle, for the kind of message each text is meant to deliver: for the 'plain unvarnished narrative' of notable events some distance away in time and space; for the explanation of observations which seem at first sight incompatible with each other or with accepted beliefs; for the enlightenment which deeper understanding of what is going on can impart; or, lastly, for the new view of a familiar world which looking at it 'with different eyes' can bring.

The first category obviously applies to the pieces written before I'd had any thought of social research, still less of turning myself into a sociologist. The first short piece included in this book is a straightforward verbal account of a wartime episode: what used to be known as *reportage*. The second – reflections on life as a POW – is just as obviously limited to description. It does, though, include passages of what amounts to introspection, arising from an attempt to account for the sense of disorientation, mild and temporary though it was, I experienced after some years as a prisoner of war.

'Friends, Enemies and the Polite Fiction' and the piece on workplace cliques and cabals, the first products of the move into organisation studies, while properly speaking in the same category, do venture a little deeper, below surface appearances. Description had begun to acquire 'thickness'.[5]

Gilbert Ryle's 'thick description' is not of course one of the

four categories of description I have made up for present purposes. The differences between the various levels of Ryle's
'pyramid of learned accomplishment' – between a blink and a
parodied wink – are all equally open to observation. The
exchanges of talk identified as irony and banter in 'Friends,
Enemies and the Polite Fiction', for example, were conveyed in
much the same neutral or bland terms and tone of voice; the
distinction between the two was conveyed in the collusive or
triumphant half-smile, or simply dead-pan expression, with
which the last speaker ended. If a difference in level escapes
notice, or is misinterpreted, it amounts simply to a mistake as
to observed fact.

Inconclusive as the summer's work I had put in at Jedburgh
seemed to have been, it turned out to be far from pointless. It
was soon evident that the Edinburgh engineering concern
which I had moved on to was being run according to principles
utterly different from those which obtained in the rayon factory.
The rayon mill ran according to a strict programme: 'limits and
constants' had to be observed strictly at every stage of the
process of production. The electronics firm had a quite explicit
policy of leaving the function – and status, for that matter – of
each manager virtually undefined. What he had to do and how
he did it was a matter of constant discussion, adjustment and
negotiation with others – who were similarly placed. Yet the
two firms (and this needs emphasising) were, at the time and
by any ordinary set of criteria, both efficient and effective,
despite their being conducted according to utterly different
principles of management.

The existence of an alternative 'best practice' where it
seemed to be generally assumed – by those who worked in
industry as well as those who studied it – that there was only
one, pointed to a major discrepancy which called for explanation. Moreover, quite apart from the basic difference in the
equally successful management structure and practice of the
two firms, there were other discrepancies, some of them quite
striking, between the pictures of factory organisation I got from
interviews with different people in them. There always are discrepancies, as I was able to say with some confidence a good
deal later. 'But the question presented by these discrepancies is

not "Which version is right?" but "How do these differences arise? How is it that these different versions of the same set of circumstances have arisen in the minds of people who have to co-operate with each other in the very circumstances they view so differently?"' ('Sociological Explanation', p. 167).

The reason for this new source of enlightenment is embarrassingly simple. Such empirical studies as I had carried out previously had involved interviews, but they had almost always been with local government councillors and officials, chief executives of business firms and the like – individual persons, each one in a different organisation. Now, for the first time, I was interviewing people in different positions within the same firm.

Sociological research begins in description, and the quality – accuracy, comprehensiveness, as well as 'thickness' – of the description makes a great deal of difference to what may be accomplished. Explanation itself, however, when it comes to it, is something entirely different.

Explanation is commonly framed in causal terms. It is the empirical basis of causal explanation that Hume famously challenged, arguing that the connection between cause and effect is a matter of expectation founded on past experience. The challenge has never been refuted. As Russell puts it, 'So far as the physical sciences are concerned, Hume is *wholly* in the right; such propositions as 'A causes B' are never to be accepted, and an inclination to accept them is to be explained by . . . habit and association.'

What preoccupied Hume and later empirical philosophers was the basis of belief in the necessary, logical, connection of cause and effect in the world of nature and human affairs. In so far as the connection is universally accepted it is of course a matter of habitual association. It is when the connection is challenged that explanation is called for – as in the case of the Copernican-Galilean revolution in cosmology. Similarly, when it comes to the everyday world of nature and human affairs, the need for explanation arises, or is called for, only when there is misunderstanding, or when explanation that has hitherto proved acceptable and unquestioned turns out to be wrong. And this is also, and particularly, the case with those studies which, like sociology, are concerned primarily with human affairs.

It is this consideration which lies behind a passage in

'Sociological Explanation' and is central to its argument: 'Sociology seems at any one time to be pursuing not so much the right kind of knowledge but the right kind of question, not definitive information but fresh hypotheses. Anyone who has done research in any field will testify to the truth of Agnes Arber's remark that the difficulty in most scientific work lies in framing the questions rather than in finding the answers. What is not so often insisted upon is that questions do not suggest themselves or rise at the bidding of the specialist student with a little time on his hands. They arise from doubt. Doubt, in turn, arises from the existence of an alternative where none was previously suggested. It arises from a discrepancy between facts, or between intended and achieved results.'

Trying to find an explanation for these discrepancies, and to other questions to which they gave rise, took up most of my research time over the next three or four years. The research project itself took the form of monitoring the progress of a scheme floated by the Scottish Council for encouraging established engineering firms in Scotland to expand into the new and rapidly growing industry of electronically controlled machinery and equipment.

About a dozen firms came into this scheme. It fairly obviously called for something more than setting up an R&D laboratory and hiring qualified staff. As the initial contrast between the Borders rayon mill and the Edinburgh electronics firm had suggested, moving into a new and innovative industrial activity and an unknown and rapidly changing market required a fairly radical change in management structure and style.

The Management of Innovation, in which the results of the study (which was later extended to cover six major English firms with interests in electronics) was built around two themes. The first was the distinction between 'mechanistic' and 'organic' systems of management. Mechanistic systems were defined as those appropriate to firms operating within a comparatively stable situation, so far as technical procedures and market were concerned; organic systems were appropriate to firms involved in rapidly developing technologies or relatively unpredictable markets – or both, as is usually the case.

However, very few out of the dozen firms managed to change their ways. So the second major theme of the book was the explanation of why it was that so many firms failed to adjust to their new situation. The answer seemed to lie in the elementary fact that people who work in organisations are at one and the same time co-operators in a common enterprise and rivals competing for advancement within it. Few of the existing staff in these established firms could regard the new venture as anything but a threat, certainly to their prospects for advancement and perhaps to their present positions. Furthermore, while careerism is largely pursued as a matter of individual concern, it may also be furthered by alliances formed with others who have similar interests and fears and who see the point of co-operating in trying to influence, hinder or thwart decisions which affect them adversely.

This is as far as I took things in *The Management of Innovation*. The possible effects careerism and internal politics had on what I called 'the working organisation' was explored in two or three supplementary papers, the first of which, 'Micropolitics', appeared in the same year the book was published. But in 1963, largely through accident, came an opportunity to carry out a study of the organisation of the BBC. I seized on it because I wanted to test out the ideas I had developed in studies of medium-sized industrial organisations in the setting of a quite different kind of organisation: large, non-industrial and preferably non-commercial.

One difference, which has immediately and strikingly apparent, I had half-expected. In business concerns of all kinds, especially those in manufacturing, management ('administration') is an integral part of the working organisation; often enough, it sees itself as 'the organisation'. But there are also organisations – hospitals and universities are the most familiar – in which the administration is seen (or was seen at that time in Britain, at least) as rather detached from the working organisation proper. The BBC pattern was much closer to the university than to the business model, as I had thought it might be, but it had developed a fairly idiosyncratic system of its own.

Careerism flourished – not least because of what seemed to be its deliberate encouragement by the Corporation. BBC staff numbered over 20,000, and was growing. All appointments, including those created by promotions, were advertised internally, filling the notice-boards which punctuated the corridors of all BBC buildings. All appointments, furthermore, were made according to a procedure designed to ensure equal opportunity and impartial judgement. The result was a career system of exemplary fairness; it was also a system that took up a great deal (some said the greater part) of management time, invited perpetual speculation and discussion, and set a level of preoccupation with one's present position and future prospects far above anything I have encountered elsewhere.

This wasn't all. In the post-war reconstruction of the Corporation, the then Director-General had adopted internal competition as a cardinal principle for the tripartite structure of the new programme services in radio. The authoritarianism which had characterised BBC administration in Reith's days before the war had given way to a chronic diffidence and tentativeness. Universal deference was paid to planners and to the image of the producer as the creative person – the worker at what they called 'the coal face'. Television of course spent its entire lifetime since its post-war rebirth under this post-war regime. Its 'creative workers' were, like those in radio, sheltered from the distractions, responsibilities and preoccupations of administration. Here, too, 'healthy rivalry' had generated a system of internal politics, but it had somewhat different implications. It was a good deal livelier than what obtained in radio and more openly discussed; rewards (and penalties) were weightier. In 1963, I found BBC Television a highly segmented organisation, with some individuals striving to enlarge or defend their own 'baronies' (powerful heads of departments are inevitably called 'barons' in the BBC, as they are elsewhere), and the less secure seeking protection from the Director-General's 'young lions'.

It all looked as if careerism and the internal politics system actually had management itself firmly in their grasp, both in television and radio. But so far as any consequences for the effectiveness of the BBC as an organisation were concerned, the implications seemed to point in two opposite directions.

The plain fact was that BBC Television was reaching unprecedented levels of success at this same time. Talks and Current Affairs occupied the centre of the programme planners' picture of television not only on account of the prestige and popularity of Baverstock's *Tonight* programme but because the same department had, among other things, made way for Ned Sherrin to transfer from Light Entertainment and devise

That Was The Week That Was. Later in the 1960s, the Drama department took on a new lease of life; Kenneth Clark's *Civilisation* built up an enthusiastic audience of a totally unlooked-for size; even Light Entertainment – insecure, convinced that it owed its existence (and certainly its name) to its being regarded as groundbait to attract a mass audience which would stay with the later programmes of less obvious appeal – scored its own 'prestige' successes.

If only by contrast, the radio side did look as if it had run out of steam. It had become completely overshadowed by television, so far as the newspapers, Parliament and – so far as anyone could tell – the public at large were concerned. The contrast with television may well have been the operative factor, or so I thought at the time. If 'the worlds radio producers tended to live in were created by successful programmes of the past' as they were said to do, it was a past becoming increasingly unreal and remote; people in radio – or some of them – talked of 'success' in terms of a move to Television Centre.

By the time I was ready to submit a comprehensive 'working report', Oliver Whitley who, as Controller, Staff Training and Appointments, had piloted the idea of the study through Administration in the first place, and had throughout been sympathetic to it and extremely helpful, had been appointed Chief Assistant to the Director-General. All dealings were now with the Director of Administration and his immediate subordinates. It was quickly made clear to me that their sole interest in the report was in preventing its publication. This they were entitled to do, since I had agreed at the outset not to publish anything based on the report 'without the consent (which did not necessarily mean the approval) of the Corporation'.

Nothing I had experienced during the enquiry had led me to expect anything like this. The embargo lasted until 1972 and put a damper on any inclination I may have had to elaborate on any of the ideas the study had suggested.

Later on, when 'mass communications' became an active area of specialist study, there were requests for contributions to conferences and published collections of papers. It proved possible to salvage one or two sections of the report which dealt with matters which could hardly be regarded as sensitive and have them published (first, of course, obtaining formal permission from the Corporation). Later on, I went further, to the point of writing one or two speculative ('theoretical') papers in cognate but more rewarding fields of study like leisure and consumerism; one or two of these pieces are included in this collection.

Then, in 1972, the embargo on the report on the 1963 report was removed. What is more, after some correspondence with the new Director-General, Charles Curran, I was invited back for a follow-up study. (The introduction to the book reporting the whole extended study contains a summary of the episode,[6] which I have never ceased to find utterly mystifying.)

The situation I found when I made my repeat study in 1973 was very different from that which I had encountered in 1963. The BBC had undergone fairly dramatic changes towards the end of the 1960s. Not only was there a new Chairman, a new Director-General and a whole new Board of Management but the relationship between administration and programme departments had been reconstructed yet again. Administration (now relabelled 'management') was firmly installed on top, with programme planning and programme departments all responsible to the 'Managing Directors' of Television, Radio, and External Services. A new and more rigorous system of financial control had been established. The decisive factor in all this had been the growing resentment of Harold Wilson and some of his ministers to what they saw as the BBC's hostile treatment of them at a time when the expansion of television, rising costs and inflation faced the Corporation with a yearly financial crisis, which could only be met by the government's agreeing to an increased licence fee. Hence the 'McKinsey reorganisation' – a move occasioned as much as anything by 'the need to demonstrate to the Government that the Corporation was making a determined effort to put its house in order'.

But the biggest change in the BBC between 1963 and 1973 was not the reconstructed top management, the stricter budgeting and financial controls, the new Managing Directors and their increased powers, or any other aspect of the new regime ushered in by the McKinsey reorganisation. Nor was it the unintended changes which followed on from the reorganisation: reduced 'baronial' powers of heads of departments,

increased union militancy or even the openly expressed dissatisfaction with what the BBC had become. What made the
difference was the decline almost to vanishing point of personal
involvement in the BBC and what it now stood for, the consequent breakdown of trust, the shared ethic and the intricate
systems of working collaboration based on them. All this had
been part and parcel of the 'private world' of the BBC in 1963,
and was now gone – not entirely, perhaps, but 'as good as'. It
was a difference perhaps best conveyed by people talking of
their working *for* the BBC as against working *in* the BBC, as
they had done ten years earlier.

Understanding can take different forms, or operate at different
levels. So far as sociology and cognate social sciences are concerned, all relate to the meaning we infer from what people do
and what people say. Weber gives two definitions: the direct
rational understanding of ideas, as in the case of writing 2 x 2 =
4, or of the facial expressions which manifest anger, fear and so
on; second, there is explanatory understanding, which applies to
the motive or purpose behind the action – its intended meaning.

Clifford Geertz's 'interpretative understanding'[7] takes this
second meaning further in that it claims to penetrate beneath
the actor's (or speaker's) intentions to purposes and motivations
which, though prompting, or guiding, his actions, are hidden
from him. Action is 'read' as symbolic of some aspect or other
of the actor's culture.

Understanding of the kind I was trying for in this protracted
BBC study is something else again, and difficult to convey in that
it involves an uneasy balance between shared understanding
and distanced neutrality.

The lengthier empirical researchers I undertook later are all
founded on interviews (as well as observation, of course). But
they went some way beyond, or deeper than, interviewing procedure followed in the earlier researches. Now, a good deal
of interviewing time was taken up with trying to convey
some understanding of what I was up to. To quote from the
introduction to the BBC book:

> I should perhaps say, of the interviews themselves [some 300
> altogether], that the term may be a little misleading; they
> followed neither the method of the professional journalist

(whether accoucheur or wrestler) nor the standardised procedures familiar in social surveys. Although I tried, by the end
of a conversation, to see that I had obtained comments or facts
on the points I thought relevant or interesting, I used no standard sequence or form of questions; and my ideas of what
was relevant or interesting information tended to change,
to . . . What each interview, which could last up to three
hours, had in common was a lengthy prefatory statement
about my interests and objectives in making the enquiry . . . I
usually followed this up by now and again interjecting half-
formed impressions or interpretations which had already
occurred to me, usually illustrating them at some length from
previous research or other experience. In general, therefore, I
followed the procedure natural to ordinary discourse, which
means that the whole study was conducted [largely] in and
through these interviews; almost all the interpretative and
explanatory ideas put forward in this book occurred – or,
often, were suggested – to me in interview, and none of them
has not been discussed, developed, or amended during interviews, or subsequently in talking with people who were or
had been members of the Corporation.

What I was now aiming at, in short, was a *shared* understanding:
an account of the structure and functions of the organisation
and of the values, motives and purposes of the people in it
which would square with what those same people saw for
themselves. It also amounted to an attempt to engage the
people I interviewed as willing co-operators in the enquiry – to
involve them in the furtherance of the study. Hence the constant need to make clear what I was up to, and what I was
making of the information I had gathered so far. How successful the procedure turns out to be depends on the competence
and experience of the researcher, of course, but more especially
on how non-threatening and interesting the researcher can
make his enquiries appear to the people he meets.

The manifest purpose in all this was to expand my own
range of observation so as to incorporate what the man or
woman opposite me had to say about the things, happenings
and activities I was interested in. But it was also, I suppose, an
attempt to co-opt the people I was interviewing into my own
role as researcher, at least to the extent of inviting them to
corroborate, supplement or correct either the accounts of relationships, activities, intentions and so on I had so far assembled
or the views about them I had so far adopted, however tenta-

tively. It is perhaps a slightly tricky procedure, approximating rather to the hearsay evidence which is ruled inadmissible in courts of law. I found it extremely useful.

There was yet another element, one which has some affinity with the understanding which is claimed for hermeneutics. There is an essay by Helmuth Plessner[8] which suggests that in order to attain to a better understanding of other people and their behaviour (and, to some extent, of ourselves and our own behaviour), we have somehow to distance ourselves from the familiar, taken-for-granted world of everyday experience and look at it 'with different eyes' – to become 'exiles from the familiar'. He cites the example of an emigrant on a visit to his native country. One step beyond this is the kind of understanding which comes when something which was part of a familiar, or at least well-known, world is missing. (Which could perhaps be construed as one more instance of the *Hound of the Baskervilles* syndrome, when something becomes conspicuous by its absence.) It was this that I experienced on my return to the BBC in 1973.

When I had first gone into the BBC, there had been what appeared to be a striking difference between what seemed to be the normal way of working and what one finds in a factory. Here there were thousands of people – engineers, scene-shifters, directors, actors, stage-managers, porters, lighting supervisors, accountants, cameramen, secretaries and so on – all doing specialised jobs which often related to each other very closely indeed: what they were doing had to dovetail in with what other people were doing, or had just done, in a meticulous and precisely timed way. None of it seemed to be *managed*. Indeed, in formal terms, the members of any particular working group, in or out of the studios, could be answerable to any number of different managers, all of them remote from the scene of action. So far as the central operations of producing and transmitting programmes for broadcasting was concerned, moreover, what they were engaged in amounted to a kind of collaborative working which required a high degree of sensitivity and social skill as well as, and beyond, a demonstrable technical competence.

Each separate task called for an intricate and complicated system of synchronous or serial collective action – of the performance of different tasks in complete concordance with each other. It was akin to what, at its superlative best, one finds happening in an operating theatre between surgeon, anaesthetist and theatre nurses (and treated in almost the same fateful terms). Commands, directives or prompts are hardly ever necessary. Emergencies, when they arise, are signals for the immediate performance of appropriate and complementary tasks by all the members of the team. No one tells anyone else what to do; no one needs telling. The same is true of the performance of their different tasks in complete concordance with each other of the expert crews who man fishing vessels or racing yachts, by established ensembles of actors or acrobats or musicians, gun crews, football teams. Over and above the trained skills involved, that is, those tasks that require co-operative and co-ordinated effort depend for their successful performance on complete and shared knowledge of the joint task, continuous awareness of each other person's presence and of his participative role, sensitivity to minimal signals, and, of course, trust.

Spectacular, well-publicised and essentially small-scale team efforts of this kind are the product of the training, practice and coaching undergone by naturally talented or dexterous individuals. When the same kind of collaborative effort, or something approximating to it, can be relied on to be routinely available in a large organisation like the BBC or a general hospital, it bespeaks features of organised collective action so widespread as to be taken for granted among a large proportion of the adult population. For each short-term, ad hoc, collective activity derives from a capacity for collaborative working which extends in a systematic – *dependable* – fashion throughout the entire organisation.

The most important feature of the BBC in the early 1960s, as I was now able to appreciate, was not the startling salience of careerism (and what seemed to be its deliberate encouragement by the official appointments procedure) or the uninhibited prosecution of internal politics and interdepartmental rivalries (this time, seemingly, the consequence of deliberate policy), These could, in 1973, be seen as side-effects – even symptomatic – of something a good deal more significant. For almost most, if not all, individuals I met in 1963 seemed to be devoting themselves – and consciously so – to individual ends and values which were consistent with those of public service broadcasting without being necessarily derived from them. This was indeed understood well enough at the time, as I found when I went back to the interviews I had recorded then. As one senior official on the Personnel side of Administration remarked, 'My job is to encourage attitudes which will pull out of the staff more than you could justify by any of the criteria which exist, say, in the business world ... What you have in mind ... is to get the best out of people. This is an increment you don't pay for,' (later on, he went so far as to say that it was 'something management isn't entitled to') 'and because of that, it's invaluable.'

Such consistency between the BBC's ends and values and those of its staff as did obtain was not the result of some happy accident. Nor, for sure, was it something created by personnel managers. No doubt senior people in the BBC did see it for what it was, and tried to preserve it and even foster it – in the 1960s – but the truth of the matter is the reverse of what the man I have quoted was claiming. Indeed, this is discernible in the way he said what he did. For it was the ends and values of the BBC itself which were the product of the combined efforts and ideas of the people working in it, not the other way round.

The special commitment, motivation and working relationships which proved so suited to the work the BBC existed to carry out had been brought to an exceptionally high pitch of refinement in 1963. They are not to be thought of, I should emphasise again, as an appropriate, tributary response to an efficient structure of management control, or even as some voluntaristic system of action called forth by the manifest need for such organisational processes. They were rather the preconditions of the effective operation of this kind of organisation – the fabric of individual involvement and relationships through which both organisational structure and operating procedures have to work.

The afterthoughts which the second BBC study had provoked were touched on only briefly in the book which came out of the whole protracted episode. It already had too much of the character of a palimpsest to make it feasible to do more. What I settled for was a further study, this time of the organisation of the National Health Service in Scotland, which I picked on because it seemed the optimum setting for the further development of the ideas sketched out briefly in the preceding section.

The NHS study turned out to be unexpectedly abbreviated rather than protracted; I myself became the object of investigation and analysis by NHS consultants and had to advance my retirement a couple of years. Before I did so, however, I had managed to interview a sizeable proportion of staff at all levels in three major hospitals in Glasgow, Dundee and Edinburgh. In this I found ample evidence of the existence of organised collective action as a support system for collaborative working; it was in fact better articulated and more positively expressed than what I had found in the BBC.

This is not to deny the existence of careerism or internal politics. In hospitals, as in the BBC and industrial concerns, there are differences of opinion about 'how things should be done', or of conflicting 'ideologies' concerning policy decisions on capital expenditure, the support available for different specialisms and departments, and so forth. The question that arises of how organisations keep going at all and manage to achieve even a semblance of effectiveness has only one answer. 'What is to be done' is an agreed procedure which emerges out of a constantly renewed process of negotiation between the people directly concerned – at whatever level the question arises. This is clearest in hospitals, where there is an over-arching consensus about the goals the organisation is there to attain – namely, the care of patients, their restoration to ordinary social life or, at the least, the relief of suffering. Commitment to patient care is an explicit part of the hospital ethos. There are, naturally enough, occasions which lead one to suspect the sincerity of protestations about such commitment, and other occasions when commitment seems to find expression in rather odd ways. It can be used as a weapon on both sides in industrial disputes; it can be invoked in criticism of administrators, doctors, nurses, domestic staff, cleaners, laboratory technicians, trade-union officials; it can be adduced as a reason for opposing any change in the *status quo*, or for advancing or challenging claims for rights and privileges. It is also true that allegations of lack of commitment, insincerity, or of professions of commitment used to conceal naked self-interest are the stuff of the internal politics of hospitals, just as they are of the BBC, universities, government departments and business concerns. But the very fact of commitment to patient care being used in the ways I have mentioned is also testimony to its strength, comprehensiveness and unquestioned validity – just as it is, *mutatis mutandis*, in other kinds of organisation.

Since then, all too obviously, hospitals, the central institutions of the NHS, have proved just as vulnerable to the onslaught of managerialism as the BBC was in the early 1970s – and has proved to be more than once since then. Which is not to read as invalidating what has been argued here about the fundamental character of organised collective action. Organisations are, as Kenneth Arrow once said, instruments of collective social action which provide individuals with the means whereby they can attain their own individual ends and realise their own individual values. All workplaces contain an extraordinarily large and diverse number of modes of social exchange, social interaction and conversational conduct, all of them carrying some of the moral weight of institutions or conventions. It is these which subtend work relationship – which make them, in fact, 'workable'. The specialisms that technological development and the division of labour have introduced into collective social action create involvement out of the demands they make on ingenuity and skill, each growing its own vocational interest and appeal. So that in so far as organisation is a *process* through which individuals are enabled to produce – i.e., make what they do available to others, to socialise their work – organisation is an essential instrument for the accomplishment and realisation of individual ends and values. As against this, when organisation is merely a *structure* which allocates individuals to different parts of the total task which the organisation exists to perform, organisation is the scriptwriter of roles to which individuals find they have become committed. Even in this latter case, this special human capacity for interpersonal concordance remains the essential prerequisite of all human organisation, including – though this is almost always missed – power structures and authority systems.

It is this last set of considerations which has engaged my own research interests over the past ten years or so. The last paper in this collection was written at the very beginning, as a preliminary canter – not so much over the ground I meant to cover but around some interesting territory bordering on it.

NOTES AND REFERENCES

1. *Local Development in Scotland*, A report of the Committee on Local Development (Chairman: Professor A. K. Cairncross), appointed by the Scottish Council (Development and Industry), 1952.
2. *Local Government and Central Control*, A West Midland Group Study, Routledge, 1956.
3. T. Burns and G. M. Stalker, *The Management of Innovation*, Tavistock Press, 1961, p. 1.
4. J. Littlejohn, *Westrigg*, Routledge, 1964.
5. 'Thick description' is a term coined by Gilbert Ryle in a lecture he gave in 1968. It denotes the multiple layers of meaning which can accumulate on any physical act, gestural or facial, which lends itself to being employed and construed as expressive behaviour. The illustrative example he uses is the way we attach a quite different meaning to, say, a wink, as against a blink. There is a difference we all know to exist between the involuntary twitch of one eyelid, a nervous response to some irritation or nervous impulse and directed to nobody at all, and a wink, which is a signal, a coded message to someone in particular. Yet they are, to all appearances ('objectively'), precisely the same. It is in the *meaning* we read into the one and into the other that the difference lies. Nor is this all. A third possibility is for a wink to be parodied; a fourth for a novice to practise winking before a looking-glass; a fifth for a parodist to 'take off' someone else's wink.

   These different meaning-levels, with each meaning so very different from the others, build up into what Ryle calls a 'pyramid of learned accomplishment'. None of these 'higher-level' winks can be brought off (or even attempted) without knowledge of, or skill at, performing and reading precisely the same physical action at a 'lower' level. (See G. Ryle, 'The Thinking of Thoughts: What is "Le Penseur" Doing?', in *Collected Papers*, vol. 2, Hutchinson, 1971, pp. 480–96. Brief summaries are given in C. Geertz, 'Thick Description: Towards an Interpretive Theory of Culture', in *The Interpretation of Cultures*, Basic Books, 1973, and in T. Burns, *Erving Goffman*, Routledge, 1992.)
6. T. Burns, *The BBC: Public Service and Private World*, Macmillan, 1977, pp. xiv–xvii.
7. C. Geertz, 'Thick Description: Towards an Interpretive Theory of Culture', in *The Interpretation of Cultures*, Basic Books, 1973.
8. H. Plessner, 'With Different Eyes' (1953), trans. A. L. Hammond in T. Luckmann (ed.), *Phenomenology and Sociology*, Penguin Books, 1978, pp. 25–41.

1

Calamity Bay:
Greece, 26–29 April 1941

This piece was written – in draft, at least – while I was a
POW in Germany. I brought it back with me when the
International Red Cross arranged the exchange of severely
disabled POW's, plus attendant medical staff, in December
1943. It was my second wartime piece; I'd written one in
Finland in 1940 – also straightforward 'reportage' about a
night-time excursion fairly typical of the kind of thing the
section of the Friends Ambulance Unit stationed north of
Lake Ladoga was called on to do. This second piece was
very like that one. I now find it a little embarrassing to
read, but I have included it in this selection to serve as the
departure point for the 'learning process' outlined in the
Introduction.

Ahead, the lights up the next loop stopped their lifting and
rocking, stared still, and went out; the back of the staff car in
front crept back at me. I pulled up and switched off the engine
and lights. It looked like being a long wait. A strong light
wavered up behind us and stayed, filling the inside of the cab.
It stayed on, level over the piled kit and the dozing men in the
back; it was discomforting, and besides, there was Jerry to
think of. I got out, feeling the fatigue as awkwardness, and hot
dryness of skin, and went back.

'I should switch off,' I told him. 'It looks like being a long
one.' He turned the switch. Down the road one or two other

From *Penguin New Writing*, no. 19, October–December 1944, pp. 9–22.

remaining lights went out, and the noise of running engines stepped down into silence as they were turned off one by one.

'Near the top yet, do you know?' I looked up the black mountain to where a few torches were playing among the tree trunks.

'Somebody's gone over up there, looks like. I couldn't say how far we are.' Far below, on the floor of the plain towards Argos, more lights twinkled tinily in a straight row. Above them, hanging in the middle of the night, the big transport was still burning in the sea and smoke clouds; that was at Nauplia, fifteen miles away.

I lit my pipe and walked up the line. Our other vehicles were there all right. I looked in at the cabs. Faces turned towards me, but nobody spoke. I went back and got in.

'The others all right?'

'They're all together, about thirty yards ahead.'

'Want a change?'

'Not yet.'

'Don't put us over the edge, cock.' It was pleasantly warm inside, after the bitter cold out on the road. I dozed off.

The lights from the car behind woke me. Engines were running again, and there was movement ahead. I started up, and after a minute or two, moved off, following the tail light in front, in first gear, never faster than five miles an hour, pinned inextricably into our place in the brigade column we had met turning on to the road two miles outside Argos.

At a guess, the distance from Argos to Kalamata is about 80 kilometres. It took us twelve hours' driving to cover it. The sun was up by the time we halted. The road was narrow, a fog of dust hung over us, and thick hedges of prickly pear stood high on each side. We could see nothing of the place except the ridge of fells running to the south along the east of the bay. There was a lane branching up to the left by us, so we pulled our vehicles out of the line as it was being closed into the right hand hedge, and started up it. The track was narrow and difficult, but we climbed for five minutes before we reached a village where the road ceased, or became small spaces between the buildings huddled together on the side of the hill. We managed to edge down a little gully of a path which led to an untidy hollow where the communal well was situated. The cover was excellent, there was water for tea and washing, and there were trees at the top of the hollow, behind the village, where we could sleep.

We went down to the well, a wide, substantial affair, and washed and shaved leisurely. There were a few women there, drawing water or washing clothes; they lent us buckets, or themselves poured water over our heads and shoulders, all with that mannerly and quiet good nature which we already took for granted.

The hours of the morning drifted remotely past. We cooked underneath the string of cypresses, whose branches took up the woodsmoke, dozed on the worn red soil, raked over our kit for bits of chocolate and biscuits, repacked the ambulances so that they could be used. Overhead, high up for the passage of the mountains, the bombers shuttled, and the noise of their salvoes came up faint, but distinct and silencing, from the empty town. Two or three times, perhaps, a Bren thumped off at them from the olive groves below, and men here and there took potshots. Fighters and guns were lost or gone.

There was nothing for us to do, and sleep we could not. The accumulated fatigue of the last days and weeks sustained a parched fire in our skin, our heads, our bones, and we had continually to be attending to little familiar jobs and saying familiar remarks, unnecessarily. We were at last insensitive to what was happening, sucked into the strict present, waiting minute by minute for this to pass. Everybody, when passing each other, grinned slightly and ironically in companionship.

And tunnelling into and confusing all this came the two unworded, unrealised essentials. The first matters most now, the second dominated then. The first builds up from the sheerly sensory aspects of Greece, of the Peloponnese especially, which have a vigour and robustness, in merely the ash-green olive and the turnip-green cactus, in the sea glinting, in the voluminously empty reaches of the mountain slopes, all white rock and burnt grass, in the dilapidated houses, which demand continually increased awareness; and reaching up from this awareness was a further one of a fusion, in all the things around, of similar qualities into a fresh and morning vitality, a further awareness of the imparting of an extra-sensory tone which at this time, in April, achieved an incandescent insistence. Then, second, there was the retreat: this was the end: we could smell the sea: nobody knew anything.

At three o'clock I walked up to the village. The sun was strong, striking heavy shadows from the buildings. There were no separate houses, but seemingly four or five tall square blocks of masonry, rubble, wood and plaster in which living quarters had been mined; windows were few and small, stuck haphazardly over the faces of the buildings. I was looking for the taverna, and found it inside a black doorway. The room was crowded with men in dark clothes sitting on odd stools and chairs. Against one wall was an open charcoal hearth, standing well off the floor and looking like a small shoeing smith's forge. Coffee was being brewed in thimbles of copper stuck on the ends of sticks and rods and thrust into the burning charcoal. I stood, clumsily avoiding the woman tending the fire, and feeling grossly foreign in battle dress. I uttered the Greek words for 'coffee' and 'please,' but apparently nobody heard. I tried resined wine, but the woman, bustling with bellows, handing out coffee holders, or standing stock still, watching the men, apparently could not see me. I looked around the room: the men were old, mostly, their faces showing little and pale, with the eye sockets, the nostrils and mouth, the cheeks blocked out by the darkness into which everything in the room was sunk; they sat still, the light patches which made up their faces constellated in unaccusing passivity, the conversation stacking up evenly between them. None of them saw me, their gaze turning unheedingly across me. I went out. I could not understand, nor can I guess now, what those old men felt in my presence, what they thought of the events they were living through, what they were saying.

When I returned to the hollow (khaki and braces, litter of tins) there was tea again, and news. The two officers of the unit had gone down to the road and had found the headquarters of our Group Area a mile towards the town; embarkation would be taking place for certain after dark; we should be moving down nearer HQ and the town at dusk so as to get our place in the queue; we were to get some sleep now.

Sensibly and obediently, we lay down again under the cypresses and stared into the thin shabby limbs of the trees. In Spain there must be a retreat of the unverdant and impenetrable landscape into itself, so that a clear, bitter noumenal world is set over and against experience; here the object composed itself for experience, presented itself as a surrounding for human life.

The bombers stopped long before evening, and when we assembled there was already a great deal of movement on the roads. Nobody seemed to have any idea about the situation north of us; we supposed the canal was still held, although the awakening rumours gave it that Argos had fallen. Here and there, trucks had already been tipped over, and their crews were dismantling and smashing the engines, loosing off shots into tyres and ripping them with bayonets; several PU trucks were on the move, swirling down the road into the town, their desert camouflage still reminiscing under the coating of dust, with the men squatting in the back shouting and laughing again with the inescapable feeling of a joy-ride. We went down with the traffic a few hundred yards from the town, turned into an olive grove, the engines crowing and roaring and a dozen men shoving each vehicle in turn over the newly-ploughed earth through the branches into positions as dispersed and covered as was possible.

Units had been appointed times when they were to move off. After dark, traffic on the road increased, and the noise of trucks crawling, checking and accelerating as the drivers felt their way along, without lights now, became almost continuous; voices shouted up and down the line interminable question, direction and answer; voices efficient, robust, exhausted or peremptory, Australian, New Zealand, or English, shouting exactly the same things through the hours, the same shouts above the unbroken wailing of bottom gears. Our turn came just before midnight. We held a break in the line and handled the vehicles out on the road, the olive branches whipping and drumming uproariously on the metal bodies. The end of the queue was just beyond the bridge when we caught up, and we followed into the town, and along between the quiet houses, the streets and squares, the grey plane of the façades bounding, by their hovering, springing, plunging horizon, the near, familiar pattern of starlit night. Every door and window was shut and shuttered.

We stopped by a big warehouse. A few officers and NCOs stood along the street, speaking directions in loud and steady tones to men as they arrived – park all vehicles well into the

side of the approach, do not smoke, do not smoke, leave plenty
of passage room for traffic, keep walking at an even pace.
'Turn right. Turn right. Turn right.'

We went forward, our feet stumbling loosely on the unseen
flags, our kit lumped on us, and inside us a burst of relaxation
and relief as all the precautionary attitudes and insurances
against disaster were dismissed: these few steps were absolutely
the last stage: here it was, quayside, embarkation point, working organisation: finally and above all, there – a couple of
hundred yards away – was a ship's light, masked but plainly
and for seconds holding in a lighted sphere a gang-plank and
the deck gear of a small man-o'-war.

'This way for the booking office.'

'Charlie? You there? Charlie? Where the Christ Almighty
have you got to? Charlie? Charlie?'

'I should worry; we'll be warm enough on board.'

'Number Two, RASC? Bill Morgan! Number Two, RASC?'

'. . . Sister Street. You know, that dirty big ride . . .'

'. . . patrolled with I tanks, and then there's two squadrons of
Hurricanes at Argos. Seen 'em.'

It was hard to see it at first. We just came, in straggling
dozens and scores, to a line of figures in the darkness, all facing
to the left. We tried to move around them, and saw then that
they were in a queue. It was quite unreckoned for, and shocking.
We got to the end, and there, with the light coming off the
water, we could see it, and it was up to twenty men deep and
two hundred yards long, a great, packed rectangle of thousands
of men. They stood very still, not talking, not smoking; there
was an occasional cough, and over the top of the block there
played a continual little motion as men raised themselves on
their toes to look to the front. We waited, banking on a move
forward five minutes from now, a quarter of an hour, count
five hundred.

We stayed where we were. After a long time there was a
good deal of noise, lights showed briefly, a lamp signalled
towards the bay, and then we heard the ship's screws beating
away from us. The next one might be a big ship, and they
would surely start on our queue then.

Then there was another long time before we knew that the
short space left until dawn meant that nothing more would be

in, before, too, the order came for all MT drivers to get back to their vehicles and turn.

We got out of the town, the streets alive with trucks pouring through, two abreast now, overtaking and weaving, flicking full lights on and off and blaring horns at jams and turnings. We'd been there, thousands of us; we'd seen it all; it all went like clockwork; we'd had it. But all our bad temper and fear, the shouting and the noise, the breakdown of orderliness meant really the return to normality; we felt as we should have expected to feel in such a situation, and the feeling was the sort that could be vented in talking and swearing about it. For evacuation here was proceeding, we had seen that, and it was controlled and supervised. There was an immense reassurance, too, in the sight of the Navy.

On the outskirts of the town we pulled over to the right hand side and slowed. As the headlights morsed up and down our line we could see, extraordinarily, a column of refugees – men, women and children with soldiers in Yugoslav uniform – all well together and walking well, for all their extra clothes and the suitcases and bundles. They must have left a train which had been halted some distance outside the town, and they were hurrying along to get on board the ship which they were sure was waiting for them; or perhaps it was that they had to keep moving south. There were several hundreds of them. The vision was so hallucinatory, so bitterly hopeless, and so sheerly daft, that we laughed at them. We never saw them again. It could be that they did after all get away, for we knew nothing except that we had been turned back.

Well, we proceeded over the bridge and found our olive grove again. It was a bad place, this roadside field so close to the bridge, so most of us raked out bully, dried figs and biscuits, filled our water bottles from the tanks of drinking water in the ambulances and struck off through a gap in the cactus to find a ditch farther from the road. The next field was an empty paddock, and we settled down along the further side and slept.

We slept very well, too, that morning, for when we awoke the sun was high and planes were cruising above the fields on the other side of the road. They were very low, not a hundred feet off the ground, and moved slowly, dropping small AP bombs and machine-gunning. They kept this up for a good spell, concentrating on a smallish area. After they had gone some of us collected small branches which we laid across the ditch and spread with grass and twigs. When this was done we crawled underneath and felt much safer. There was still nobody else in the field, and so long as there was no movement about us nothing would happen beyond casual sprayings. But there was never an interval of more than ten minutes or so for many hours, and the casual spraying, from gunners whose heads and shoulders we could see so plainly, was very frequent and at times very close, holing the cactus pads above us. It was a good ditch, three feet deep with a steep outer bank, and the moments of enfilading fire were brief. But the special terror of air attack comes from the qualities of the sounds planes and their weapons make; machine-gunning from the air sounds different from any other automatic firing, a series of irregular crackles, as though of the winding up of a cheap clockwork toy of giant size. It seems, too, that the plane is moving so steadily, and that the gunner must have such perfect sight of everything on the ground, that to put a dozen bullets into each separate man should be as simple as spearing a dead leaf with a walking stick.

In the afternoon the lulls became longer, and people took to strolling about the fields. O. returned from one of these trips and said he had found a cottage with the people still there; it was on the railway line, which ran parallel to the road a hundred yards or so further away. We listened, but there was no sound except of voices, and I started back with him. We kept alongside the hedges, and flattened out under them when the planes came back our side of the town. Their yellow noses and wing-tips showed up very brightly against the blue and brown of the mountains.

It was a biggish house, with a garden of vines and a wide shanty-built veranda on the side fronting the railway. The fat woman who stood at the edge of the shade with sewing in her hand smiled at us and waved us towards chairs. An old man, his grey hair and moustache streaked with thick black hairs and a strong, handsome face moulded also in a gracious smile, moved out from inside the kitchen door. We all sat.

'You boys been America?'

'No.'

'I was there. Nineteen hundred twenty-eight I come home

to my family. New York, Detroit. I drive taxis, work hotel.'
'You still speak good English.'
'You boys English? Bloody Germanoi.'
The planes were quite near again, and a salvo of small stuff
dropped away up the road. The old man turned and spoke to
his wife, who called through the kitchen door. They both
smiled encouragingly at us again, and in a few moments a girl
came out with a tray and glasses of syrups. The old man took
the tray.
'Here you are, boys. Help yourself. Cheerio!'
We thanked him as we were able, and then he told us more
about America, about the skyscrapers and the speakeasies and
the Pullman cars, and about working hard and earning good
money, while his wife stood just inside the shadow of the roof,
looking up from her sewing now and again to listen to the
English speech and to smile at us. We stayed close on two hours.
When we got back, most people seemed to think that Jerry
had finished for the day: there had been a longish break, and
the evening before he had stopped about the same time. It was
past five, and little groups of officers and men were standing
about all over the paddocks and groves by the road, eating,
and brewing dixies of tea on primus stoves. Near our car a few
officers were finishing off two or three flasks of whisky, and
they called the pair of us over and gave us a couple of drinks.
Everybody was talking a lot, about near escapes during the day
and about how the Navy would be in for the whole bunch of us
that night because Jerry couldn't be far away now.
Anyhow, our lot would start early this night and make sure
of getting well placed in the queue. I got some food down, and
packed valises and haversacks while O. went off to the Group
Area HQ for final information of the arrangements. He was
back in a very short time. No MT was to be used this time;
most vehicles had already been put out of action; movement
into the town would begin at half-past six, and our small group
of sixteen could start in as near the head of the column as we
wished. So we finished up in a hurry and then sat by the roadside, smoked cigarettes, and kept our eyes on the gap along the
road which led to the grove where HQ was.
Files began forming before 6.30, one on each side of the road.
At the same time, a staff car pulled up by us. Two ambulances
were wanted to collect casualties back along the road.

We got two vehicles out on the road, four men were detailed, and the rest of us moved on. By this time the files stretched as far as we could see into the town. The sun was still up, and we saw now, walking up the rise towards the bridge, more of the locality than we had yet been able to glimpse through the cactus hedges. We saw the stretch of plain across the top of the bay between the mountains, which closed together behind us, climbing to the high buckled ridges in the centre of the Peloponnese. The floor of the valley was a thick, rich, brocaded green in the evening sunlight, and the white walls of the farmhouses scattered over the fields completed the textbook illustration of prosperity.

The white stone bridge crossed no water, but a wide shallow bed of rounded rocks and pebbles glowed creamily between the grass banks. There was not much damage in the street beyond, but its utter dereliction stared lividly out at that countryside. We passed on into it, and then, immediately, the files up the street began to break up, the movement travelling back quite slowly, as though we were a burning fuse; men stopped to listen before running for cover. I made across an empty patch of ground between the houses straight into a deep culvert. It was perfect cover, the banks rising steeply as I squeezed along after the others in front, and a concrete lining strengthening the bed.

By the time I was a dozen yards in, the first salvoes were falling. They had obviously spotted our movements and concentrated on the entrance to the town. The force amounted to some twenty-five bombers, and they circled around in formation at about 500 feet. They stayed for an hour, machine-gunning while the bombs fell, kneading us against the earth with their fugal screaming, and punching our bellies furtively with the tremors of the ground when the explosions slammed. Dust sifted down on us.

Five minutes of silence we let slip past before walking back slowly to the road. The lines reformed. I looked for the rest of the unit; and was bewildered to see them all there. Nor did anybody else mention any casualties; everybody had found good cover, and the bombs had been so many that they must have been lightweight. The march recommenced.

In the next street it happened again. This time I followed a crowd into a cellar, and we sat around in the half light and talked about how the Navy would be there, and how we'd all make it. Whistles gave the All Clear this time, and we climbed out quickly and joined the already-moving lines.

The route followed the boundary roads of the town round to the south and back along the shore to the harbour. Down every side road men were trickling down from the hills and assembling at the side of the route. There was one plantation of cedars where a detachment of RTRs stood paraded in threes while their officers addressed them. Ahead of us we could see the OC of the Group marching alone, a tall, thin, elderly man with precise, taut features, who kept up an absolutely even pace, thrusting himself firmly along with a shooting stick.

The last light lay on the bay as we came up to the harbour. We could just see a dead mule which had been dropped on to the pavement opposite. The saplings along the promenade looked blown and untidy as we passed under them. Chunks of masonry were sprinkled along the road. We had no idea at all where this spot was, in relation to the quayside of the night before. All the time, working inside the mass of an army, all references and relations are to the things also inside; nothing outside – countries, people, new qualities and new values – is noticeable except as the army comes to them, and you gradually stop looking at anything outside. Where we were might have been a different town altogether from that we had left in the morning.

The queue which had started five deep thickened slowly as the thousands came up behind. Most of us sat down and watched the seaward end of the bay. Somewhere at the back of us a crowd began singing songs like 'Underneath the Arches' and 'Somewhere in France', very softly. At the head of the queue, a few yards away, there was a field telephone working. The stars multiplied.

Why we began that night again with such complete assurance I do not know. With us at the head of the queue, in a good position, confidence remained longest, but after midnight – when I took a turn along the road – the ranks behind had dwindled, and most of those left were asleep on the ground. The RCS sergeant in charge of the field telephone turned up and found the post unattended; he went very quietly round from man to man until he discovered his signaller, and then proceeded to tear him off one; his voice of furious outrage rang along the quayside.

O. drifted over once again to the group standing around the OC. He called us up together when he returned.

'Well, it's certain by now that there's nothing coming in to-night. He's been telling officers to disperse again to the hills outside the town.'

'To-morrow night?'

'I think he's pretty sure in his own mind that evacuation is off altogether, but of course he's not going to say that. There's no wireless here.'

There was a considerable pause while we accepted all this.

'We shall wait here in any case until the ambulances turn up. This is the only place they've been told to find us.'

We drifted apart and lay down. O. came over to my tree, and began talking about the possibility of getting further south to one of the villages on the tip of the peninsula and trying there to pick up a small craft that would take us to Crete. The map showed a road right down the peninsula. There were moun-tains to cross, but the distance was short enough to give us a chance, on our own, of reaching the east coast. It was the best gamble we could make. We waited impatiently for the ambu-lances to come so that we could get back to the other vehicles.

They turned up at last from the nowhere of the town, and with information which removed the need for decisions. Hours of searching for a dressing station had landed them at about midnight at a large public hall in the centre of the town. Walking wounded they met told them they had been directed there by Greeks. The whole floor of the hall was covered with beds, all occupied by British wounded. The only staff working there were two doctors and three nurses – Greek civilians.

We got inside the two ambulances and drove off to the hall. It faced on to a square, and imposed – in the blue darkness – an impression of imminent bulk and dramatic perspective which later daylight treated as spurious; but the hall is still incorri-gibly stagey in memory, and it was after all, when night removed its shabbiness, the dirty broken windows, and the shops at its side, a simple and honest structure, well propor-tioned. At the back of the portico there was a row of glass swing doors. I pushed through these and the curtains behind them.

At the other end there was a platform. Just in front of this there was a doctor bending over a bed, with two nurses standing by. A candle and a torch lit the group, reflecting quite brightly off their white costumes, and gleaming faintly along to us and the walls over the shiny traces in the bedsteads, sweating hands and faces, kit brasses and enamel mugs. We squeezed in, all of us, and the officers went along to speak to the doctor. They conversed in French, their whisperings filling the hall with intermittent jets of pattering sound.

That was the finish, really, when that conversation started. Afterwards, we were taken to a small, newly-built clinic, where we slept on the floor along the corridors until daybreak. Then we went in to work. There were just over two hundred patients in the hall, and about a hundred and twenty beds. Most of the floor space between the beds was filled with stretchers, or with men lying on the floor. Behind the platform there were two or three small rooms, a kitchen with a very large fireplace, a library, a small yard. The hall had obviously been used for some time before these last days had filled it with British casualties, but what its purpose had been, and how it had been changed to its present one, how the biscuits which made up the first breakfast of porridge got into the kitchen or the large Red Cross ground flag on to the square in front, how all the patients had got there, are questions that are hardly worth asking even now.

There was no bombing at all that day, and the town, empty and silent again, looked hollow and fragile among its creeping shadows.

But we had withdrawn from all that business. We kept working all day, and we recognised with no more than curiosity the German entry in the two rounds fired from a light gun and the one burst of machine-gun fire. That was all there was, that, and a brief inspection from the main door by a tall young Oberleutnant who ordered everyone to stay inside.

Late that night men came down from the hills again on the chance of the Navy coming in. They found the Germans in the town and a heavy field gun in position on the quayside. They stormed the Germans with Bren guns mounted on trucks, cleaned them up and took the gun. I have heard the story many times, and it is quite true; I believe one man was awarded a

VC. But I was asleep in the clinic a couple of hundred yards away at the time.

At eleven o'clock the next morning the capitulation had been made, and some of the patients were out in the portico watching the thousands of men being herded past at a half trot up to the first Sammellager.

2

Men and Barbed Wire

Soon after getting back from Germany, I was asked to meet
Dr A. T. M. Wilson, then a colonel in the RAMC, a member
of the Army Psychiatric Unit. He was working on the planning of 'rehabilitation camps' for the enormous number of
POWs who would, it was thought, soon be released by the
advance of the Allied forces. A good number had already
been returned from North Africa and southern Italy, and a
pilot venture had been started up in the Midlands. He
asked me to visit the place for a few days. Most of the time
was spent in my talking about my experience as a POW
and also about my reactions to repatriation. There was,
naturally, some follow-up to this, and I met one or two
other members of the Army Psychiatric Unit, most of
whom had belonged to the Tavistock Clinic. I wrote up a
full-dress statement for their benefit. Later on, I expanded
and embellished it somewhat, and published it as 'Men
and Barbed Wire'. Wilson had belonged to the Tavistock
Clinic and, after the war, set about creating the Tavistock
Institute of Human Relations; I kept in touch with him and
the Tavistock Institute for several years. I didn't know it at
the time, but this marked a first step in the direction my
career followed in later years.

It is just over a year since I came back from Germany. I suppose
that should mean that the years of prison life there should now
be visible in perspective. But perspective, in this as in all else,

From *The Fortnightly*, new series, no. 940, April 1945, pp. 272–7.

contributes no meaning. Forgetfulness and emphasis, anecdote-derived, have contrived to refashion that existence according to the patterns that literature and the traditions of behaviour admit. I can see, now, a process of liberation that began with the final search outside the main gate on a wet autumn afternoon and ended with the cheering crowds and the pipe bands in Leith harbour. The men I knew, and all the thousands within the barbed wire, can easily show themselves, now, as cheerful, irrepressible squaddies. And what marks of that time are on me for good are indistinguishable from old habits.

The spectacles remain, of course. The spectacle of Kalamata – the long, silent queues along the quayside at night, waiting for the destroyers; the Stuka attack by the bridge; the ten-thousand herd of prisoners shuffling and trotting through the centre square; the New Zealand major storming and cursing at the German Town Commandant; the old, rotten, chewed corpses at the sea's edge. The spectacle of Dulag Korinth–the cooking fires in the dusk; the market at the gate; the crocodiles of men spoking out from the cookhouse; the ordure-smeared scraps of paper fluttering everlastingly about the camp; the machine-gun fire along the wire at night; the undiminishing queue at the two condemned wells; the sleeping pits dug in the firm sand. The spectacle of Frontstalag Salonika – the two-hour check-parades on the centre square; the bed bugs and the lice; Olympus across the bay; the dysentery patients with shreds of flesh between their skin and bones; Feldwebel Keminade; beri-beri: such things are easy to remember, and they have been easy capital for conversation. And at first they were just that, fixed and dead like old photographs. The months, though, have given them increased meaning, whenever I can think of them in sum; the images have a vividness still which can set going a consciousness of what it was like to be alive at those times.

Liberation was not a process of weeks: it was a moment. It was when I boarded a Bakerloo train and started the last stage of the journey home from Stalag VIIIB. Instantly, and with bewildering completeness, the forty-five months of my absence dropped clean away. Here it was, Forhan's for the Gums, Diagram of Stations, I am the Phonotas Girl, the salmon-coloured paint on the doors and fittings, the double, dental row of lights: a pattern so familiar that it must signify the real and normal world, a recognition so immediate that it must signify the utter unreality and insignificance of all that had happened since I had last seen it. I was glad of this, for I should be able to take up where I had left off, perhaps a little better at doing some things, certainly slower and clumsier at others; there would be all those wartime regulations to find out about; it would be interesting reading up the history of the war, amusing to compare it with camp rumour; I would have to find out what had happened to my friends and to London in the Blitz; it would be amusing to be mildly lionized by acquaintances. The noise of the train grew more reassuring.

Since that moment, I have had to acknowledge an increasing awareness that the business of returning, of beginning where I had left off, of catching up, is not so simple. Quite largely, I think, this feeling of discrepancy, of incompatibility between myself and people at home was initiated by the weeks of answering questions which insisted on the peculiarities of my experience. I had continually to cast unformed judgements into words and say what it felt like to be back, what sort of life we led in prison camps, what I thought of the Germans. There were lectures and articles which I read, on the psychological abnormalities of prisoners of war and refugees which I have not been able to assure myself were incorrect or exaggerated. I would catch myself being grotesquely hearty or fatuously dumb.

Perhaps this is becoming a little too personal, a little over-dramatised. What I want to convey, however, is necessarily derived from personal experience, although I believe that it is shared by other men who have returned from prison camps, and, I believe too, by refugees and 'liberated' people. There is the ballooning emotion that comes when freedom is sensed as an actual experience, and with it the feeling that the return to familiar surroundings is all that is necessary for a return to normal life; there is an increasing consciousness of estrangement and abnormality.

What happens when a man becomes a prisoner of war, what happens, conceivably, when people have their country occupied by an army of enemies, is a revolutionary change in his make-up as a social being. He does not leave his friends, the people he knows, and go into prison, where he, uniquely, is thrust into a hostile environment and where he must fight an essential battle to maintain his selfhood, where he can, defending it, regard himself as cut off from normal society, from real life. He has with him instead the society that he knew as normal and real, and it is towards this society, towards his friends and acquaintances themselves, that he has to reorder his attitude.

It is difficult to think back to our state of mind during the first days of captivity in Corinth. We all, I suppose, based our ideas of German prison camps on press versions of Dachau horrors; we envisaged lives flattened out under relentless discipline and omniscient organisation. We expected the worst, and prepared for it. There would be a time of tough and bitter experience, and we had to get through it as best we could. So, when we departed – as most of the ten thousand of us did – from customary ethical standards, we did not feel that we had jettisoned decency for good and all, but that we had pocketed such things until the time came for employing them again.

In fact, conditions were extremely bad just at the beginning: no food was issued for the first three or four days at Corinth. The wounded and sick were segregated and cared for, after a fashion, so that there were no obvious claimants for sympathy or generosity. The job was to keep oneself alive, and nobody had anything to spare for anybody else. There were exceptions, of course, as there always are; close friends remained together, and food that had been saved or scrounged might be shared with the man one 'mucked in' with; but apart from the existence of such cobbers and muckers, society around each prisoner would be regarded by him as a cunning enemy: people you had liked and trusted for years, and with whom you had shared a number of dangers and excitements would be watched suspiciously while they divided up the rations; fights over this occasionally took place.

On the positive side, this meant that life resolved itself into a perpetual intrigue for food. Even when things were a little easier, fear of future shortages, fear of jealousy, or of importunate begging hardened each man's selfishness and cunning into permanent features of POW life. The campaigns and humiliating shifts directed in the Dulags towards cadging food from men who went outside the camps to work or who had other means of getting extra food were resorted to later in the Stalags for privileged jobs, better quarters, fuel, or protection by a 'racket-king', as well as for potatoes and sugar. For most people, this business of scrounging, wangling and ingratiation was the really serious business of life; it is possibly the aspect of prison life in which most danger for the future life of the prisoner of war lies.

The other notable break with normal standards of living which occurs at the start of captivity and which tends to be better adjusted as time goes on and conditions improve, rather than to become more definite, is the almost conscious and deliberate rejection of common decency and cleanliness. This is perhaps an inevitable consequence of bad living conditions – although for most of us they were no worse than those of the retreat through Greece, when almost everyone managed to keep clean and tidy – but it went beyond the mere negatives of not washing or shaving, not keeping one's clothes clean; within a few days, the crowded barracks at Corinth camp swarmed with lice, to compete with the bed bugs that infested them already; a curious index of this deterioration was observable in the enormous increase in spitting. Lack of privacy was absolute, of course, and latrines were a stretch of sand pitted with shallow trenches; but most men neglected the most elementary principles of hygiene even to the extent of only kicking sand, and one was liable to come across excreta in the most surprising places. Flies, and dysentery, were thick in the air.

At Salonika there were inside latrines and running water, and this side of things improved. But the problem of barrack cleanliness remained, and of the primary chores that any community necessitates, and which were not done. NCO's placed 'in command' of a barrack by the Germans, uncertain of the extent to which they could exert authority in any case, quickly became, or were made, aware of the anomalies of their position, and were usually afraid to issue orders. Certainly nobody was fool enough to volunteer for such jobs. All arrangements affecting order and cleanliness, therefore, were deferred until an outraged and contemptuous guard imposed them as orders.

And this aspect certainly does have its long-term effect. The resentment aroused by such scenes with guards, and the connotation that all work, inside as well as outside the camp, comes to have as 'work for Jerry' introduces a positive and obstinate element into a previously apathetic or a social rejection of cleanliness and order. Also, the bludger, the *débrouillard*, can invoke right feeling and military duty on his side, and does so, frequently.

Throughout the period of the Greek Dulags, the great herd of men which had been driven through the streets of Kalamata on the morning of 30 April 1941 remained, for the most part, a herd. Dirty, unshaven, undisciplined, shiftless, grubbing continually for bits of food and cigarette ends, indecent, selfish, we must have provoked by our appearance the bullying and occasional irresponsible shootings that stirred wretchedness into a fierce misery.

In Germany, in the permanent camps, the Stalags, conditions are very different. The camps are planned and organised for their purpose. The German rations themselves are slightly better, and are regular. Camp administration and guards are recruited from older men and from those unfit for active service – apart from the few Party men. But most important of all, the International Red Cross services come into full action, BRCS parcels of food, undreamed of in transit camps, arrive, correspondence is permitted, parcels of clothing, books and tobacco can be sent from home. In response to specific needs, and following the forms set down by the Geneva Convention, organisations have to be arranged between prisoners and camp authorities for distributing Red Cross supplies, for corresponding with Red Cross authorities at home and in Geneva and with the Protecting Power in Berlin; football leagues are started; the inevitable classes in German grow into established schools with enormous curricula; makeshift concerts and entertainments grow into dance bands and a permanent theatre.

However, the prevailing mood is still to 'see it through,' and not to 'make the best of things'. The organic community life that emerges is short-term: the recurrent and arbitrary suspension of all social functions, standstill orders, the complete vacuum around the community, the impossibility of imposing more than fractional alterations on a rigid environment – all these hedged social existence with provisos, regulations, taboos and fears. They provoked, too, defensive attitudes of cynicism or of 'sense of humour', and a blank inability to think of workable improvements.

For individuals, routine was a vitally necessary protective

device. The disposition of our food into the constant proportions of the daily meals – the bread ration made three thin half-slices for supper, five for breakfast, and two for lunch – the turnabout at cleaning our quarters and washing up after meals, and all the other minutiae of daily existence were ordered not so much for efficiency's sake as for the sense they created of living in a normal, familiar world. Similarly, the perspective of the barrack-room from one's own bunk, the crackpot shelving nailed up around it, the location of one's friends and enemies about the camp, the character of the compound guards, the time for the issue of Red Cross parcels, the stains and graffiti on the walls and neighbouring bunks were all familiar constellations whose removal or disturbance affected the foundations of existence. Consequently, to have to change quarters involved a tremendous emotional upheaval. Such an order was issued not infrequently, and entailed merely our removal, much at our own pace, from one barrack to another, perhaps in the same compound. All barracks were identical in design, variations in the physical conditions of different parts of the camp were for the most part trivial, and the time and labour needed for removing and settling down might well have been regarded as the welcome occupation of a day or two. But no; for days and weeks after a move – and before, if we suspected it – we would be consumed with savage resentment of the German authorities; crises *de nerfs* would alternate with long spells of melancholy brooding; we would avoid people on whom we relied normally for half-an-hour's conversation; the vistas of the war would prolong themselves interminably.

We acquired, in this reaction to our environment, a special set of psychological moods according to which we lived. These modes determined our ways of thinking and the matters which occupied our thoughts, the orientation being always away from what would disturb or worry us. For example, my own reactions towards the war became entirely technical and impersonal. The reading of the *Deutsche Allgemeine Zeitung*, the winnowing of rumours, the endless discussion and prognostication of events, absorbed a great part of each day, but the devastation of towns in the West and the slaughterous battles in Russia, Rommel's advance and Stalingrad, affected me only in terms of their historical significance – an attitude impossibly abstract now. Dejection and pessimism came, but not from allied reverses, or from the impact of German propaganda; they were consequences of periods of military inactivity.

Again, we talked enormously, but we avoided that perpetual discussion of common acquaintances which can become the dominant topic among a group of people; incompatibilities and dissatisfactions in personal relationships cannot be faced when those relationships are indissoluble and close, so that the only protection was not to acknowledge the existence of such difficulties. Talk was the one great amenity, and filled a great part of each day; in such a huge, leisured and stable community, the opportunities for social intercourse and for getting acquainted with scales and categories of living other than one's own were illimitable; there can be few prisoners whose horizons have not been considerably extended in these directions. Inherent in this conversational traffic, though, are the same dangers as there are in too close a confinement within the bounds of any social class. Everybody in a POW camp has a contemporary background and a recent experience practically identical with everybody else's. Back in normal society, the repatriated prisoner can often find himself rather lost in talking to people without that background and experience, much as products of the worst public schools find themselves lost when they have to do with a working man.

In permanent camps, racketeering and bludging, although they persist as whole-time pursuits, tend to become less obtrusive, an inevitable consequence of the greater stability the community has, and of the respectability such stability affords. In the long run – and this counts in the years of Stalag life – most men adopt an habitually ingratiating manner towards those in useful positions, and will do far less for other people in general than they did before they were captured. The occasional memory – and the occasional consciousness of their continued existence – of these developments in oneself is one of the more disturbing legacies of POW life. Perversions, sexual or criminal, were not, I think, widespread, but they were practised fairly openly and without challenge. A curious and revealing circumstance was the existence, for most of my two years in Germany, of a Stalag razor gang who intimidated British WOs in charge of certain camp affairs, who engaged in one or two quite bloody exploits, among minor bullying and rough-housing, without, so far as I know, any counter move being made by the thousands of us who knew of them. This is, perhaps, the extreme case to which was applied a governing principle of social relationships in prison camp – the right of the private individual to make himself a public nuisance.

Apart from the qualifications which I am trusting any reader to make for himself, this account, besides reflecting the incoherence of unassimilated experience, would be absurdly grim. Of course men, even when they become prisoners of war, do not cease to be rational beings; I do not mean to suggest that virtue and right conduct are expensive luxuries; I certainly do not think of myself or of other returned prisoners as fit subjects for psychiatric treatment. Most of us – I certainly – have had extremely valuable experience in prison camps; I met a large number of interesting people; many very funny things happened; there were many enjoyable times; a pleasant sort of easy friendliness existed; I had time to read; I had time to think. What I have been trying to record are the reasons I can find for a feeling; a feeling of our lives as having been lived according to modes utterly different from those I had felt, thought and behaved in before, and from those I am still working myself into now, after a year.

3

Friends, Enemies and
the Polite Fiction

This and the next article are companion pieces, the first-
fruits of the new perception of social behaviour which
came with the almost simultaneous encounter with two
entirely different industrial organisations, one a rayon-mill
in Jedburgh, in the Scottish Borders, the other an electronics
firm in Edinburgh, heavily engaged in research and development. This second firm was the mainstay of the Scottish
Council's 'electronics scheme' (see Introduction, pp. 10–11).
Some of its staff also co-operated in two or three other
research studies, in particular the self-recording exercise
mentioned in 'Sociological Explanation' (pp. 157–77 below).

Social interaction of any kind requires some degree of consensus.
This is true only if the word consensus sheds its connotation of
empathy, of emotional rapport, and is confined to meaning
agreement on the terms of which interaction takes place.
Consensus may thus be defined as the tacit delineation of
mutually accepted norms of behaviour. Since it takes two to
make a quarrel, a quarrel requires consensus in this sense. The
examination of certain situations in which consensus is purpose-
fully manipulated may illuminate its significance in interaction;
the primary object of this paper, however, is to relate the analysis of interaction to more general sociological categories, and
thereby to develop further insights into the process of social
interaction.

From *American Sociological Review*, vol. 18, no. 6, December 1953, pp. 654–62.

Most of the commoner terms in the literature of sociology suffer from confusion and ambiguity, but none probably so much as 'status' and 'role'. We shall, however, start from the definitions stated by Parsons:

> A social system is a system of processes of interaction between actors. . . . Each individual actor is involved in a plurality of such interactive relationships. . . . The participation of an actor in a patterned interactive relationship . . . has two principal aspects. On the one hand, there is the positional aspect – that of where the actor in question is located in the social system relative to other actors. This is what we will call his *status*. . . . On the other hand, there is the processual aspect, that of what the actor does in his relations with others. . . . It is this which we shall call his *role*.[1]

In this rendering, 'status' has a locational, almost non-behavioural, reference; 'role' denotes the behavioural aspect of participation in the social system. The attractiveness, and the dangers, in this use of the terms, lie in its derivation from a basic paradigm in intellectual manipulation – the graphical expression of a binomial. There is, of course, the convenient rag-bag of 'personality' into which items not covered by the terms can be stuffed and packed off to the psychologists for sorting, but even so, there are specifically social elements in the individual's social behaviour which are not comprehended within either term. Some of these elements are dealt with in this paper; meanwhile, the words 'status' and 'role' will be used to indicate the locational and action elements in social interaction.

The roles that an individual plays in different social situations may sometimes be present as possible alternatives in the same situation. A man may invite workmates or colleagues into his home and meet them in the same situation as that in which he enacts the role of husband and parent. The roles of husband and of parent may themselves overlap in this way in different situations within the home. At work, the member of the staff of a factory who is in a clique-relationship with some other members may find a similar overlapping, or juxtaposition, of the two roles. When the ambiguities in such situations becomes stressed, the fictive character of roles emerges into obviousness and a false social position has to be resolved by some declaration pointing to association with one of the groups – an affirmation of one status – and rejection of the other. But since such declarations carry with them a threat to a status in which the individual is involved, and which therefore constitutes a value to him, they are with rare exceptions covered by entry into a form of joking relationship and emerge as banter.

To use banter is to play at being hostile, distant, unfriendly, while intimating friendliness. It is a style of interaction used when two roles are presented to an individual and he decides to retain the status appropriate to both, while, as he must, acting out the role of only one. Banter, then, becomes a style for managing children taken by parents or teachers when other adults are present and forbid the adoption of a role attaching exclusively to their status as teacher or parent. It is frequent among adolescent boys and girls when they are together and there is a desire both to retain the security of the individual's status in his own peer-group and to assume a sexually attractive role towards the opposite sex. It is used by married people and intimate friends in argument, when each is concerned to maintain both the status of an intimate and the status of membership of a larger group whose prestige – as masculine, or as feminine, or as educationally, socially or economically powerful – weighs in the argument. In every case, the relationship with the group dominant at the occasion of interaction is retained; it is the other relationship which bears the episode of banter, as of less social significance at the time but nevertheless requiring safeguard for the future.

Status positions may be structured according to the esteem, and so the rights and privileges, accorded them in society; in effect, this is equivalent to structuring in terms of the security within the total environment offered by a status. But in a society in which status may be gained, and therefore may also be lost,[2] the occupancy of a status has constantly to be tested and proved. In social organisations which are instrumental in character – armies, factories and working sub-communities and the like – status changes are frequent and status is the dominant and most clearly determined value. In such organisations small group membership is of importance to the individual, both in cliques to provide mutual validation for status and in cabals to extend each person's control over the status-gaining process. Situations are therefore constantly arising in which a clique-membership status is presented in interaction situations which also involve the status of membership in the organisation as a whole. In certain areas of interaction, when clique and sub-community statuses come near to equivalence in importance, banter becomes the prevailing style – it is almost impossible to behave in any other way in messrooms and canteens. The following account illustrates the sort of occasion which gives rise to banter; it is representative of many such occasions in this organisation. It may be remarked, in parenthesis, that considerably less security was attached to organisational status in this particular concern than in most, largely because of a policy of 'allowing responsibility to grow with the person' and an associated policy of neither discharging nor downgrading; it was therefore necessary to check continually the security (i.e. the location in the esteem structure) of one's status and the adequacy of role-playing to find out whether the disguised adjustments to the organisation which were the equivalent of bowler-hatting were not taking place around one. Membership of cliques and cabals therefore becomes of primary importance.

> At the end of a foremen's meeting, the supervisor (Foreman A) of a department of skilled workers asked for a reconsideration of the earnings of two men who consistently failed to earn a bonus although their work was of a very high standard; they were both unmarried and were not worried about not making bonus, but he thought the special care they always gave jobs merited extra money, even though they were not liable to be met with demands to repeat jobs which had produced unsatisfactory articles. The chairman's view was that the provisions of the wage system met the case since the firm did not need articles produced to meet higher tolerances than were enough to meet design requirements, and that if men were prepared to spend time doing this rather than in producing more in the same time, the factory lost as well as the men, and should certainly not have to pay more for doing so. There was by now fairly general discussion. At this point the supervisor received support from a departmental manager, one of a number of young men who had risen fairly rapidly in the firm. This man argued that the firm frequently needed work done requiring special care and that it should provide a financial reward to those who constantly employed it and who would be called upon on such occasions. The counter-argument, which was that such occcasions were known to be allowed for by rate-fixers, came from another member of the same clique (Dept Manager B). Both

became fairly involved in the positions they had taken up, and the discussion became warmer than any previous exchange in the meeting. The end came like this (as recorded on tape).

Foreman A: You get this type of person in every department. You get the type that prefer to turn out a high-class job and not bother about making bonus.

Chairman (to Foreman A): Your men aren't complaining about this, are they?

Foreman A: No, only the rate-fixer puts a time on the job, and they're taking time in excess of that.

Chairman: Well, they're below average then. And they're quite happy about not making bonus, and we're quite happy, at the moment, to have our machines run at a low utilisation rate. If the time comes when we're short of machines, then we'll have to consider doing something about it.

Foreman A: That's all I wanted to know – the general policy. (Long pause – a feeling that the subject had not really been disposed of)

Dept Manager B (restating his previous argument): If we really had the class of work suitable for this type of man, then surely the men would earn bonus.

Dept Manager A (resuming argument): What do you mean by this class of work?

Dept Manager B: The high-class work that these men seem to be prepared to do. (Several voices)

Chairman (easing off): We're getting on to a rather thorny subject now. High class . . .

Dept Manager A (raising voice): No, no. Supposing these two characters got married or came up against it – the sort of position most of us are in – their output would probably double at the same quality. Meantime we can't do much about it, but the existence of these two people in the factory has been quite justified.

Dept Manager B. (grinning): Because of their low machine utilisation?

In the case of this interchange, the socially dominant group was clearly the meeting, which represented indeed the factory organisation itself for those present. It was necessary for departmental managers both to act out roles appropriate to their special status in it, which, as they were members of a young, rapidly promoted group, comprehended a special degree of involvement in the welfare of the firm and a capacity for ready judgement and apt verbalisation. On the other hand, the intimate and valuable relationship within the clique had to be safeguarded. Short of prearranged rehearsal of serious argument, which too would have had the character of play, banter was the only way out.

The two-fold nature of the banter relationship seems to indicate that 'status' is not entirely adequate as a description of a social location. It is implicit in the usage of the term that there should be incompatibility to some extent between one status and another, as there is between one role and another; if two roles are not incompatible, in any sense (i.e. do not contain within their range of permitted behaviour acts which would be inappropriate to the other) then they are, of course, one and the same. Here we have a type of situation in which a dual status is possible. The fact is that, in the interaction situation, a status is the 'membership of a group and of a particular category' claimed by the individual and admitted by the group. The admission of the claim is conveyed by consensus, its rejection by the withholding of consensus.

In all societies, the joke is the short cut to consensus. And it is the characteristic double understanding of the joking relationship that allows of the maintenance of two status positions through the same unit of social action, through performance in the same 'role'. It allows consensus to exist on two planes, so to speak, when consensus, and the member relationship it subtends, is almost by definition an element exclusive to one relationship at a time; the friendly ridicule of banter is an act of overt exclusiveness which, by sharing the joke with the excluded 'victim', includes him in a special relationship with the actor. The effect is to maintain undamaged the status pattern – the nexus of memberships – pertaining to an individual.

There are other occasions when what we may call a primary status membership of a socially dominant group is threatened by the simultaneous presentation of an alternative, secondary, status membership, which on its side is not valuable enough to be safeguarded. However, simple rejection of a relationship is damaging to the primary status, implying a disregard for values which is dangerous to the esteem structure in which the primary status is located. The style normally used in rejection is again one which encases the act in a form of joking relationship. To use irony is to play at being friendly – at maintaining a member-relationship – while intimating enmity, rejection. In this case, the element of reassurance in the joking relationship refers to the status occupied in the group more socially significant to the occasion – the joke is shared with them at the expense of the other. With both banter and irony the first object is the defence of the primary status against the threat of the simultaneous presence of another; to accept the secondary status is to abdicate from the other.

The child, ridiculously exaggerating the strength and prowess of another, establishes a joking relationship with his peers and safeguards his position in the esteem structure of the group when it is threatened by the secondary subordinate status offered in the overweening demonstration or claims of the other. The force of the irony lies in the convention which disguises hostility in a style overtly connoting goodwill, helpfulness, friendliness.

A declaration of enmity is in fact a rejection of a secondary member-relationship to accept which would threaten the secure occupation of a primary membership. But the outright declaration of enmity would provoke a conflict which would, whatever the loss or gain which came out of it, damage the primary membership. It would damage it because consensus between an individual engaged in a conflict and those not so engaged would be impossible.[3] The entry into irony, by establishing consensus along the line of the primary relationship through the shared joke, allows the rejection of the secondary relationship without danger to the primary. The ironic style comes a good deal into interactions engaging persons whose status is insecure or vague, and is operated especially by persons in motion through esteem systems. It may often be sequentially related to banter. There comes a period in the career of the social or occupational success when the status in a group or clique or cabal useful and significant at an earlier stage has to be safeguarded on occasions by banter, and a later period when it has to be rejected by irony. The behaviour of successful Trade Union leaders and industrialists who become successful politicians may follow such a pattern as may that of women making successful marriages, children emerging from street playgroups, schoolboys being made prefects, students being appointed to the University staff. It is displayed typically in some middle-class treatment of Negroes and Jews, in the treatment of some adult children by parents and of some parents by their adult children. Fundamentally, its use is in those situations when primary status has to be protected without disrupting the social organisation in which both primary and secondary statuses are involved. A second illustration, drawn from the same milieu as the first, may demonstrate more clearly the operation of this particular style of manipulating consensus.

> The manager of a small branch factory of a large concern was at the head office talking over current difficulties of selling his particular product with the sales manager and the general manager. The branch had been through a difficult period of building up production, and the rather unexpected shrinkage of the market was causing its head some concern; the discussion was therefore being carried on seriously, that is, each assumed an equally serious attitude in advancing his views. The office was closed, and there was consequently less pressure for decisions as a result of this particular discussion, but there was obvious unity in the acceptance of the purpose of the discussion and of its importance. After some time, the chairman looked in. The chairman was a man of fairly wide industrial interests and with a growing public reputation. He listened in silence for a minute and then turned to the general manager and said, 'But, Frank, I am right, aren't I, in thinking that sales of this particular job don't matter so much? You were saying, weren't you, a couple of days ago, that you weren't worried about selling this particular job. We had plenty of use to make of the space if it was scaled down.' After the embarrassed pause which this entry provoked, the chairman rephrased the statement, using his normal, rapid, rather emphatic delivery, but winking broadly at the branch manager and the sales manager. These two became involved in the amusement which continued through several variations of the same theme, to none of which, naturally enough, could the general manager find any sufficient response. In the end, the general manager entered the amusement and the situation dissolved. There was, of course, no attempt to reconcile the attitude of involvement displayed by the general manager in the earlier part of the discussion with the markedly dissociated opinion betrayed by the chairman.

The ironic elements in the situation were the sharing of the joke with the others present, including the observer, and the superficial attitude of association with the general manager in clarifying the situation. According to the present interpretation, the chairman was engaged in rejecting a secondary status implied in a high-up, policy-making, clique relationship between himself and a man in a subordinate position in the concern, and asserting a primary status clear above all three other members of the organisation present, a status, that is, in which association with the sales manager and a branch manager could be treated by him, on occasion, as equivalent or primary as well as secondary to that between himself and the general manager. Had he kept silent, he would have accepted the clique relationship implied in the secret knowledge.[4]

This sort of occasion occurs as one among many. To treat it in isolation is to give it, as far as the actors were concerned, an utterly disproportionate significance. Other occasions would, in fact, display quite other or even contrary significance for the status of the people involved. Interactions between members of an enduring community take on a regulatory or cybernetic character, especially when, as in an industrial concern, status changes are frequent.

Second, the occasion for the use of the safeguards operating through banter and irony appears only when two discrete status positions are presented to an individual simultaneously. It was perfectly possible for the clique members to occupy unreservedly and securely their status positions within the clique when interaction situations included only other members of the clique; it was similarly possible for them to act out the roles appropriate to their status within the larger groups of the organisation in the absence of other members of the clique. And it is quite possible for no need for safeguarding to arise even though the clique and the major group is represented in the situation, provided that no threat to the primary status emerges from the situation.

We carry with us the capacity for acting out a number of roles, for occupying a variety of status positions. A function of that capacity is to keep the roles and status positions discrete – to act out a role in which we follow modes of behaviour more or less inappropriate to other roles. The foregoing sections have reviewed the procedures usually followed when this inappropriateness becomes actually embarrassing. Normally, of course, roles are acted out in separation and without any of the embarrassment, social or moral, which may result from their juxtaposition in the same interaction situation.

In terms of social structure, cities are arenas for status-gaining or status-changing activity. They can be so by virtue of the discreteness of social institutions in them, a discreteness which is demonstrated in the functional differentiation of urban areas and in the demarcation of clearly defined sectors in the life-space of the individual. Prestige or status can be improved much more easily in one sector than in all, in one institution than in all. Occupational promotions are worked out separately in terms of improvements in class status, in prestige within the clique and so on. The embarrassments usually attendant upon change of role which may have to be overcome by banter and irony are in fact mostly avoided by resigning from one milieu or group and gaining admission to another. Status gains, that is, are not usually registered within the same groups, but by movement between groups. Urban society, because of the discreteness and multiplicity of its institutions, provides perpetual opportunities of escape from the embarrassments of a new or challenged status.

For instance, in interviews with some fifteen members of the executive grades in a factory in a large town, it appeared that more than half had moved house within two years of obtaining their biggest rise. In most cases also, the rise in occupational status had itself involved a substantial lateral move in the organisation, and in some, a move from one city to another.

In terms of a cultural tradition framed in terms of community status, this discreteness of status positions looks as if individuals in different status positions behaved as though they were different persons. This characteristic of urban society has given rise to a number of speculations about its schizophrenic nature. 'As if' behaviour in urban society is so functionally necessary that it has to be arranged for even when two different statuses are occupied in two groups with virtually the same membership. In those cases cited above in which there was still overlapping between, for example, neighbour-group and work-group, the shift in occupational status was treated by an 'as if' arrangements until a move of residence could be made. As one man, who had risen rapidly to the position of deputy departmental manager but who still lived in a housing estate near the works, put it, 'Jock's all right in the cinema queue, but it's Mr Cullen on the shop floor. If any of them call me "Jock", then I know they're trying to start something.'

The conditions affecting similar situations in small communities are different. There is no possibility of maintaining groups so discrete that status changes can be made in one sector and then validated in others. Thus status gains in occupation, sport, political and church groups, in clubs and associations, and even through marriage tend to remain isolated. In contrast with the city-factory executives, men who had risen to foreman, department manager and higher ranks in a small town factory all retained first-name relationships with the work people – not only those whom they had previously worked alongside, but newcomers also. The only cases in which promotion had been followed by a change in residence were those facilitated by the existence of a group of 'firm's houses' reserved for managerial staff. It was noticeable that people at managerial level recruited directly from large cities tended to use, in their relationships with work people, the behavioural cues and status symbols current in urban society, and also to remain conscious of their stranger status for periods of up to twenty years residence in the town.

'As if' arrangements of another kind are therefore necessary in local communities, this time being directed against the acknowledgement of a particular status dissociated in rank from the community status – the position occupied in the esteem system of the whole community. In terms of the present analysis, this indicates that no break in membership is permitted; consensus has to be maintained in all interactions between members of the community. (Thus, while banter is permitted – indeed a frequent – style, irony is not permitted, and when used isolates the actor, not the victim, from the primary group.)

> During one period of field work in a factory in a small town, I had occasion to transcribe certain figures and other records kept in the office of a departmental manager in a factory. One afternoon, a conversation with the manager led to his talking about the effects of promotion on the behaviour of different men in the factory, and eventually, to something of a diatribe against one particular person who had moved up into an executive position the year before. He had tried to get support for his promotion from everybody, had blackened the man who was leaving and whose post he hoped to fill, had gone into local politics on the same side as the divisional manager, had displayed unpleasant anxiety when the time came for the decision. Now, despite his fulsome affability, he was unpopular with his colleagues, was looked down on by those lower down as a talebearer, and so on. All this was delivered with gestures and emphasis distinctly more lively than previously in the conversation, which ended with this episode, both of us

returning to separate desks. Later in the afternoon, he telephoned the man of whom he had been speaking; there was a question about the allocation of a morning's time put in by a shiftworker in one or the other of their departments. The whole matter, which could easily have been one of dispute, was handled with the greatest mateyness and ease; first names were used, there was appreciably no sense of effort in maintaining the demonstration of friendliness; there was no over-emphasis, nor, on the other hand, any discrepancy between facial expression and words or tone of voice; each other's account of the facts was fully accepted and agreement quickly reached.

Inside the space of one hour, my companion had displayed quite marked enmity and equally well-marked friendship towards the same person. There was, as far as I could judge, no suspicion of awareness that there was any incompatibility between the two episodes – both were acted through as natural expressions of two distinct roles.

In addition to the safeguard styles of banter and irony, and the means of avoidance possible in urban society, there exist the devices of 'as if' arrangements by which difficulties in interaction encountered by the discrepancy between status positions occupied by the same individual may be surmounted. 'As if' arrangements may be subsumed under the general heading of polite fictions. The arrangements are in general directed toward the exclusion from the terms of interaction of any status occupied by a participant which is incompatible with the establishment of the consensus necessary for participant membership alongside the rest of the group.

Role displacement – the substitution of an entirely new, incompatible role for another – is as familiar a feature of the careers of most people as physiological change, and occurs as a well-marked aspect of the process of socialisation. But what also occurs in socialisation is a change in behaviour within the same role. While expectations of behaviour change with roles when the child moves out of his position in a family situation to the street group or the school or the extended family, expectations also change when the child reaches certain ages; actions greeted with the pleasant attention of laughter or affectionate remonstrance at eighteen months may arouse much less pleasant responses at three years, and violence at a later age. Socialisation can indeed be seen as a process by which society continually raises standards on the role of the child in this way.

The shift of behavioural patterns within the same role is

typical not only of the socialisation process, but also of other constellations of institutionalised behaviour. In Scotland, where Sunday is marked out with special behaviour and symbols by a significantly large proportion of the population, role-behaviour in the family, the extended family and in the residential sub-community, undergoes considerable change of a cyclical character. Other changes are also regularly observable at other times in the week – for instance, on Saturday afternoon, and at special periods in the year such as the summer holiday and festival days. It is not possible to regard changes of this sort as extensions of some role, since there is implicit in them the same inconsistency with the normal, everyday patterns of behaviour. There is, in fact, the displacement of behavioural features which is normally associated with change of role.

In small communities, social situations of different kinds (at work, in the public house, in church, at sport, at home, in clubs) so often involve the same group membership that, as Kaufman has shown,[5] status positions in each of them are merged in, and indistinguishable from, a generalised community status. Nevertheless, institutional behaviour varies with each different situation encountered by the individual in a small community, and not merely with the overt purpose of the group.

In all situations that admit of typical, institutionalised, behaviour, such behaviour has to be validated consensually. Change from one form of behaviour to another, whether through a cycle of status positions or through a cycle of institution, denotes a change from one application of consensus to another. The establishment of consensus is mediated by the exchange of behavioural cues, sometimes obvious – as in the case of children when emerging from the school gates – sometimes extremely subtle – as in Quaker business meetings, in which unanimity has to be achieved and voting procedures are not admitted. What is conveyed *through* such behavioural cues is the new range of permitted behaviour and its further modal definition through approval and disapproval. The outcome of the establishment of consensus is membership, not merely of the group involved in the interaction, but of a type, a category identified with some precision in the schema of the social system with which a person socialised into it operates. The congruence of such classificatory schemas in an interaction through consensus allocates a status to the participant individuals.

The classificatory schema is more refined and detailed in respect of behavioural categories lying close to the individual, that is, more familiar, than at the periphery. Social distance straitens behaviour in interaction because the categories involved are peripheral to the individuals concerned, and are prescribed by a minimal range of norms. Interaction of this kind runs to stereotype behaviour or more properly, cliché behaviour. Foreign visitors to a country are often disconcerted to find not only that they are being treated as stereotype English-men, Americans or Indians but that they are in fact behaving like stereotype Englishmen, Americans or Indians. At the other extreme, interaction between persons socialised into the same classificatory schema either through membership in the same local community or through long intimacy is prescribed by a maximal range of norms and runs to spontaneous behaviour.

Spontaneity in interaction springs from a consensus so comprehensive that the behaviour possible in the circumstances is no less than what each socialised individual would condone or approve in himself. Thus spontaneous interaction is determined by the existence of a consensus applying to all norms of social behaviour of the system into which the individuals concerned have been socialised.

Between spontaneous and cliché behaviour in interaction lies an array of possible categories of action identified in common usages 'role-playing'; such categories are marked by a restrictive, delineating quality, with criteria to distinguish appropriate from inappropriate behaviour. The criteria are of two kinds. One applies to the place in the value system occupied by the institution in which the interaction situation occurs; the other applies to the places in the esteem system occupied by the participant actors. With the first kind, institutional behaviour gains in complexity and in variability the higher in the scale of value it lies. One may, for example, compare the variety of forms of religious action in the Middle Ages, especially the inclusion of spontaneous activity in art forms of poetry, music, painting and dancing with the relatively specific nature of religious action now. The higher the place occupied by an institutional form, the greater the number of social norms relevant to behaviour in situations occurring in the institution. As for the second criterion, it has been sufficiently established that the esteem system of a group, community or society, is structured according to the social norms prevailing among their members. In G. C. Homan's words, the persons coming closest to achieving the group norms hold the highest social rank.[6]

The norms which apply to any particular interaction are a selection from the whole range applying to the whole social-ised behaviour common to the participants, the selection being determined by the institutional character of the interaction and by the rank of the participants. The way in which the norms are mediated into action – the way in which people make them-selves aware of how to act in the situation – is by the operation of consensus. The classificatory schema referred to above may then be viewed as a hierarchy of consensus subtending the norms of behaviour into which individuals are socialised. Differences in the social behaviour of a person can be regarded as differences in the *number* as well as the *kind* of norms involved in the situation. Cliché behaviour involves fewest norms, requiring little consensus. Spontaneity involves most norms, requiring maximum consensus. Between these two extremes lies social action involving varying ranges of norms determined by the values accorded to the situation and the participants and requiring an appropriate degree of consensus.

The phenomenon of the 'polite fiction' appears now as an intrinsic element in social behaviour. Status exists as member-ship first of the group in which the position is occupied and second of a rank order in the esteem system; status is realised only in such membership. The prerequisite of membership is consensus extending through the group in interaction. Con-sensus is necessary at whatever normative level interaction occurs, subtending the range of norms to which behaviour in it relates. In passing from one interaction to another, the individual moves from one status to another. This usually involves both a displacement of membership and a shift in the range of social norms engaged. Both changes must be validated by the estab-lishment of consensus in the new situation as in the old. This is accomplished naturally and with complete freedom in most cases. But, as we have seen, occasions arise when the member-ships involved in two separate, although proximate, situations overlap. There is then presented a dilemma situation of two possible ranges of norms of differing coverage, each with its appropriate level of consensus. Such accidents are quite frequent in most individual's lives. When two people with a fairly intimate relationship allowing for an approximation to spontaneous behaviour are joined by a third acquaintance, the change to a new consensus subtending a more restricted range of norms is almost always automatic and unthinking. Not to execute the change, or to revert to the previous consensus and normative level is, in any society, bad manners, an affront to the newcomer which lies in rejecting the status-membership claim implied in his presence. It may well be, of course, that experience of occasions on which such rejection has occurred accidentally or intentionally, or when cues have been misinterpreted as rejection, arouses some fleeting sense of artificiality in making adjustments of consensus in this way. More definitely, 'as if' arrangements in which the two status memberships are occupied on different occasions in a group with the same participant members induce such a sense. In military service, the dual nature of the relationship of a superior officer or NCO with the group immediately under his command is given acknowledgement in the phrase 'on parade, on parade; off parade, off parade'.

Embarrassment arises through the failure to establish or maintain consensus about the range of social norms affecting behaviour in an interaction. It is potential typically in situations in which two statuses are presented simultaneously. Two devices are commonly used to avoid embarrassment. In one kind of situation dealt with in this paper, the status alternative to that occupied by a membership of the group dominant in the interaction is lower in the esteem system operating for the group; the ironic style admits of rejection of the lower status while safeguarding consensus through a joking relationship with the dominant group and the primary status within it, a consensus that might be broken by a display of bad manners. In the other kind of situation reviewed, the secondary status presented is also rejected, but safeguarded for the future, again through the joking relationship. We have called the two styles irony and banter, with some sense of straining ordinary usage, because the meanings of the two words contain, without precision it is true, the implications of a consensus withheld from the recipient in the case of irony,[7] and shared with him in the case of banter.

NOTES AND REFERENCES

1. Talcott Parsons, *The Social System*, Tavistock Publications Ltd, 1952, p. 25. It will be noted that Parsons does at any rate drop the dubious element of expectation usually brought into the definition of 'role'.
2. It should be emphasised that we are here using the term purely in its 'social location' sense, not in the sense of the 'situations vacant' column or of the census.
3. Although consensus may be replaced by loyalty, in which the consensus itself has become institutionalised, and the relationship safeguarded.
4. See K. H. Wolff, *The Sociology of George Simmel*, The Free Press, 1950, pp. 330–8.
5. Harold F. Kaufman, 'An Approach to the Study of Urban Stratification', *American Sociological Review*, 17 (August 1952), p. 430.
6. G. C. Homans, *The Human Group*, London, 1951, p. 179.
7. Fowler, in distinguishing the correct usages of humour, wit, sarcasm, irony, etc., presents them in an interesting table, in which the aim or motive of irony is identified as 'exclusiveness', its province as 'statement of facts', its method or means as 'mystification' and the audience as 'an inner circle'. (H. W. Fowler, *A Dictionary of Modern English Usage*, Oxford, 1926, p. 241.)

4

Cliques and Cabals

It will be apparent, I hope, that this is not simply a re-vamping of the observations which provided the empirical material for the previous paper 'Friends, Enemies and the Polite Fiction', but what I suppose amounts to a sociological analysis of it as opposed to a socio-psychological study. In any case, the findings are *categorically* distinct, although they are also, I trust, compatible. It is in fact quite frequently the case that the same observational material can yield more than one coherent set of analytical findings; usually, though, it is more convenient, or less confusing for the reader, to settle on different settings or different groups of people for different analytical purposes.

We are familiar with the idea of the clique, the group of inti-mates who are drawn together by similarities of age, attitude – by any manifestation of shared sub-cultural norms. The groups differ in desirability, exclusiveness and importance, but mem-bership is always a matter of choice and election – one doesn't think of neighbours or kinsfolk or workmates as a clique. Around this description is a distinct penumbra of depreciation that goes with the term; we rarely, unless we are being brazen about it, own to being in a clique – it is always of the cosy relationships displayed by others that we use the word, and in

First published as 'The Reference of Conduct in Small Groups: Cliques and Cabals in Occupational Milieux', in *Human Relations*, vol. 8, no. 4, 1955, pp. 467–86.

doing so rate the value of membership in it deliberately lower than would the people in the clique. 'Cabal' has similar connotations of a special set of shared norms and of disapprobation by others, but it is used with special reference to groups seeking power, or exercising it in a secretive, and therefore illicit, way. 'Confidant' is reserved for a special form of the pair of friends, with secrets as both the basis and the content of intimacy.

While the distinctions between these three kinds of group are available in the common-usage terms clique, cabal (or caucus), and confidant, such distinctions have been ignored in the literature of sociology.[1]

For some time past, however, they have proved useful to the writer in distinguishing certain types of behaviour in segregative groups characteristic of working organisations. But an attempt to reintroduce such commonplace insights into statements about situations that would be acceptable to sociologists leads to a reconsideration of the function of such groups and the contrast they offer to larger membership groups and to reference groups.

The analysis presented here treats groups not as autonomous social forms but as necessary corollaries of certain kinds of conduct. They are actual assemblies of persons used by the individual to gain ends that are private, if not peculiar to himself, in the same way that reference groups, ideologies and so forth are invoked by the individual at an abstract level to realise certain specific ends. What we have to say about cliques and cabals, therefore, is related conceptually to interpretations of reference group behaviour and of other categories in which the status and conduct of the individual and their connotations are sociologically of first significance.

MEMBERSHIP GROUPS AND REFERENCE GROUPS

The development of ideas about reference groups has taken place at the same time as a theoretical development in social anthropology that appears to have very similar connotations. Lineages are now being treated, by some writers, as networks of relationships arranged in staged ramifications from the individual which exists in conceptual terms rather than as an ineluctable datum of social life in primitive society. A lineage, according to this view, is a frame of reference for the jural status of an individual. Specific relationships, and the actions they endorse or prohibit, which are relevant to the gaining of specific ends, are brought above the threshold into interaction as they are required. For the individual, the relationships of kinship are the embodiment of a set of normative elements, invoked by him when faced with situations requiring sanctions for conduct.

This seems to me to be the implication of Fortes's review of the methodological significance of kinship studies in his 'Structure of Unilineal Descent Groups' (1953). He says: 'I do want to make it clear, though, that we do not think of a lineage as being just a collection of people held together by the accident of birth. A descent group is an arrangement of persons that serves the attainment of legitimate social and personal ends. These include the gaining of a livelihood, the setting up of a family and the preservation of health and well-being.' There is a similar implication in Leach's study of kinship terminology (1945). The relevance of this shift[2] in the theoretical view of kinship structure taken by social anthropologists to concurrent developments in the general theory of reference groups (Merton and Kitt (1950), Newcomb (1952), Sherif (1948)) is fairly obvious and will be exploited in the first part of the paper.

The new theoretical and research strategies made possible by these two concurrent developments in social anthropology and social psychology are not confined to work in the more generalised fields of social structure, social control and social process. Their impact is equally fruitful in the field of interaction, since they may enable studies to proceed outside the experimental room, once there is formulated a set of concepts that will allow a valid classification of behaviour into what is determined by membership of a group in interaction and what is determined by reference to other groups or categories. The contribution of this paper to such a formulation is the proposition that these two sociological forms are not dichotomous. Neither can be treated as a residual category of determinants when the other has been fully explored. Just as reference groups allow the individual to pursue ends in interaction with the sanction of norms other than those 'given' in the situation or manifest in the behaviour of others present, so do membership groups allow the individual to retreat from the controls and norms operating in a larger social milieu[3] through the media of reference groups.

So far as the study of groups in natural settings is concerned, there is no observable tendency to discriminate categories or functions, even where common usage, as we have said, gives a lead. Lloyd Warner, indeed, applied the term to all informal associations in 'Yankee City' (Warner and Lunt, 1941, pp. 350–2) and earlier (pp. 110–12). He apparently includes under the rubric of 'clique' involuntary (neighbour, kin) as well as voluntary groups. While he defines it as 'an intimate non-kin group, membership in which may vary in numbers from two to thirty or more people', he goes on to say: 'The clique may or may not include biologically related persons', and 'It may be composed of employees of a factory, an ethnic group, the adolescents of a neighbourhood or school, or of the members of a fraternity, political organisation or church.' Homans finds an astonishing identity of structure and function among all groups (1951). The procedures of sociometry define a clique as any group of three or more members all of whom make mutual choices of each other when naming the persons with whom they prefer to associate in any specified activity (Moreno, (1953)). Roughly the same criteria were applied to the identification of two cliques among the fourteen men observed in the Bank Wiring Room researches at Hawthorne (Roethlisberger and Dickson, 1939). Sherif writes: 'Under the strain of adolescence one's stability is shaken with crisis, insecurity, and frustration in various degrees. Caught in this situation, adolescents gravitate toward each other. They try to find comfort in their own intimate relationships. They share secrets. They develop common tastes in movies, books, dancing, adventure, in relation to persons, groups, etc. With all of these common ties they form a group, a clique or gang, of two, three or more, with the unmistakable properties of an informal group structure' (1948, p. 332).

This indeterminacy that attaches to the term when it is rendered almost synonymous with group appears to increase when the concept of 'group' itself is divided into membership group and reference group (Sherif; Merton and Kitt, op. cit.), which may be identical but are sometimes mutually exclusive and sometimes non-comparable social forms. 'Comparing himself with his unmarried associates in the Army, he (the married man), could feel that induction demanded greater sacrifices from him than from them; and comparing himself with his married civilian friends he could feel that he had been called on for sacrifices which they were escaping altogether. Hence the married man, on the average, was more likely than others to come into the Army with reluctance and, possibly, a sense of injustice' (Stouffer et al., 1949). The reference groups include not only groups ('unmarried associates') to which the 'average married man' *cannot* belong, but impersonal social categories (single men) along with membership groups (married civilian friends).

It is at this point, however, that the common-usage distinctions that sociology ignores begin to re-emerge as pertinent. Merton and Kitt (op. cit., p. 86) point out that the norms or attitudes appropriate to a reference group other than the 'in-group' may be equivalent to 'nonconformity to the norms of the in-group', and go on to exploit Sherif's thesis of the strain on the individual and on the 'in-group' itself of 'discrepancies between the two, i.e. the cases in which individuals actually live in one group but aspire to belong to, or are made to relate to, another' (1948, p. 106). In their discussion of 'The American Soldier' material to which Merton and Kitt's essay is devoted, attention is restricted to cases of actual or potential secession from the membership group, and the implications this has for the functional theories on which Merton's treatment hinges. There are, however, adjustments other than secession that are marked by explicit references to the norms of larger or more remote sectors of society than the immediate fellows of the individual. In the first place, it has been found that the overt reference to the norms of such larger groups occurs in the main where situations confront the individual with a choice of inconsistent roles (Eisenstadt, 1954), or when some new demands are made on the individual (p. 202). Second, although Eisenstadt relates these findings again simply to movement through the social structure – social mobility or socialisation – Bott has gone on to relate the suggestion, in Eisenstadt's essay, that the reference group is *invoked* by the individual in order to resolve a dilemma, to Leach's parallel treatment of myths as serving the purpose of validating the status claims of the narrator (1954, p. 265). 'People use class reference groups for making both comparisons and evaluations in the widest social context, but their usages vary according to the immediate social situation and the specific purpose of the comparisons and evaluations' (Bott, 1954, p. 268).

This traffic of references from the present situation made by the individual is not one-way. Just as reference groups other than the primary group existing here and now for the individual are invoked in order to enable him to resume or maintain control of the social situation in which he finds himself, even in the sense of 'explaining' the situation to himself or another (e.g. the interviewer in the cases analysed by Bott), so there are primary groups themselves that are entered for the sake of the support they afford in social situations. I want, that is, to regard clique, cabal and confidant pair not as particular structural forms, not as topographical features randomly scattered about the social landscape, but as media of specific kinds of behaviour designed to control specific kinds of situation. Not only do membership groups act as the media for socialisation for the individual, through which he can tap the resources of the wider society for sanctioning behaviour and formulating the norms that he wants operative, they may also exist to afford retreats from the norms of the wider society when they involve demands the individual cannot meet.

To put it rather more straightforwardly: if we are observing behaviour of people in a particular milieu – say a factory or a university department – we shall find certain conduct definable as in accordance with the norms of the milieu; other conduct will be acted out as sanctioned or governed by the norms of groups or categories outside the milieu – by reference groups; other behaviour still will be sanctioned or governed by the norms of groups forming particular social enclaves within the milieu. Reference-group behaviour, that is, can invoke groups smaller than the milieu and enclosed by it, as well as groups larger than the milieu and embracing it. We shall have reason to modify this statement later, but the two-way direction of reference, the instrumental nature of group membership, and the determination of the behaviour typical of the group by the contemporary social situation in the milieu are all essential elements.

OCCUPATIONAL CLIQUES AND CABALS

As I have said, the utility of the common-usage terms that form the subject of this paper appeared first in connection with research in factories. The distinction between the two forms of group first made itself apparent by following, in the most striking manner, the age-grading of management and supervisory staff in a factory.

Most members of the top management set were a year or two each side of forty years old. So, at the period of the big initial developments in the techniques on which production is now based, most of them were about twenty-five years old. The higher management group tended to regard twenty-five as the age when people were at the top of their inventive ability; older members of the group entertained doubts about their continued value to the industry and the firm beyond the age of forty. This idiosyncratic form of age-grading was reflected throughout the organisation as a value element in the ascription of personal status, in the sense used by Marshall (1953), and deepened the rift between those members of the firm, management and workers, who had grown up in the traditional milieu of the engineering industry, with its stable skill structure and standardised functional roles and those who were occupationally native to the new engineering. With the peak of the age-grade structure below forty-five years, to be markedly older than one's colleagues at any level was presumptive evidence of failure of some sort; just as subordinates who were younger as well as of lower rank constituted a bigger than usual threat to status security.

The members of the management organisation were in any case markedly insecure. The firm was in a rapidly expanding industry, and the degree of elasticity that the situation appeared to require was achieved by a refusal, partly a matter of conscious policy, to define status and functions. The norm was promotion; and the way to promotion lay not only in making the best of the tasks that were handed to one, but by perceiving and acquiring responsibility for new tasks, and, frequently, by encroaching on those of others.

The insecurities aroused by this situation produced a wide variety of responses in behaviour, especially a number of devices designed to increase relative security either by trying to acquire more control over the situation through promotion or by increasing the insecurity of others. In one respect, the response was specific and distinctive. Over a period of some months, it was possible to distinguish groups of intimates who – in the canteen, in the corridors after lunch and after the factory stopped at night – constantly gravitated together into collusive-looking conversations. Some of the groups were of older men, others of younger; to all appearances, they were otherwise similar in the status of members, in activity, in structure. But this identity ended there. There were distinct differences in the content of conversation, in the attitudes displayed and ultimately in the uses of membership.

In the groups of older men, the conversation reflected a tendency to contract out of the situation as far as they could. Their lack of acceptance of the novelties in the situation, their peculiar position in the age-grade structure, their previous experience and qualifications led them to concentrate on making their functions better defined and led them into those functions that had more definition; management of the production of the 'bread-and-butter' lines was in the hands of noticeably older people. But these positions were also out of the main run of career opportunities – they had, to this extent, resigned from the race. Their cliques had a specifically protective, reassurance purpose, the reassurance expressing itself in a critical dissociation from the firm; features of the organisation – the bonus system, rate-fixing, progress meetings, the formal communication system – were mentioned depreciatingly as 'the way the firm does things'. The factory's chief product was scrap; the place was full of youngsters from universities who knew nothing about industry and yet told experienced craftsmen what to do; the craftsmen who were made laboratory technicians were spoilt for good work thereafter. Most of the direct criticism of the lack of definition of status and function came from the older group; they thought of their jobs in contractual terms, being employees of a firm in which they were prepared to do certain specified work and to undertake specified duties, in return for a salary, rather than in terms of responsibility shared with colleagues in a professional group for the discharge of the common task that the whole firm was set.

Younger groups in the factory included many who were without formal qualifications; they were more mixed, both in their occupational derivation and in their attitude to technical qualifications, than older groups, who made occupational qualifications (as engineers, draughtsmen, skilled tradesmen) much more central to their status. The younger executive generally felt he was doing better in the organisation than he would in other firms. He had spent his career-formative years in the firm. He was favourably placed in the age-grade system. Thus he identified himself and his interests much more with the firm, and felt committed to the organisation. He did not on that account accept 'the ways of doing things' that were criticised by members of older groups but, instead of citing them to demonstrate dissociation from the organisation, rather discussed them as features of policy emanating from this or that person and subject to improvement or change if sufficient pressure or persuasion were applied. The characteristic direction taken by his response to insecurity, that is, was towards improving his power over the situation in which his insecurity arose rather than towards withdrawal from it. For example, there was a distinct resemblance between the situation of an older office manager and a young departmental manager, both of whom saw their jobs and responsibilities as having lost importance in recent years and both of whom complained openly of the absence of titles, of the absence of formal definition of responsibilities and tasks, of the absence of a 'sort of family tree that shows you where you are in the organisation'. Yet the older man discussed the matter in terms that reflected a view of himself as the helpless victim of a system – contrasting the system, and the position of people like himself in it, with what obtained in other firms – while the other referred to unspecified ways in which he and others in a 'propaganda group' were trying to 'improve things'.

The formation of mutually exclusive groups by older and younger managers and supervisors was a noticeable feature of the social system of the factory. Those groups, composed of the younger sort, that accepted the system and values of the present organisation while trying to improve their situation in it: such groups I identified as cabals. Others, composed of older men, dissociated themselves from the system, and, while they were by no means without hope or prospect of further promotion, had come to accept a view of the odds against themselves as pretty high: jobs 'outside' – in other firms – were mentioned as among the possibilities for the future by older men, never by younger managers in the factory.

CHARACTERISTICS AND SIGNIFICANCE OF BEHAVIOUR IN
CLIQUES AND CABALS

It was the groups of older men for which the term clique seemed more proper. They were distinct not only from cabals but from other formations, notably the interest-groups, such as that composed of a number of juniors who attended evening training courses or lectures together, and whose association was 'legitimate' in terms of the factory organisation, of the industry at large, and of society itself, since they were in common pursuit of technical proficiency (see below, pp. 83–4). It is the peculiarity of the clique and of the cabal that membership is not legitimate, or not quite legitimate; that their experience and participation in them are, to however mild a degree, infractions of the rules and the order prevailing in a particular milieu.

The milieu, the social area, is, therefore, related to the clique in a determinate fashion; and this we find to be so in other settings than the factory. Cliques in factories, offices and universities; in clubs and societies; among street neighbours, school-children, service units and others are known as cliques only in relation to that specific status. If one distinguishes cliques from cabals in the way proposed, then the role that involves clique membership is one that accommodates a degree of failure in the status. The clique in the factory then appears as an organised retreat from occupational status.[4]

Failure and insecurity, terms that have been used earlier in this paper, are both extremely difficult to employ consistently in this kind of analysis. Nobody, of course, accepts fairly and squarely the fact of having failed to perform adequately in a status to which he laid claim. He furnishes himself and others with assurances that he in fact succeeded but the system was rigged against him, or that failure is not final, but an episode in a progress towards success, or that the status is one he has not really claimed, or one in which it would be vulgar to succeed. There are other devices, too, by which the annihilation of a self-image can be avoided. Some of these have been enumerated by Goffman (1952). But all these devices need collusion – the fact of not having failed needs the testimony of some other members of the same culture. It is this kind of collusive mutual support that is provided in cliques.

Insecurity is just as slippery a term. It is properly a doubt about whether or not performance in a role is really controlling the social situation as it is meant to do. It is not so much ignorance about the reaction of others involved – a condition that we recognise as smugness or self-assurance or plain ineptitude – as knowledge that in some connections one's actions directed towards controlling the situation (i.e. other people's further action, especially in regard to oneself) are only partially successful. Insecurity, that is to say, is based on knowledge, and the behaviour typical of the insecure is that which is made in an endeavour to increase control of the situation either directly or covertly but in any case illegitimately, according to the code prevailing for other participants. It is often possible for membership of a group to promote such illegitimate control, either by the fact of membership or by allowing for strategies to be practised in co-operation with others. Such groups are cabals; they offer the possibility of illegitimate control and thus of success.

DOMINANCE AND COUNTER-SYSTEMS

Before we proceed to some account of the characteristic forms of behaviour in cliques and cabals, some observations are necessary on the style of behaviour peculiar to cliques and, to a lesser extent, cabals. The collusion that is sought in membership is not only the exchange of tokens of esteem more or less false according to the currency of the occupation at large. Also involved is intimacy, a lack of the constraint or guardedness maintained in the occupational milieu, an intimacy that, being obtainable only within the shelter of the clique, makes for a comfortable, expansive friendliness. Furthermore, the support given by the clique to the individual consists largely in its *differing* in many ways from the milieu in which it exists. It appears to act as a system running counter to the larger system of the organisation of society itself.

As individuals in our society, we know that there are a number of different levels of behaviour appropriate to the degree of mutual knowledge existing between the people present. This is something rather distinct from the differences in roles. It is related more to the idea of social distance and strangeness. The more socially distant two individuals are, the more straitened their behaviour is in each other's company. Restriction of behaviour implies a resort to modes of speech and action that are widely accepted – a lowest common denominator of conduct. Freedom of behaviour, on the other hand, is understood to allow of more possibilities – of a wider variety of actions 'in the circumstances' than would be open to us in a less-known social environment.

For each individual, then, we can postulate a range of levels of behaviour extending from spontaneous to restricted. These levels correspond to degrees of intimacy in relationship – the more intimacy, the more openness. Moreover, we can relate these levels to the ways in which individuals orientate themselves to situations by referring to the norms they think are held in groups other than the one immediately present (Eisenstadt, 1954), Restricted behaviour will be appropriate to situations in unfamiliar milieux. Here the relevant norms for the conduct of the individual will be those thought to be most widely held or most widely valued in the society to which he belongs; spontaneous behaviour will be appropriate to situations for which the norms are held to apply to the immediate milieu of the individual.

The behaviour of individuals in the same broadly defined categories – the urban professional class, the lower working class, university students – tends to gravitate to one level in that range when they are with other members of that class, to other levels with members of their families, to yet other levels when they are with clients, or welfare workers, or members of the university staff, and so on. Among these levels there is normally one that bulks very large in the individual's total range of activity. In the case of individuals in occupations usually designated as middle class, that main level in their range of behaviour is fixed by their occupation. So that a salesman, a factory manager, a bank official or a university lecturer will not so much tend to maintain his occupational role – as it often seems – on a good number of occasions outside his occupational context, but will, rather, tend to behave at the level of spontaneity or restriction and with the degree of intimacy or distance customary in his occupational role.

The spread of a particular level of behaviour – or style – outside the milieu in which it is appropriately connected with a

specific role can be described as dominance. Since cliques
appear to be refuges in social areas in which importance attaches
to failure and success, they exist also as retreats from the dominant manner. We can say that in so far as a person performs
successfully in a role important to him, he will be satisfied to
use the style he has developed for it inside and outside the role.
But sometimes an individual fails, or is doubtful about his success, or has rejected his occupational role because it has become
devalued, or because it is a second choice anyway. The failure
will seek to opt out of his occupational role in collusion with
others – he will want to present the occupational role as being
less important to him. This can be done only by establishing a
level of intimacy that will allow him to act more spontaneously
and to find more spontaneous, less restricted reactions to his
behaviour in others. In this way, by putting success, so to speak,
in quotation marks, the greater intimacy and 'naturalness' prevailing in the clique affords a status to its members that can be
regarded as more desirable than the occupational status from
which the individual temporarily retreats; it is indeed superior
in that wider tolerances for conduct and the securities of
friendship endow the status with a higher 'reality' value.

The function of retreat is emphasised by the fact that the lead
in cliques is taken often enough by the comic, or by the man
who has made the clearest rejection of his occupational role
and can indulge in most open criticism of the structure and
manner of the occupation, and of people successfully performing in occupational roles.

The clique thus appears as a form of counter-system, a characteristic element in our society in which patterns of behaviour
appropriate to dominant positions find their response in countervailing patterns of conduct developed among the less privileged or less powerful positions. It should be borne in mind
that elements of conduct usually labelled 'sub-cultural' are not
merely different from the 'culture' recognised as dominant but
are contradictory (e.g. the significance of the family in working-
class and middle-class life). Working-class culture may be
interpreted as a 'counter-system' to middle-class culture, and
not merely as a variant sub-culture, a dialect form of the standard culture. It maintains itself by constant hostile interaction
with the dominant culture. The *élites* of such counter-systems
are the persons offering the most striking contrast available, so

far as norms and style of behaviour are concerned, to the appropriate dominant group (among working men *vis-à-vis* adults, school-children *vis-à-vis* class teachers, etc.). Of special interests in this connection is the general thesis advanced by W. R. Bion (1950) concerning the choice of leader by psychotherapeutic groups at times when he, the physician, dislodges himself from the leadership status ascribed to him. 'The new leader is, in my experience, without exception, a thoroughgoing psychiatric case' (p. 397) . . . 'the group, when left to spontaneous behaviour, chooses as its leader . . . its most ill member' (p. 399).

Criticism – usually expressed ironically – of the occupational successes and of the system in which such people are successful is the basis of the consensus existing between members of the clique, and the content of most conversation is often a repetitive sequence of comic anecdotes about successful persons or, even more pertinently, about people striving too earnestly to be successful. These unfortunates are twice damned. Not only do they accept their occupational status and their role and the constriction of behavioural manner unquestioningly, but they fail to establish any control at all over their position relative to others – they can't make the grade. The comic manner is directed exclusively outwards; within the clique, people treat each other seriously except on occasions when outsiders are present and banter can be used on a fellow member, and except where the clique is fortunate enough to possess a butt – somebody to whom clique membership is all-important and who is prepared not only to reject occupational success within the clique, but to forgo it outside the clique in order to take the lead in promoting spontaneous behaviour and intimate relationships. But the norm is a sarcastic or cynical disavowal of the values implicit in the occupation, an ironic criticism of the working of the system and of the people gaining higher occupational status or working to secure their present one, and gleeful derision of the failures earnestly striving for success and unaware of their designation.

The ironic criticism prevalent in cliques is a heightened form of gossip, which is a much more common institutional form. In essentials, gossip is passing judgements – disapproving, depreciating or condemning – on the behaviour of others. It is an indispensable instrument for fixing one's own occupational prestige, or for finding an acceptable style. Collusion in gossip offers the guarantee that, because one is united with at least one other in judging A to be deficient in technical knowledge, B to have made a stupid gaffe, C to be too sycophantic, D to spend too much time chatting in the canteen, the speaker and his hearer – compared with those others – are at least free from such faults. In gossip, speaker's and audience's status claims are underwritten, relative to those of people being discussed. In cliques, gossip criticism is normally couched in ironic terms, so that a joke is shared among the clique members at the expense of the outsider (Burns, (1953). The sharing of a joke is a universal shortcut to consensus, the clue being that laughing is a standard, universal and undifferentiated acknowledgement of incompatibilities in a situation that can be known only to those with at least the same sophisticated knowledge of the situation as is available to the speaker. The laugh indicates (a) common knowledge, (b) collusion with the speaker and the others laughing.[5]

Associations established in gossip are usually too indeterminate and impermanent to be called clique relationships; although there are always, among colleagues, distinctions drawn between those with whom one individual can safely gossip – i.e. be assured that his own relative status will be sustained by the comparison – and those with whom it is too risky. The behaviour typical of cliques is related to a need not so much to underwrite an occupational status as to gain reassurance about a status that is suspected to be lower in esteem than that to which initial claims may have been made, or lower than that of occupational peers.

Clique relationships are devised to fulfil their functions in a variety of ways. In another factory, for example, there was observable at the level of management immediately below the general manager a fairly marked absence of effective communication over many aspects of their work, together with a notable degree of sociability before and after lunch, and at other nonworking times. The chief executive was extremely authoritarian and inclined not only to restrict the functional responsibilities of his immediate subordinates, but to anticipate or set aside decisions when appealed to by men lower down the management hierarchy. Senior members of the staff complained of not being 'real' works managers, development engineers, office managers and so on. Their personal status was lower than what they felt to be normal to their occupations, and they were not able to discharge their functional roles effectively. Among other things, it was comparatively useless working out a system of communication with colleagues, since effective communication – i.e. the request for, or the undertaking of, specific tasks in response to shared information about requirements – was impossible; nothing could be done except through, or in association with, the factory manager. In reaction to the shrinkage in their status that this implied – a shrinkage patent to their own subordinates – they had developed a collusive withdrawal from responsibility displayed in shared jokes about the factory and about the members of staff seeking a profitable cabal relationship with the chief executive, and in sociable conversations about topics at some remove from their occupational interests.

In the clique, intimacy is institutionalised. There is a special style of behaviour recognised as appropriate to interaction between clique members; there are recognised topics which hinge on the gossip motifs, or which reinforce the latent rejection of occupational success and of the system in which success is secured. Content and style are frequently ritualised in catchphrase greetings, or more elaborately in patterns such as that mentioned by Logan Wilson (1942). 'In lesser colleges and universities where advancement is often largely a matter of seniority, the "dead wood" and otherwise objectionable members of the faculty provide a favourite indoor game for private faculty parties. This pastime is known as "Firing the Faculty". Each participant draws up a list of colleagues he would discharge if he were president, the winner being the person providing the list with the largest number of names found on other lists.'[6]

The clique appears to serve as a system of mutual defence for a set of people who are conscious of failure in a dominant role. The method of defence is to establish standards of reference by which the norms defining success in the role may be discounted. The new standards of reference are not, of course, peculiar to the clique; they are imported from other milieux, real or fancied, in which more sophisticated evaluations of success are made. But the norms of the clique are realised through interaction within the clique, given potency, for the time being, in excess of the norms prevailing in the dominant milieu of the occupation or organisation by their implication in more spontaneous behaviour: they must be 'more valid' because they are attached to 'more natural' or more friendly behaviour and relationships.

We have discussed the process by which failure according to the criteria prevailing in a factory – an organisational milieu – may be redressed. Redress is accomplished by treating the norms prevailing in the factory as a peculiar inversion of those obtaining outside, in the wider milieux of industrial occupations. It may be observed of clique behaviour in, say, academic, literary or artistic milieux, that such reference to a further, an 'ultimate', a 'true' set of norms – prevailing somewhere outside the milieu in which a status is being claimed – may be carried to any extreme. Where standards are in any case special or eclectic, clique reference may be made across the void of the milieu in which the clique exists, and in which failure has been indicated, to true criteria as resident in norms existing in posterity, 'in the eyes of God', or *sub specie aeternitatis*. These are perhaps more truly the last refuge of the individual who has failed to achieve the success or recognition to which he laid claim.

Cliques are never long-lived. In every case, the degree of intimacy and the content of discourse tend to become routinised, since they are defined largely by reaction against those prevailing in the dominant status. When this has developed far enough for it to become manifest to the clique that they are members not of an independent system with superior worth attached to its conduct and values, but members of a counter-system, sustained only by opposition to the major system of the milieu, then the greater validity ascribed to the clique judgements is seen to be spurious, and the clique breaks up.

CABALS AND THE LEGITIMACY OF SUCCESS

In its outward forms, which give the meaning to the common-usage term, the cabal differs little from the clique. But the identity is, as I have said, superficial. The gossip foundation is there, in occupational cabals, since it is the main content of non-technical communication between colleagues. But it is much less ironic, much more an attempt to plot and in particular to modify the prestige ratings – the personal status – of persons throughout the organisation. The cabal member strives to arrive at an estimate, continually redefined, of his own position in the esteem system, and to manoeuvre that position favourably for the future allocation of power and rewards.

The essential points distinguishing cabals from cliques are: (1) there are real status distinctions involved between cabal members. Leadership is important, and proximity to the leader is important; (2) the function of cabal membership is neither to redress occupational failure, nor to gain reassurance, but to promote further occupational success outside the cabal; (3) the relationship of the cabal to the outer milieu is not one of withdrawal or rejection, but of power, in which the cabal attempts to restructure situations and values in the interests of its members.

Often enough, membership alone is very useful. Membership of the right groups in political, literary and some professional worlds is sufficient to gain an unearned increment of status or prestige. To be in a cabal relationship with a powerful person in an organisation like a factory also means the possibility of access to information that is a secret from colleagues, and thus a source of power to oneself.

Cabals tried to capture important people in the factory by supplying information concerning the factory to them or by positioning themselves so that the information about the factory was usually checked with them. One of the most powerful cabals in the factory had established a practice of calling on a chief executive close on finishing-time. The occasion of the call would be entirely legitimate, but would also serve as a lien on the all-important half-hour of relaxed chat about affairs in general that could take place in the empty office building. Cabals sought the adoption of strategies and policies that would bring themselves more power – and more security. It was therefore particularly valuable to have intimate relationships with someone of higher or more secure status in the factory.

Persons in middle and lower management ranks would bring into prominence any intimate association with other people of high prestige in the organisation. A department manager, asked to give the names of people with whom he most frequently communicated, included the general manager and the production chief among the first three; a later study revealed that these occupied the twenty-third and ninth places respectively in order of frequency of meeting them.

People in a cabal are militant about their occupational status; the last thing they are doing is withdrawing from that status, or resigning claims to promotion or success. What they are doing through this institutional form is either manoeuvring a higher status than they are aware their technical performance in an occupational role is gaining or maintaining for them, or so altering the system in which status positions exist that status positions of those outside the cabal will be devalued.

Cabals are, of course, no more permanent than cliques. Some individuals make better use of their membership than others, and the structure is broken by their defection. One executive supplied a life-history of a cabal over a period of some years. It had begun years earlier when the factory had been in the throes of reorganisation after the war. At that time, one large department responsible for design and inspection was being closed down, and the man in charge was trying to get into the position of chief of the production side – works manager. This meant a campaign between him and the titular works manager, each having one or two junior people on his side. 'Now at that time,' said my informant, 'three of us, Mac, Alan and I, we made a sort of makeshift discussion group which was also a propaganda group for new methods, new ideas for improving the situation in the factory. Then some early developments started up and Mac was put in charge of this and I came into it and so did Alan, who was in the former works manager's camp. Mac tended to rely on me, technically anyway, because I had been in the new production chief's camp, and Alan and the other chaps were getting squeezed out all round. After a year or so, Mac was appointed in charge of a new factory being started up, so the job of running the new development was shared between Alan and me.' Now, of this new work, the speaker had got by far the more significant share, and up to a year previously had been fast building up an empire, with junior executives, three cars at his disposal, trips across half the world, responsibility for a large part of the factory production and so on. Then the whole thing had collapsed – the job was shelved *sine die*, and he was back on small-time development work alongside Alan. He ended up, 'There's always been con-straint between us, and this business of putting us in the same room together is some idea of trying to get over it. Well, of course, it doesn't. We tend to keep clear of each other.' The two other members of this cabal had been promoted very rapidly, and on a more secure basis, and were now in charge of sizeable production units elsewhere.

The speaker, at the end of a period in which he had been conspicuously successful and then very unlucky, was still at the level of his former colleague. In material terms (even in salary) this was no failure – his failure was entirely relative to his expectations from membership of this particular cabal. What was crucial to the speaker's situation – which was in fact extremely painful to him now that he was left isolated – was that procedures were fairly openly acknowledged that were illegitimate in terms of the occupational norms of the organisation.

Cabals exist for success. The norms governing the attainment of success are, however, not those prevailing in the milieu of the organisation; these are such as may be validated throughout the membership of the organisation, and thus relate to technical proficiency, achievements, acceptability to peers, subordinates and superiors, which can only be validated publicly and over a period. Members of cabals pursue success. In this they are governed by norms attributable specifically to the behaviour of the most successful persons in that milieu. Reference from the individual member is thus to the cabal, and therefore across the milieu of the organisation to the small group who have achieved success and with it the power to control the achievement of others.

Thus behaviour in cabals accommodates itself to the norms that manifestly pertain to the behaviour of successful persons in the same organisation. In both particulars, behaviour is strictly 'other directed', in Riesmann's phrase. Mannerism as well as manner is taken over, achievement or failure is registered according to the significance it will have for 'the boss'. So in the factory, an oddly indiscriminate use by the chief manager of the phrase 'fair enough' to signify assent was reflected in the speech of some executives subordinate to him, but by no means all: the line of demarcation followed precisely the lines of cabal attachment. So, also, at the end of an unsuccessful attempt by two members of the staff to complete negotiations for financial support by an outside organisation, the representative of the latter – knowing the factory well – suggested that what was bothering them now was what Mr J., the factory manager, would say; they did not see that it was funny, but agreed.

Yet in no sense, so far as I was aware, did members of any of the cabals use means to obtain promotion that entailed deliberate falsification about themselves or others, manifest sycophancy, any damage to the organisation or inefficiency in its operation. Indeed, as was mentioned earlier, their membership at first appeared determined by age and position in the structure of management. Why, then, were their members 'unpopular' and regarded as seeking success illegitimately?

In a society like ours, in which power, rights and privileges are distributed with systematic unevenness throughout institutions arranged in hierarchic order, it is assumed that socially useful qualities qualify individuals for higher positions. The society maintains itself, to some extent, by allowing better qualified persons to reach higher positions than their parents. It is therefore necessary for competition for accession to higher positions to be promoted in every institution of instrumental importance to society. An equally necessary corollary is that a sufficient variety of devices must exist by which the great majority who do not succeed[7] may nevertheless maintain fully their title to be members of society. It must also distinguish between legitimate and illegitimate forms of success. The medium of success, in terms of promotion in rank or of prestige, is election by peers or, more frequently, selection by superiors. In the latter case, which is appropriate to the present discussion, legitimate success must be such as accords publicly – throughout the system concerned – with the basic assumptions of society.

Now this latter condition – by which success is regarded as 'deserved' in terms of the qualifications of an individual known to all members of a system and admitted as highest among his peers, and most appropriate to the new position – can hardly ever be fulfilled. The amount of information required for the success to be fully legitimised in this way can rarely be made available to everybody, and the concomitant designation of rivals as failures prevents universal approval being feasible. Thus success is rarely fully approved as legitimate. It is so regarded when certain conditions are present or interposed: when competition is on an agreed, formalised basis previously accredited by the society as in accordance with its basic assumptions (examination, selection board procedures, tests) or when the successful competitor has interjected special conditions that make selection of him more difficult – a request for special rights or privileges.

The seeking of success by the satisfaction of the norms manifestly attributable to the selectors, therefore, renders cabal behaviour illegitimate. Neither condition for legitimacy is observed, and the existence of the cabal as a group, with collusive arrangements among its members and with one or more persons in or near the position of selector, manifestly flouts the interest that other members of the system have in the legitimacy of their success. By treating senior executives as the reference group underpinning the norms of the cabal – an 'ultimate' reference in the reverse direction from that involved in clique behaviour – the groups of younger executives no less than those of older men behaved in disregard of the norms of the milieu.

In the case both of cliques and cabals, the people who compose them tend to seek more enduring associations than they find in these forms. This kind of association has to be above all reliable and durable – one has to be sure of getting reassurance, or applause, or comfort, or absolution from having done the dirty on somebody. A confidant relationship is therefore commonly formed outside the group. The confidant role is often conferred upon someone of distinctly lower prestige, a younger person (but, if so, one who is in another career line), someone who is fixed in his present position – the good, steady bloke, or someone even outside the milieu concerned. The archetypal confidant relationships are between the smart, attractive girl and the plain, dowdy friend, and between husbands and 'career wives', as they are known in the United States. Confidant pairs, however, are clearly required, and known to exist, in most occupational milieux. They are mentioned here since they may be regarded as necessary appendages to clique or cabal membership. In the confidant relationship, the closest intimacy (i.e. 'naturalness', 'reality', as contrasted with the distance and artificiality proper to the dominant manner) is sought as a guarantee of the individual's moral rightness in inverting the norms that ascribe failure or illicit success to him.

Alliances of this kind are founded on secrets – the support looked for by the superior partner can be supplied only if there is a degree of intimacy built up that will allow the discussion of fears, doubts and actual incidents damaging to the self-esteem of the superior partner. And the intimacy and the knowledge that reassurance will be forthcoming are bought by passing secret information – about the senior and others at his level, and about the organisation in which his junior is involved. The price also includes some public surrender of superior status – 'best friends' will wear identical clothes and accessories, the career wife will be introduced into some meetings of colleague groups, a subordinate will be Christian-named on a formal occasion. But even more than this, intimacy in the confidant relationship is assured by the passing of information about the speaker so damaging that betrayal is not feasible in the situations that ordinarily obtain in our society. The clue to the confidant relationship lies in the fact that it bears self-revelations that would be too embarrassing between people of equal status, and that the revelations normally flow in one direction only.

SUMMARY

1. In success-oriented milieux, there exist needs for reassurance about possible failure and needs to improve chances of success by illegitimate means.
2. Informal groups in the management organisation of a factory appeared to distinguish themselves according to the age of their members. This distinction reflected in turn assumptions about the greater suitability of younger people to the needs of the industry. Membership of the groups appeared to offer compensations to older people and improved chances of success to the younger.
3. Compensation for failure offered by cliques required reference to norms outside the milieu of the organisation. Validation for illegitimate improvement of chances of success through cabals required reference to the norms of the most powerful group in the organisation – the top management.
4. For most men in the middle classes, their occupational role is dominant; relationships in the dominant milieu are formalised and conduct straitened, relatively to relationships and conduct possible in small groups. The release from constraint offered by membership of cliques and cabals ensures

support for the norms to which behaviour in them is referred, since greater intimacy and wider latitude is seen to guarantee a higher validity, more reality, for the norms of the clique and cabal. Greater intimacy and validity, which sustain a higher degree of consensus, are contrived by the constant use of a joking style.

5. The characteristic form of conduct in cliques and cabals is a variant of gossip. In cliques, the variant form is ironic criticism of the successful, the would-be successful, or the system in which others are successful. In cabals, the variant form is appraisal of others in an attempt to arrive at the latest definition of the position of self in the esteem system, and to manipulate that system in one's own favour.

6. The clique exists as a counter-system, maintained as a countervailing pattern of norms and values over and against the pattern prevailing in the milieu, and especially in the dominant group, and serving to sustain rejection of the dominant milieu in ways appropriate to organised social living.

7. The impermanence of cliques and cabals, and the ultimate inability of membership to provide continuing assurance of the rightness of the norms to which reference is made in them make for the creation of confidants out of persons external to that milieu, or part of the milieu, in which competition with others for success takes place.

NOTES AND REFERENCES

1. So far as I am acquainted with it, Strodtbeck and Hare in their 'Bibliography of Small Group Research', *Sociometry*, 1954, vol. XVII, no. 2, list 1,407 books and articles. There are, of course, many references to clique behaviour in works that could not properly be included in such a list.

2. A shift not altogether completed by Fortes, who says, apropos of the 'jural fiction' of allowing a slave to succeed to property rather than allow it to go to another lineage by default, that 'the aim is to preserve the existing scheme of social relations as far as possible'.

3. The term 'milieu' is used to denote a social system or part of a system through which a person is free to move by virtue of a specific status in it, e.g. a factory, a household, an occupation. More particularly, the word refers to the boundaries of the social area within which occupancy of a particular status permits movement. Thus, in the same hospital, a kitchen worker, a physician and a patient are members of different, though overlapping, milieux.

4. Thus, relating what is said here to what is still the most elaborate analysis yet reported of behaviour in a factory working group – the Bank Wiring Room observations of the Hawthorne studies (Roethlisberger and Dickson, 1939, pp. 508–10) – the second of the two sub-groups identified among the fourteen members of the

group is a clique in the meaning attached to the term here. The first group (A), which more closely approximated to the norms of the whole group and of the operatives in the whole plant, has characteristics – notably the inclusion of the inspector – that would appear to identify it more properly as a cabal. However, no more than guesses can be hazarded here, since it is very doubtful whether, among the working class, dominance can always be ascribed to occupational roles.

5. At a recent conference, a passage of debate about the relevance of statistical methods was ended by one of the contestants quoting a remark to the effect that statistics were like bikinis – what they revealed was interesting, but what they concealed was vital. The ensuing laughter established the last speaker as the winner of the point at issue, since the laugh was naturally taken to signify association with him in the contest; the discussion was dropped at that point.

6. For the occupation of university teaching and for one organisation (presumably only part-fictional), there is a full description of a set of such topics and the style appropriate in Kingsley Amis's novel *Lucky Jim*, which is about a university assistant who is a failure as an academic man; the overwhelming sexual and other successes the hero enjoys outside his occupational role, and the comic deflation of academic endeavour and achievement, excellently reflect the reinforcements of fantasy and ironic criticism that clique membership supplies to the individual.

7. These considerations, and some others concerning failure advanced in this paper, owe much to the suggestions by J. Littlejohn on the significance of failure as a social fact, and to a recent discussion with Professor R. M. Titmuss.

BIBLIOGRAPHY

Bion, W. R., 'Experiences in Groups: VI', *Human Relations*, 1950, vol. III, no. 4.

Bott, E., 'The Concept of Class as a Reference Group', *Human Relations*, 1954, vol. VII, no. 3.

Burns, T., 'Friends, Enemies and the Polite Fiction', *American Sociological Review*, 1953, vol. 18, no. 6.

Eisenstadt, S. N., 'Studies in Reference Group Behaviour: I', *Human Relations*, 1954, vol. VII, no. 2.

Fortes, M., 'The Structure of Unilineal Descent Groups', *American Anthropology*, 1953, vol. 55, no. 1.

Goffman, E., 'On Cooling the Mark Out: Some Aspects of Adaptation to Failure', *Psychiatry*, 1952, vol. 15, no. 4.

Homans, G. C., *The Human Group*, London: Routledge and Kegan Paul, 1951.

Leach, E. R., 'Jinghpaw Kinship Terminology', *Journal of the Royal Anthropological Institute*, 1945, vol. LXXV.

Leach, E. R., *Political Systems of Highland Burma*, London: G. Bell, 1954.

Marshall, T. H., 'The Nature and Determinants of Social Status', *Yearbook of Education*, 1953.

Merton, R. K., and Kitt, Alice S., 'Contributions to the Theory of Reference Group Behaviour', in Merton, R. K., and Lazarsfeld, Paul F. (eds), *Continuities in Social Research*, Glencoe, IL: The Free Press, 1950.

88 *Description, Explanation and Understanding*

Moreno, J. L., *Who Shall Survive?* New York: Beacon House, 1953.
Newcomb, H., *Social Psychology*, London: Tavistock Publications, 1952.
Roethlisberger, F. J., and Dickson, W. J., *Management and the Worker*, Harvard University Press, 1939.
Sherif, M., *An Outline of Social Psychology*, New York: Harpers and Bros, 1948.
Stouffer, S. A., *et al.*, *The American Soldier: Adjustment during Army Life*, Princeton University Press, 1949.
Warner, W. Lloyd, and Lunt, P. S., *The Social Life of a Modern Community*, Yale University Press, 1941.
Wilson, L., *The Academic Man*, Oxford University Press, 1942.

5

The Cold Class War

A 'squib' – provoked, I imagine, by my alarm at the recrudescence of the 'Keep 'em down' mentality typical of the early 1920s which I thought had been buried by the experiences of the war and the post-war years. It was a bit premature, as one can see now. The full-blown reaction came twenty years later, and has lasted a great deal longer than the comparatively brief spasm which accompanied the lock-out of the printing industry in February 1956.

A recent political cartoon in *Punch* showed a dark wintry landscape. From the ruins of a factory stepped a black-overalled figure; thick-booted, bullet-headed and overpoweringly strong. In one fist wriggled a dazed-looking judge, in the other an innocent-faced workman; a trade union official, no higher than the boot he was clutching, ridiculously strove to hold back the destroyer. The cartoon is a lucid presentation of the contemporary middle-class image of the worker. The proletarian peril is back with us again, irrational, hostile, nihilistic, getting more and doing less, making each wage increase the preface to a wage demand, refusing to accept the need for higher production, breaking agreements, flouting the law, rejecting elected leaders, enjoying the benefits of full employment and housing subsidies and health services, and threatening the economic system from which the benefits derive.

From *The New Statesman and Nation*, 7 April 1956, pp. 330–1.

How has this image been created? First, there has been a
marked change in the relation of the Labour Party to the working class. For the first forty-five years of its existence, the party
was fighting against social injustice, inequality, war and the
abuse of power, from which the working classes were the
principal sufferers. At the same time, it attracted the political
support of middle-class individuals and groups who were
dissatisfied with a social system which gave them insufficient
rewards, made them insecure or frustrated their talents. The
protest was real enough; and, when power came, many of the
wrongs were redressed. But with power came the party's accession to the 'establishment'. The function of the Labour Party, as
The Times said at the last election, is now to put forward an
alternative government to that offered by the Conservative
Party. We are all familiar with Labour's search for a new programme; what we do not see so clearly is that the Labour Party
has steadily lost its identification with the working class and,
more important, the working class has been losing its principal
means of political expression. The Labour Party, like the
Conservative, increasingly speaks *to* the workers, not *for* them.

Second, there is the change that full employment has
wrought in the power-structure of British society. Wages and
prices have risen and the worker has more power in all his
dealings with the institutions of organised society. He now has
a greater measure of choice in his daily activities and his career
than at almost any time in the past; the possibilities, of course,
are limited, and there are many decisions that he must take or
leave; but the increase in his power is real and it is felt – the
ability to spend money either on a TV set or on holidays; to
move from one job to another; to increase earnings by playing
the bonus system or working overtime, or to take a day off, to
move to a new house or to stay put. In all this there is one overriding constraint on the worker: he can choose only between
the possibilities which other groups and institutions present to
him. Yet in one field, as a member of an organised group of
workers, he can exercise a positive control over institutions and
standards: he possesses sanctions to coerce others, perhaps his
employer or, if need be, members of his own group. The middle class has a simplified and dramatic view of such sanctions
as the right to strike; these, it believes, should be used only as
measures of self-defence against a threat to employment or

subsistence. And it has been confused and appalled at its application to inter-union disputes, to demarcation problems, to wage differentials, and to the disciplining of individual workers.

The fact that the working class, as such; is largely inarticulate – and that the middle class controls the press and the radio – permits the fabrication of the proletarian bogy-man. It also promotes a certain recklessness, a desire at all costs to make 'them' listen and, if not to understand, then at least to realise that the workers must be reckoned with. This has appeared most clearly, perhaps, among the dock strikers who are 'on their own' in protest against the three large 'establishments' – political party, Dock Labour Board and large trade union. And the image of the bogy-man has contributed in part to the third conditioning process – the conception of management as the manipulation of workers. The more the worker is seen as an irrational, hostile, unpredictable power, threatening the wanton sabotage of the system which supports him and the rest of society, the greater the need to understand this power so as to control it better; to study the behaviour, attitudes, motivation and aims of workers, so that they can be better harnessed to the requirements of the management.

It is fatally easy to lapse into obscurantism about this; studies of people as workers are just as proper and defensible as studies of people as parents, voters, consumers or in any other role. What concerns us here is not the morality of such studies, but the current view that effective management springs from the knowledge, intuitive or learned, of how to control workers. This view is supplanting an older one, which saw management as essentially an assembly of technical skills such as costing, time study and progress control. While few managers have this new knowledge, any more than most managements fully understand and apply the techniques of the old 'scientific management', they are inclined to see their job in terms of 'managing men'; to talk of the 'human factor', to look for qualities of 'leadership', 'stimulation' and 'getting on with people'. It has become a kind of missionary endeavour, in which the men are converted to the true faith of productivity, incentive schemes and automation. Finally, there is the resentment of the middle classes. Relatively, their power and their share of rewards and privileges have all diminished. They feel that they are victims now, and their resentment is finding some cautious political expression. But beyond this resentment there is anxious bewilderment. They cannot understand why, now the workers have security, they do not behave like rational, normal people, why they do not become middle-class themselves. A family with a steelworker, a turner and a couple of assembly hands can take forty pounds a week back to a slum house in Govan. A study of a mining community reveals that miners, even when earning fifteen pounds a week, spend their money on sprees and outings rather than on buying nice new houses, with nice gardens, nice furniture and nice clothes to wear in them.

So, to the respectable middle class, the behaviour of the workers seems delinquent, a wilful disregard of standards of behaviour which workers know to be proper or desirable, but disregard through stupidity, irresponsibility or original sin. There cannot be any understanding until the middle class realises that the workers may have different standards, judgements and codes of behaviour. The existence of sub-cultural differences is a sociological commonplace. But apart from those differences which serve to identify social status they have not received much attention. There is more to it than china statuettes and standard lamps, saying 'pardon' and not saying it, pigeon-fancying and bird-watching.

There is, for example, the restriction of competition in working-class life to outlets – to games and sport, argument and abuse, manual dexterity, gambling – which for the middle class are essentially non-serious play activities. Competition for jobs, for promotion, for higher pay or privileged positions; competition in sexual attraction, competition for power, the serious concerns of the middle-class adult, are disapproved of. Only success in terms of luck is permissible; there must be no damned merit about it. How could it be otherwise? Workers are at the bottom of the social system. Continually told by their 'superiors' that they are less worthy, they are forced to feel themselves perpetual failures in a competition for success which begins at the age of five and lasts until middle age. Yet they are all born into a society which depends for its survival on the movement of those with the socially desirable and socially useful capacities into positions of power and prestige; social mobility, in turn, depends on the acceptance by everybody of success as important – all important.

So what of those who fail, who fall from favour at the first stage of selection, who score low marks, who fill the modern secondary schools, who become rank-and-file workers? In their own sector of society and increasingly as they get older and hardened to their class position, success must be devalued as improper, as bought by sycophancy, by cheating, or at best by chance. How otherwise can such men believe in themselves, carry on as effective persons with recognised membership of society?

The essence of working-class life lies in this emptying of fundamental meaning out of the institutional systems which are shared with the dominant sections of society. The family in the middle classes is truly the basic social unit. All earnings of the parents are family income; all successes are expressed in terms of house and furniture or of provision for wife and children; immense amounts of time and energy are devoted to expressing social status and personal character and values in terms of wallpapers, cars, gardens, entertainment and the proper rearing and educating of children. But in the English urban working class the family has little of this overwhelming importance for the life of the individual. There is the essentially contractual bond of the parents, with weekly payments made by the man in return for his wife's cooking meals, looking after the home, rearing their children and providing sexual gratifications. An elementary fact of budget surveys is the unrelatedness of the father's earnings to what the wife gets; there is almost a national norm for the sum handed over, and there are certainly local norms, with little variation between a labourer and a skilled fitter.

There is a similar deflation of other aspects of the family, for it is outside the family that we find the characteristic institutions of the working class. The houses belong to the women, and the friendships that link them run, across the generations, through the homes of married sisters, mothers and daughters, aunts and cousins. The social milieu of the child is the street, where the play groups and gangs preserve an autonomous cultural tradition.

It is the groups of men which underpin the other non-family institutions. For the man, attachment to his mates carries with it moral imperatives of a kind that the middle-class man feels only towards his family and his own occupational success.

Loyalties are involved which are simply unknown in the middle class except in stylised situations which are not part of the serious business of life – in team games, in associations built on acquaintanceships formed in school, regiment or college. Working-class loyalties are, however, matters of deep involvement, of dependence and easy intimacy, and there is strong pressure on individuals to conform to the standards of the group. This shows up most explicitly in industry. The limitation of production rates by tacit agreements among workers has been familiar ever since the Western Electric researches of twenty-five years ago, but this is only one way in which the massive machine of non-competing, controlled, working-class solidarity makes its impact on industry. The line between the management and the worker, the widest social barrier, is so drawn that it includes in management all but the rank-and-file workmen. To succeed occupationally is to abdicate from the working-class.

Working-class manners and institutions are deliberately maintained to show that the worker repudiates middle-class values. Working-class culture is a counter-system, maintained by and maintaining the millions who, more and more explicitly, are marked off for failure to make the social grade. The sustained raspberry at the system, that Orwell heard in working-class humour, is only one of the expressive rejections that the workers have to make of the middle-class world above them.

It is hard to say how long working-class culture can survive recognisably in its present form. The worker is now surrounded by dilemmas. He has more money, and there are new models of conduct and values in the élite worlds presented to him by the cinema, TV, advertising and the other mass communication industries. The rehousing programme is breaking up all the non-family social institutions peculiar to the working class, and it is leaving the individual with the choice between some imitation of middle-class family life, a depressing isolation, or new forms of community-officered neighbourliness. At work, incentive schemes and productivity campaigns are beginning to break down the traditional practices by which groups of workers set their own pace and output. However he treats it, there is a real moral issue here for each individual worker. Is it right or wrong to produce more and earn more than his mates?

Perhaps working-class culture will disappear with the present generation of adults. Perhaps a revolutionary change is occurring in the structure of British society. But the least likely outcome is the production of a universal middle class. We may be developing a true mass society divided into specialised élites and population masses, who will be marked off only by financial status. At present, it seems most likely that we are creating new and more rigid divisions. As social mobility occurs at younger ages, and as the dominant class develops cleverer techniques of social manipulation and control, the differences between the 'successful' and the 'failures' may become more and not less pronounced.

6

Micropolitics: Mechanisms of Institutional Change

This was meant not so much as a supplement to *The Management of Innovation* as to explore and emphasise the significance of internal politics a little more thoroughly. It is a familiar element in the life of all large organisations – including universities. For the most part internal politics is simply careerism writ large, although it often assumes importance when there are disputes about the strategy being pursued by the organisation or contemplated for the future. More significantly, it plays a large part in decisions about the response to be made to substantial changes in the circumstances in which an organisation exists, and can be all-important in decisions about the alterations in structure which may be needed to meet the new situation.

Political theorists have made no bones about identifying working organisations as political systems of a kind. Hobbes appears more than once to regard bodies within the commonwealth as subordinate civil orders, whether limited by law, custom or charter, and so politically serviceable or benign – the muscles of Leviathan – or savouring of unlawful or secret designs, and so debilitating or malignant – its worms or wens. Currently, there are frequent passing references to conceptual similarities between forms of organisation and decision-making in government and in business. Such remarks are usually in the form of Merriam's: 'Only confusion will be created by trying to draw

From *Administrative Science Quarterly*, vol. 6, no. 3, December 1961, pp. 257–81.

too sharp and exclusive a line between political and other forms of organisation . . . On the contrary, clearer view is gained by frankly recognising the fundamental similarity between them.'[1] Leoni, at the end of his paper on the distinction between political and economic decisions, admits that 'in a broader sense the decisions of boards of directors may also be called political'; i.e. fall within his definition of political decisions as 'group decisions reached according to some coercive procedure.'[2]

The tendency to regard corporations as somehow, or in essence, political organisations of the same kind as states, though of a diminished order, has been reinforced by the study of administrative systems, which, since Weber, has applied the same terms of authority, legitimacy, domination, subordination and so on to political, ecclesiastical, military and economic institutions.[3]

There is, however, one distinction between the greater and the lesser forms of political organisation in the connotations of the use of the word 'political'. It is best conveyed, perhaps, by the difference between the English 'politician' and the French *'politicien'*, which is distinctly pejorative in sense. In universities, industry, associations and working organisations of all sorts, the used is used exclusively in this second, pejorative, sense.

Consideration of the distinctions that exist in scale, generality, comprehensiveness and so forth between organisations called and deemed political and other organisations may help develop insight into the nature of political activity. For, in dealing with the political element in the life of corporations, one is compelled to attend to the fact that politics, political organisation and government are all a particular mode of behaviour.

There seems to be, in the case of political studies no less than with other social sciences, a reluctance to develop the notion of politics as what we experience it directly to be, as a mode of doing; instead, exposition is almost always in terms of structures. What really exists, writers seem to assume, is political anatomies frozen into stability. Change 'happens'. Political ideologies are developments of this same categorising proclivity, the abstract structures – communist, democratic, totalitarian – being presented as the forms to which present structures should be accommodated or from which or into which they should be changed. The point that I am trying to make here is, I believe, substantially the same as that made at length, and much more elegantly but in somewhat misleading terms, by Oakeshott in his much-discussed inaugural lecture.[4] Not only political ideologies, as he suggests, but other structural models of the institutions and modes of political activity are abstractions from the activities which they are intended to explain and guide; more important, they are representations of static forms, not of processes.

If, however, we follow Oakeshott's return to the consideration of politics as an activity, it is surely in the hope of finding something more enlightening than his 'activity of attending to the general arrangements of people'. The promise of reward in the study of political activity in corporations such as universities or business concerns is that it is recognised in them as only one kind of activity among many. Administration, manufacturing and teaching are not political. They may, however, become involved in or coloured by politics. And the subject of this essay is the colour which politics gives to action – what makes certain kinds of conduct recognisably political.

There is one large, but easily penetrated, obstacle in the way of discussing the internal politics of corporations. People do not regard themselves as politicians – or as acting politically – except, of course, on occasions when they are led into accounts of successful intrigue and manoeuvring, when they bolster their self-esteem and reputation by projecting the whole affair into the safe social context of a game or a joke. Normally, either side in any conflict called political by observers claims to speak in the interests of the corporation as a whole. In fact, the only recognised, indeed feasible, way of advancing political interests is to present them in terms of improved welfare or efficiency, as contributing to the corporation's capacity to meet its task and to prosper. In managerial and academic, as in other legislatures, both sides to any debate claim to speak in the interests of the community as a whole; this is the only permissible mode of expression.

It is backstage, so to speak, that the imputations of empire-building, caucus log-rolling, squaring and obstructionism occur. The linguistic division, which is also a moral one, is particularly marked in universities, where mutually exclusive sets of expressions exist for discussion in faculty meetings or committees, and in bars, common-rooms or parties. In the first, the only legitimate reference is to the needs of students and the advancement of approved branches of learning. Allegations or even hints of careerism or pressure-group politics are treated as entirely improper in faculty meetings, yet may be entirely legitimate and acceptable in other settings. Indeed, in certain gatherings it might be imprudent, without perhaps being socially suicidal, to impute more high-minded motives than self-interest and aggrandisement to reformers and claimants for more resources.[5]

Political conflict within management has the same dual code of terminology and value. Rival groups are charged, in gossip sessions, with incompetence within their own sphere and with ignorance of areas outside it. The direct, and intended, consequences of such allegations is to reduce the relative influence of the rival groups in future debates about the growth or transfer of departmental duties and responsibilities, about patronage, about promotion and so forth. This kind of criticism is, however, regarded as unfair *because* it has such consequences. In more formal meetings, criticism of others is tolerable only when its author is manifestly free from such concerns, and even then the suspicion that he is prompted by some obscure interest may attach to him. The acceptable argument, again, is one which is rigorously in tune with the commonly acknowledged needs of the concern. It has also to assume that the membership of the concern works entirely as a co-operative working community.

In fact, members of a corporation are at one and the same time co-operators in a common enterprise and rivals for the material and intangible rewards of successful competition with each other. The hierarchic order of rank and power that prevails in them is at the same time a single control system and a career ladder. And this dualism reflects the order prevailing in society at large. There is a sense in which a national society is an organised, co-operative system. Nevertheless, complicated and highly organised societies depend for their survival on maintaining a flow of the best-qualified people to the top places in society, where the best talents are most needed. To do this, a complex system of educational and occupational promotions open to merit has been set up in most such countries. But beyond this, it is essential, if members of such societies are to enter the race and compete as best they can, for them to regard success in the society's terms as the highest personal goal in life. This indoctrination is usually fairly successfully carried out. It is enormously strengthened by the material rewards offered, and very often success is seen in terms of material rewards. However, in the nature of things, few people can actually succeed out of the total numbers who have to try. Thus, a western society is composed of people almost all of whom are frequently confronted with the possibility of failure. In many cases, therefore, people will try to increase their chances of success by illegitimate means and will impute the same means to others who are or may at some time be in competition with them.

Yet while there is the dual linguistic and moral code attached to the co-operative and competitive aspects of society and its constituent systems, there is also a sense in which we recognise both kinds of value, incompatible as they may appear to be in the discussion of immediate issues concerning the distribution of rewards and resources. Both advance toward the agreed goals of an organisation and personal ambition can be seen as components of the moral system on which conduct in society must be based if the kind of social order we have is to survive. It is, in fact, this ultimate conjunction which 'legitimises' career success. While this may be admitted grudgingly in the academic world, in business there is a prevalent level of discussion at which both kinds of reference are acknowledged as valid and compatible, a level at which initiative, drive or enterprise may be seen as both in the interests of the self and of the firm. The answer the candidate for an executive position is expected to make to the managing director's stock question 'What kind of position are you aiming at?' is 'Yours'.

In business, we may note a further level at which the interests of individual organisations are reconciled with those of groups of organisations that are ordinarily incompatible. What I have in mind here is something other then the disregard of differences in the pursuit of common aims such as trade exhibitions and negotiations with trade unions or government departments; it is rather the emergence of a higher morality in which the active pursuit of the individual firm's own commercial ends is held to serve the interests of the industry or of the country, both of which depend, in turn, for their survival on the percolation of the best-equipped members of the community up to positions of power.

From this point of view the moral legitimacy of action is a relative matter; it can be appraised only in the context of the milieu. A senior member of an industrial development laboratory, in the presence of colleagues from his own department, can describe how he removed documents relating to labour costs from the estimating department after office hours, so as to prepare an estimate for a contract and so demonstrate how much more capable development engineers were of preparing such an estimate than the estimating department. He could do this in the knowledge that his colleagues approved his action, which, after all, had been done on their behalf. In the same way, a managing director can say: 'If an inventor has secured a patent or a process in our field and his invention has merit, we buy the patent if he is willing to sell it for a reasonable sum. But if he tries to hold us up, we refuse to buy it and 'invent around' his patent, which we can easily do after we have examined the plans which he has submitted to us for sale.'[6] In both these cases, an appeal could have been made to the legitimacy of a dishonest act when judged in the context of the larger interests of the firm – in more effective estimating in the first case, and in the interests of the community in the lower cost of an innovation in the latter.

It is the feasibility of reconciling the systems of values and of interests that distinguishes political action from other kinds of activity, characterised as delinquent or deviant. The utterances, the moral values and the goals of rival groups, even in a revolutionary situation, are comprehensible in this sense; if they are not, then opponents can indeed be said to be criminal or insane. But the reconciliation may not be actual or feasible in present circumstances, or it may be potential and dependent on a change of circumstances. In other words, political conflict may take place within the framework of a system of beliefs that is in some ultimate but quite conscious and explicit sense shared by the contending parties; or it may be about the reconstitution of the framework – about changing the 'rules of the game' themselves.

We return to the discrepancies noted between the public and private terminology of debate in corporations, between the corporation as a co-operative system and as a population of individuals and groups competing for success, between the values of individuals as members of small combinations and of larger. How does this appear in terms of the individual, rather than of the systems of which they forms part?

In the first place, individuals get jobs in corporations because of their utility as resources of physical strength, manual dexterity, craft skill, social skill, business experience or technical information. But they remain persons, nevertheless, with private interests, ambitions, goals and values, most of which are irrelevant to their utility as a resource, many of which may be incompatible with those of other members of the corporation, and some of which may be incompatible with those of the concern itself. For most of their working lives, the distinction between them as resources and as whole persons can remain concealed. Functionaries who limit their social conduct and demeanour to the strict requirements of their task are regarded as either fearsome or pathetic automata. But for all of us there are times when the distinction between our employers' view of us as sources of usable faculties and information, and their fellowship in common humanity becomes disconcertingly apparent: when we present ourselves as candidates for appointments, or when promotion vacancies occur, when there are salary increments which are not automatically available, or when we ask for resources for our personal enterprises.

In between such revelatory occasions, the distinction, while latent, remains alive in our persistent efforts to improve our chances, when the time comes, for betterment. These efforts may be made individually or in combination. But since what counts in an organisation is the individual contribution as a resource, it is manifestly more effective to argue the claims of the resource itself. In doing so, we almost inevitably find ourselves contesting rival claims and promoting the interests of others who share with us in providing the particular resource with which we have identified ourselves – with our particular academic discipline or with our kind of business expertise, with youth and energy or with experience and *savoir-faire*, with technological flair or with commercial enterprise, with research results or with teaching ability. Behind these alliances of resources lie the combined self-interest of persons. More, in combining with others, it is their utility to us and our own utility to them as resources in pursuing that self-interest which forms the basis of the commitment. In an extreme but familiar case the favour enjoyed by an individual or a combination, from a professor or from a divisional manager, would be regarded in a realistic sense as a resource; in the case of combinations it has often provided the cement binding an active caucus together.

So far, the discussion has assumed the standpoint of the individual as the focus of a system of commitment, action and values. Yet it is just as usual for historians and sociologists – even those who escape the stigma of historicist fallacy and perhaps some who apply it to others – to regard political action as an epiphenomenon, as the manifestation or instrument of grander and more occult movements in human affairs. The manoeuvres of individuals in pursuit of their own interests are seen as responses to economic, social and psychological forces. These are generated by the new expectations put upon them by changes in the constitution of the society in which they live and in their particular position in it.

Political action, even on the scale with which we are concerned, often does seem predetermined by more extended, external sequences of events, of which the actors seem to be unaware, at least as having a direct bearing on their actions.[7] A simple and direct instance of the infusion of actions and events by an historical trend may be found in the way in which new capital resources are allocated to different sections of a business concern during a period of growth.

The larger British companies interested in electronics have all grown considerably since 1945. This expansion followed a common pattern. As sales rose, production capacity would first have to be expanded as a matter of urgency. Sales forces would then be strengthened in order to 'lengthen the order book' in accordance with the expansion in output and to deal with the wider range of active customers. Office services would have to be expanded and, lastly, expenditure on research and development would be increased to ensure future survival at the same level. Of course, this cycle worked in a complicated and deliberate way, but to the people involved each move seemed to be the consequence of individual political effort. Indeed, this effort was needed. The chief engineer of one large concern, which had expanded three-fold in about ten years, saw a new laboratory building as his own personal achievement:

> About three years ago I made myself a bit of a nuisance to a lot of people because I said we couldn't possibly operate here with the laboratories that we had – we couldn't operate efficiently . . . With the old arrangements you had a communications lab, literally in that wooden hut over the way, and the electronics people were distributed all over the building – they had a room up there, the auto-lab; people were all mixed up together. First of all it was highly inefficient, and secondly you couldn't persuade people to come here. Graduates would come along and they'd say 'Can we see the laboratories?' and you'd show them a scruffy little room here, and another scruffy little room there. I said to the managing director, 'I'm ashamed of it.' To cut a long story short . . . I managed to persuade the great ones to let me have the money to build a lab and we got this magnificent building put up.

Each actual change of this kind in individual concerns may be carried through without conscious reference to the changed context, which appears to the outsider not only to have made the internal change possible but even to have prompted it. But there is more involved than a difference of interpretation resulting from the difference in perspective of actor or observer. Political action is the necessary instrument for the accomplishment of internal change of this kind, which, to an outsider observer, is the inevitable consequence of a new situation. Looked at another way, that is, the new situation may be seen as a favourable set of opportunities, a releasing mechanism, which allows people to implement political action already being fruitlessly undertaken or being held in abeyance for the opportune occasion.

What the observation of the internal politics of corporations suggests, therefore, is a dual relationship between political action and social change. Politics as the instrument of social change is one arm of this relationship; social change as the power supply or releaser of political action and of aspirations held in check is the other. But the term social change in this context is something rather more specific than a verbal invocation of vast, indescribable but all-explaining historical processes. It means either the intrusion of new resources into the conditions of existence of the corporation or the extinction or weakening of an existing resource.

Cutting across this division of external and internal change is another: political conflict of interests may take place within a system of beliefs consciously shared – the unchallenged rules of the game – or across a division of values, when it is the rules of the game which may be in dispute.

These two sets of differences provide us with an elementary system of classification of political action in its instrumental aspect. We may set the scheme out thus:

	External change *(new resources)*	*Internal change* *(altered balance of)* *resources*
Shared beliefs	A	B
Discrepant beliefs	C	D

This has provided us with four categories, which we can proceed to fill. At the elementary stage to which these conceptions have been taken, the filling will have to take a paradigmatic form.[8]

A. SHARED BELIEFS AND EXTERNAL CHANGE

When political action between groups in a corporation who share the same system of beliefs is triggered or kept going by changes in external circumstances, then it has the general effect of maintaining the two sides in a state of dynamic equilibrium. That is, no organisational (constitutional) change is involved, and no reversal of the balance of power (i.e. resources). Rather, the weight of resources committed to and usable by different sections of the corporation alters so as to affect the degree of commitment of those sections to the corporation, and thus the contractual value of the commitment as resource. The paradigm of this first category is taken from the familiar management-worker arena of the system of bonus payments. We may, in turn, take a concrete instance as a type case.

A large machine shop in a Scottish firm was manned with craftsmen who were regarded, both inside and outside the concern, as displaying high technical competence. The firm operated a system of payment for work done of the usual kind, a basic time rate plus extra payments scaled according to the speed at which separate items of work were done. The management of the firm assumed, formally, that instructions given to craftsmen in the form of drawings, planning schedules and verbal orders would be carried out at a speed determined by the craftsman's skill and his desire to increase earnings. This assumption was supported explicitly by trade union representatives, and, implicitly at least, by operatives. The basic time rate is the time estimated by a rate-fixer as necessary for a workman of average ability to complete a single part. As elsewhere, however, this estimated time was in practice fixed well below the mean time likely to be achieved.

The difference between the rate-fixer's 'normal' times and the actual average was the direct product of the balance of power between management and groups of men drawing such bonus earnings. Thus, I was told: 'This used to be a time-and-a-half shop, but during the war people got used to fantastic times. They would do a job rated at fifty minutes in ten. Now the norm is half time, and everybody reckons that jobs should give a bonus of 120.' When they were in doubt, rate-fixers would now write in times a little less than what they thought probable, since they were certain that if the time was shorter than the accepted norm of half the average time, it would be disputed, and 'they can always put a bit on; but you can never cut a time'. There was constant traffic of men from the machine shop coming to dispute times, with the foreman usually either an arbiter or an advocate for his workman. This was thought quite normal: 'You never get an engineering shop without cribbing.' If, because the material was defective or a previous operation wrongly performed, a particular machining job could not be properly done, men 'of course' worked on it and passed the part on, since they would otherwise be paid for that period at the basic time rate. The whole system was explained quite frankly, with the air of its being a normal and reasonable, though tacit, arrangement.

When earnings are determined by two variables: the extent to which a man can exceed a specified speed of work and the considerations affecting the specification of speed, and this latter variable is a matter of informal but systematic bargaining, then each individual can increase his earnings not only by working faster but also by insisting, in concert with his fellows, that jobs always take a longer time, on the average, than is allowed for. If this insistence can be concerted fairly widely among the group, they will be able to enjoy increased earnings through a reduced normal time merely by the exercise of their political power within the concern, a power deriving mainly from economic sanctions (i.e. withdrawal of their effort temporarily or finally, completely or partially, openly or covertly).

Within the limits set by the social, economic and political system of which any factory community in Britain forms a part, the acceptance of bargaining in this particular sphere serves the function of maintaining the organisational structure in a particular concern. Over a period of time there may be minor alterations in the total benefits or resources to be disposed of within the concern. Thus one particular management may be in a weaker position than others because of its comparative ineffectiveness in political situations or because working conditions are worse, or because jobs are relatively insecure, or because its need for labour is greater than that of other firms. In such circumstances the existence of bonus earnings and rate-fixed times, in which norms on which pay is based can be adjusted so as to make up for these relative disadvantages, is of eminently practical use. Weekend overtime is used in much the same way. Similarly, fluctuations may occur in the amount of work coming into the concern, or in its profitability – and thus in the amount of benefits available for all groups with a claim on them. Rate-fixed times can then be made generally tighter, as they were before the Second World War, or looser, as they became during the war, or established at some level in between, as they have been since. This kind of fluctuation occurs in addition to trends of a smoother and more explicit kind, extending over the whole industry, in basic wage-rates.

B. SHARED BELIEFS AND INTERNAL CHANGE

As in any other autocracy, the main theatre of political activity in a business concern is in the immediate neighbourhood of the boss, and such activity rises to a peak as a problem of succession becomes imminent. At these times, political action has to do with attempts to control the redistribution of the most important positions in the organisation. According to the functional classification of political action suggested, it is designed to hold the organisation in equilibrium during internal change, when the system of beliefs about the moral and technical criteria appropriate to the appraisal of the human resources contained in the system are shared throughout the system. I want to illustrate this category with the case of a large engineering works whose managing director, after spending almost the whole of his life in it and the greater part of that in his present position, was facing retirement.

Partly as a preliminary move, partly to strengthen management after a period of very rapid expansion, a management committee had been created and was declared to be the major planning and decision-making group.

The important element in the situation was the impending change: the resignation of the managing director and the choice of a successor. And the manoeuvres of the managing director and of the senior managers immediately below him were all directed toward maintaining the *status quo*, the director to maintain as full control over the relationships as possible, the managers to maintain the relationship with the director that kept them in position as his immediate lieutenants. The new management committee, was as soon as it was created, was virtually a dead letter. The original structure was retained. This was one of the simplest and the commonest forms of top management organisation, i.e. a series of single links between the managing director and each one of the members of top management. There is, of course, a constant and understandable tendency for both sides to develop this link at the expense of links with other people. It is simpler for the managing director and each senior manager to deal with one man than with several simultaneously. 'These discussions [about the need for sales effort as against engineering effort] go on within my division and with the managing director – *not* in the management committee,' said one senior manager. 'If I can persuade the managing director, that's good enough for me.'

The managing director was clearly seen as the central source of visible power ('Here the managing director is all-powerful'.) His approval, either implicit in a general and acknowledged association with the individual manager, or explicitly given to decisions or proposals, was the best possible validation of managerial action. From the director's point of view a structure which allied each senior manager more firmly with him than with colleagues reduced the absolute and relative isolation characteristic of the top position.

This kind of set-up appeared to remain as the fundamental structure of top management. 'And still today his is the hand on the tiller – there's no question about it. And if X's hand left the tiller here today, my personal belief is there would be utter chaos.' The shift of the centre of gravity slightly downwards and away from personal to committee responsibility was therefore formal rather than actual. While one informant said that a big change had occurred in that the managing director now had only six people reporting to him, as against thirty previously, another cited an instance of his 'producing ideas about redirecting effort' some stages down. Again, while one senior manager said that the managing director had had to 'change over from personal control to delegated control', the same man instanced occasions when he had instructed his own subordinates to 'go to the old man for authority'.

The steadily increasing importance of the succession problem and the preoccupation with the relative placings of candidates had its effect in another direction. Much of the consultation initiated by the managing director was thought to represent covert attempts to test people out: 'He asks me a question about something entirely in my sphere, and then goes to X and asks the same question.' The placings themselves had admittedly changed more than once in recent years. What was described as his 'hopes for people' had changed. The consequence seemed to be that no one had any clear idea of the qualities regarded as appropriate for advancement to higher positions; furthermore, people were beginning to suspect that these qualities changed from time to time.

The functional organisation of pair relationships, therefore, became overlaid by a fairly clear political alignment. Among the ten senior and divisional managers there were groups: the old guard, who had been with the firm since before the war; the young Turks, a group who had risen rapidly since their recruitment in the immediate post-war years; and the new men, imported more recently from other concerns. These alliances were aimed at improving the chances of their three leading figures for the succession, but political action was aimed inevitably at reciprocating the managing director's efforts to retain his former mastery, through the pair-relationship system. Since he was still in effective control and would retain the right to nominate his successor, the function of the alliances was to control access to him, to strengthen and coordinate claims on him, and to exert control through him.

The political alliances and rivalries were conducted, so far as

I could, judge, within the terms of friendly colleague relationships. Inevitably, however, thy brought out and accentuated personal insecurities inherent in membership in top management. The need for the support of enduring alliances such as those prevailing among the political groups was again a reflection of the relative lack of autonomy among the heads of functional sections and of the continued dependence of senior managers on the managing director.

Among all members of the top management there was enormous respect and regard for the head of the concern, for his wisdom and experience accumulated over almost the whole lifetime of the industry, and also for his commercial flair and technical insight. 'In former days, X was a general manager, sales manager, chief engineer, commercial manager, chief accountant – the lot. Being the almost-genius that he was, and still is, he carried it.' The effect of the testing-out procedures and of their reciprocal – the heightened, almost extravagant, praise accorded his qualities by his immediate juniors – was again to put an extra premium on good and close working relationships with him, beyond those customarily necessary with the executive head and arbiter of careers.

By the time the succession was eventually decided – in favour, quite predictably, of the most prominent of the 'new men' – the working organisation of the firm had become stable almost to the point of paralysis, a familiar condition of pre-succession periods. The working structure developed under the old managing director, despite surface reform, became rigidly defined almost to the point of parodying its traditional form. The firm's task itself had been conceived as a holding operation, as a job of keeping the firm going (during a period of mild recession) without any adjustment or new departures, until the interrupted growth curve resumed and business on the same technical and commercial terms as previously could again serve as a basis for expansion and survival.

C. DISCREPANT BELIEFS AND EXTERNAL CHANGE

We now consider the character of political action when external circumstances are changing, thus intruding new resources into the political system of the corporation, and there is a discrepancy in the kinds of values, purposes and criteria of achievement obtaining among the members.

The instances of political conflict used here are all taken from studies of organisational problems in the management of firms in the electronics industry. Perhaps the most prevalent of such conflicts – at the time these studies were made – was that between sales departments and development laboratories. All these firms had, after the 'defence cuts' of a few years ago, been compelled to move out from a market dominated by government contracts to one more akin to the ordinary commercial market for capital goods. This amounted to a revolutionary change in the task of the enterprise. Much of the electronics industry had its origin technically in government research establishments and financially in government contracts. Thus, the market had nursed the industry which served it; and the customer had provided, or reduced the need for, the sales tasks of market exploration and market development and of matching customer requirements by appropriate design and economical production. Many concerns therefore had not only to address themselves to these tasks for the first time in the new commercial market but to discover that such tasks existed.

The course followed by the larger concerns was to create powerful new sales departments. For an industry that exists by creating a continuous stream of innovations there is a special indeterminacy in the market, and there is an initial difficulty in identifying potential customers at all. An innovation may have varied applications. Establishing relationships that might eventually get something sold demands a multiplicity of diplomatic and technical skills and diffuse information. This problem of indeterminacy and variety was solved by splitting sales departments into product divisions. Each of these would then be linked with a development laboratory specific to its range of products: broadcasting, telecommunications, radar, data handling, computers and so on.

This course was beset with long and arduous campaigns of attrition in every firm. The acknowledgement of the new importance of selling could only be achieved by a structural change in which sales became organisationally dominant. Sales managers and senior technical managers contested the amount of influence either side was to have over the disposition of resources within the firm: about the allocation of capital for sales development and technical development; about the extent to which selling or engineering interests dominated decisions (in two larger concerns the development laboratory found its programme abruptly decimated by the overriding need to produce saleable objects in a short time); about the leadership of larger sectors of the concern, including their rivals and production; about the relative size of their empires; about the adaptation of other departments – commercial and other services such as accounting or production – to their needs; and about the appointment or promotion of individuals and the creation of new departments.

All the moves in these conflicts were patently generated by the changes in the relationship of these firms to their markets, and particularly by the falling level of government demand. Development engineers were seriously concerned about the threat of a sales hegemony. 'We used,' said one, 'to work for our customers (ministries) direct – they were our masters, really. Now head office [the sales department] are our masters.' The conflicts themselves were waged, as I suggested earlier, through attempts to 'shop' the other side (i.e. to inform on their errors or to expose their incompetence).

There is a nice irony in the resistance of development engineers – the professional innovators – to an innovating change. For our purposes, however, the point of this very summary account is that substantial structural changes took place inside firms in response to major changes in their circumstances. More particularly, these structural changes were only carried through over a period of some years and after the strenuous efforts of development engineers – who had previously played a dominant part in determining the firm's policy – to defend their position. And the structural changes were essential because development engineers appeared to be incapable of accepting a new definition of the commercial purpose of the firm.

D. DISCREPANT BELIEFS AND INTERNAL CHANGE

The fourth paradigm is of political action in circumstances of change internal to the corporation, when there are disparate views about the criteria and goals of the corporation as a whole, when, in short, there is an ideological conflict. The effect of political action (the outcome of the connected series of manoeuvres each aimed at a specific target or protective of a specific position but not necessarily strategically connected) in this instance is to alter the power structure while leaving the organisational structure (the constitution) relatively unaffected. It is an effect most familiar in terms of the circulation of élites in the larger society.

Perhaps the most interesting and enlightening political campaign encountered in these studies of industrial concerns was that successfully conducted by a development laboratory to establish its right to separate autonomous existence between a research laboratory and the production plant. All these were situated in different towns, although the intention had been to put the development laboratory and factory on the same site. Work on a new range of products based on advanced electronic techniques had begun in the research laboratory which was part of the parent organisation; the development laboratory was newly formed in order to produce designs which the factory would then manufacture.

While the distance between the two laboratories took some time to cover, it was also seen as an advantage, by development engineers. They had little doubt that separation made it easier to appraise the products of the research laboratory independently and to decide on redeveloping. It was said, for example, that the research laboratory began by believing that the development laboratory would merely take over a design that they had produced, check the tolerances, see that it could be engineered, make a prototype and send it for manufacture. According to development engineers, this 'didn't often happen; more than likely it had to be entirely redeveloped'. Even when remoteness was not seen as positive advantage, the drawbacks were regarded as negligible – 'We speak the same language and there's a good deal of frank talking on visits . . . We have to know what they're doing very early on.'

Many of the statements offered by development engineers reflect the growth of a quasi-inspection function. This function had been turned to effective political use: 'Relationships with the Research Lab weren't at all good three years ago. They couldn't understand why their brilliant circuits were criticised. Now they know by experience that they can go wrong.' Status distinctions between the two groups also became less obtrusive, possibly as a consequence of the friction between them. 'Most of the troublesome people have left – you really can't have research people who think they're God Almighty.'

Over a number of years the development laboratory struggled to insert itself between the research laboratory and the production department until a balance was struck and given titular recognition in an identical name for both establishments (invidious professional distinctions between research and development being dropped), and in the appointment of the heads of both as joint managers.

A second strategy again used 'organisational needs' to establish development engineers in complementary and equal roles with research staff. This was a system of pairing between the opposite numbers working in either establishment on the same equipment or technical item. Pairing extended down through both establishments and worked not only through day-to-day working contacts but in the all-important progress meetings. Each establishment provided the chairman of the meeting on alternate occasions, and both members of each pair from the two establishments whose work appeared in the agenda attended the meeting.

The development laboratory viewed altogether differently the almost parallel situation between itself and the factory, which had been created later and had also been sited a good distance away. This factory, it was said, had begun with dreams of being 'a genuine production factory' (as distinct from workshops operating under the direction of the laboratories) and still strove for autonomy. The production department pressed its claims for autonomy by demanding clear designs and specifications and by claiming the job of translating these into manufactured articles without the development laboratory's retaining responsibility. These claims were wholly rejected by the development laboratory.

Many of the moves and ideas which figured in the account by development engineers of their group's struggle for autonomy and equality were repeated, with the significance reversed, in the account of relationships between the development laboratory and the production department. However salutory the influence exerted on the research laboratory by a separate and remote development laboratory, having the production department so far away was 'thoroughly bad'. It was much better, said the development engineers, for the designer to 'live with the job' – to have design responsibility for equipment throughout production. Only by having development on the spot with production was it feasible to maintain this kind of control; otherwise there was a tendency for a hand-over of responsibility to take place: 'What happens is that you're constantly getting unsuspected faults arising from characteristics which you didn't think important in the design. If you got to hear of these through a production person to whom the design was handed over in the dim past, then instead of being a design problem, it's an annoyance caused by that particular person; you thought you were finished with that job and you're on to something else now.'

The whole two-sided situation is neatly expressive of the way in which political pressure is rationalised in terms of organisation. The reversal of argument was taken even to the point of explicitly suppressing pair relationships (so valuable in the set-up *vis-à-vis* the research laboratory) which had grown up between development engineers and production people: 'We've set up a liaison chap to act as a channel for communication. You can get all kinds of private arrangements between production and development people . . . Personal knowledge is no good to anyone.' The overt expression of the development laboratory's campaign for power and status equal to the research laboratory and for control over production was made in terms of the exigencies of organisation and had been by moves made in the interests of more effective working. The structure of relationships between the three establishments was, in turn, the creation of the successful manipulation by the development laboratory of its intermediate position to establish first a necessary and finally a dominant role in the whole tripartite system.

This paper has attempted to show political action in two perspectives: first as the category of personal conduct concerned with the advancement of self-interest, however that is defined, and second as the instrument by which changes in the external or internal conditions of social systems are translated into adaptive changes of these systems. The link between the two perspectives is provided in the notion of 'resource', human and material.

To live as we do, with other people, we must put ourselves out to use and make use of others. In both ways, we translate complete persons into resources, into skills, information, possessions, rights, usable by others. There are many forms of contract for farming out such resources or acquiring them, individual by individual. The terms of such contracts are the matter of politics. It is being argued here that politics are the exploitation of resources, both physical and human, for the achievement of more control over others, and thus of safer, or more comfortable, or more satisfying terms of individual existence.

Politics are familiarly an activity requiring combinations of people; individuals are to be reckoned with politically only as commanders, or as leaders 'representing' others, or as persuaders, and thus potential representatives. Less frequent, but equally familiar, are instances in which a combination confronts one man – a despot or a boss. The individual, no less than the group, is politically active. What we see in such confrontations are two manipulable combinations of different sorts of resources: voluntary commitments from persons on the one hand and material resources plus legal or traditional or extorted commitments from people on the other. Political commitment to a person or to a combination is a surrender of the independent exercise of an individual attribute – a voting right, possessions, information, persuasive power, fighting abilities, or control over further resources already committed to oneself – for use by them as a resource. A commitment of this kind is equivalent to an investment of oneself as a resource in an enterprise. The return looked for from such a surrender is the advancement of one's interests, which can range from the grossly material to the transcendental.

Politics, then, involve obligations, which are the exchange currency of resources – the ability to dispose of the capacities or attributes of others (the obligations attached to vassalage, even, were balanced against the extent and promptness of protection from feudal lords). It is here that the notion of a contract enters in, and its contemporary derivative – a view of the State, and indeed the world, as a kind of stock exchange in which one invests duties and obligations in return for rights and privileges.

But if a contract between the individual and the State, or interested groups and society, were all that was involved, historical experience would exhibit no other characteristic than the slow cyclic beat of more and less injustice, of the circulation of élites, of *mutabilitie* – the descent from golden ages into disorder and renaissance of the old order. It would, in fact, resemble the life histories of many of the corporations which make up the body of Leviathan, and in which commitments are exchanged in this way, being contributed so as to make up the human resources of business, of industry, of administrative systems and associations, in return for livelihoods, the benefits of ordered existence and other material or intangible rewards.

Yet we do know change. And while politics are always about the terms of our contract with society, and about justice and injustice, and about who are to be top people, there are manifest differences between the kind of terms possible to such contracts today and yesterday. So that politics are not only about the rules of the game – the game itself changes. It changes with the nature and extent of the resources which the game is about.

The material progress of civilisation depends on the accumulation of resources. Within this truism lies a rather more significant notion, neatly conveyed by the double meaning of the word 'resource', 'a means of supplying some want; a stock or reserve' on the one hand, and a 'capability in adapting means to ends, or in meeting difficulty' on the other. For the accumulation of resources itself depends on the prior development of information both as knowledge and as skill. And, in turn, the further development of such technical information depends on isolating, extracting and exploiting fragments from the total, undifferentiated natural order in which man lives: fire, fur, timber, corn, wool, hides, flint, metals and the like. Human resources come next, exacted from conquered enemies, women and children, the illiterate poor. Last come magnetic forces, steam, carbon chains, radio echoes and the extraordinary array of subsequent developments which more or less suddenly, more or less astoundingly, emerge from the environmental datum of human existence into perception and use as an accessory.

So, in the development of man from the primordial ecological niche, we can mark off successive stages by which he extended what was here-and-now available through the conversion of parts of the reality of nature into human resources. The essential step is man's perception of a possible new relationship between himself and a part of his environment, a new relationship in which it is seen as a potential means to his personal ends, replacing the former involuntary relationship with the world into which he was born. When the ground became arable or pasture, when fruits became provisions or seed, when trees became wood, when men and women became slaves, when galvanism became electricity, a part of natural creation became a manipulable resource. Major advances have the appearance of the piecemeal, competitive and then organised discovery and settlement of new continents, beginning with husbandry, the conversion of certain kinds of animals, plants and land into tended resources.

At each stage, as something more of the total natural and human world man started with becomes converted into a resource, so the social order is first strained and then changed. All this is familiar ground. Technologies develop and so the order of society changes. It is an insight at least as old as Montesquieu and confidently expanded by Marx from his earliest writings.

There are, however, two technologies involved, physical and social, as well as two kinds of resource, material and human. Step by step with the development of material technology, social organisation has had to become more and more explicit and rational. Bureaucratic management and government; national, urban and rural administration; communications systems; and economic interactions have all become more refined and more extensive as material technology has piled up physical resources. As ignorance or passive acceptance, imaginative insight or pragmatic skill, yielded to tested and learnable techniques, each step enabled men to manipulate others more and more, individually and *en masse,* and more and more *of* others.

The extraction of physical and human resources from the total environment, which has been the work of material and social technology, increases the stock of resources which may be committed. And since the social organisation of both technologies has usually been, and is for us still, ordered in other ways from the existing distribution of rights and privileges, of power and esteem, among the members of society, new physical and human resources enter on the social scene and become available for political commitment in ways not in accord with the existing social order. As physical and human resources have accumulated, therefore, they have of necessity widened and altered the possibilities of political action. And it is through political action, in small as in large social systems, that changes in the structure of society have occurred.

NOTES AND REFERENCES

1. Charles E. Merriam, *Political Power*, Glencoe, IL, 1950, p. 9.
2. Bruno Leoni, 'The Meaning of 'Political' in Political Decisions', *Political Studies*, 5 (1957), 239.
3. Max Weber, *The Theory of Social and Economic Organisation*, Glencoe, IL, 1947, says: 'It is indifferent, so far as the concept [corporate group] whether the relationship is of a communal or associative character. It is sufficient for there to be a person or persons in authority – the head of a family, the executive committee of an association, a managing director, a prince, a president, the head of a church – whose action is concerned with carrying into effect the order governing the corporate group' (p. 133). See also 'Domination', in M. Rheinstein (ed.), *Max Weber on Law in Economy and Society*, Cambridge, MA, 1954, pp. 322–37.
4. Michael Oakeshott, *Political Education*, Cambridge, 1951.
5. It is impossible to avoid some reference from the observations made here to F. M. Cornford's well-known 'Guide for the Young Academic Politicians'. Jobs 'fall into two classes, My Jobs and Your Jobs. My Jobs are public-spirited proposals, which happen (much to my regret) to involve the advancement of a personal friend, or (still more to my regret) of myself. Your Jobs are insidious intrigues for the advancement of yourself and your friends, spuriously disguised as public-spirited proposals. The term Job is more commonly applied to the second class' (*Microcosmographia Academica*, Cambridge, 1908).
6. Quoted by Edwin H. Sutherland, *White Collar Crime*, New York, 1949, p. 221.
7. For an example of the deployment of a larger historical trend in the inner political world of univ ersity life,, see the account of the elections at Lincoln College, Oxford, in 1851 and 1862 in V. H. H. Green, *Oxford Common Room*, London, 1957, chs vii and viii.
8. The instances cited here are taken from the author's studies of British firms in the electronics industry. See Tom Burns and G. M. Stalker, *The Management of Innovation*, London, 1961.

7

The Sociology of Industry

This was a commissioned article calling for a comprehensive review of the 'state of the art' in industrial studies. I did set out to do that, and although my own personal judgements show through on every page, it does, I think, stand as a kind of memorial to that brief span of years – from the mid-1950s to the mid-1960s – when sociology had discovered a new vocation (or rediscovered an old one) in the criticism of accepted interpretations of social behaviour and social institutions. The sociology of industry played a very minor role in all this, but it did share the same sense of discovery – of breakthrough.

The sociologist's interest in industry reflects that of society at large. He shares a pervasive, rather anxious, concern with industrialism as the characteristic institution of modern advanced societies and as the prime mover of social change in them; or he may participate in efforts to diagnose those failings of the industrial system or of single undertakings which impoverish or disrupt the lives of individuals, families, groups of people, or whole sections of society.

Such interests bear on the *external* references of the industrial system; the issues and questions lie not so much in industrial organisation themselves as in changes in social structure, in

From A. T. Welford, M. Argyle, D. V. Glass and J. N. Morris (eds), *Society: Problems and Methods of Study*, Routledge and Kegan Paul, 1962, pp. 185–215.

improvement or deterioration in welfare, and in alienating or pathological conditions attributable to industrialism.

On the other hand, he may desire to elucidate the irrational forces that operate in social systems brought into being and maintained by self-interest. Frequently, again, he may accept more or less uncritically the aim of making industrial and business undertakings more efficient as instruments of the material progress of society, or more efficient or less troublesome as instruments of private profit-making. Studies of these latter kinds are directed towards the *internal* order of industry and the situation arising within it; with very few exceptions they tend to accept the existence, values and purposes of industry and individual undertakings at their face value.

In this chapter we shall follow this general division by considering first the study of the institutional nature of modern industrialism, and thereafter enquiries into the internal structure of industrial concerns and the roles and situations prevailing in industrial milieux.

THE EXTERNAL RELATIONSHIPS OF INDUSTRY
WITH THE SOCIAL ORDER: THE SOCIOLOGY OF INDUSTRIALISM

Inquiries into the external relationships of industry extend far beyond the commonly accepted boundaries of industrial sociology and, indeed, make up most of the matter of social and economic history over the past two centuries. The demands of capitalist industry for human effort and material resources, and the increased flow of goods and services which it produces, have since its formative years occasioned the most profound disturbances in individual lives, extinguished and created social institutions, and substantially altered the structure of society. Because it has continued to demand new as well as more materials, and new kinds of human effort and skills, and because it has produced entirely new kinds of goods and services as well as more of those already in familiar use, the disturbances, social innovations and structural changes have gone on.

But there is an area central to the history of the social consequences of industrialism which received the chief attention of Marx and Weber and which, after a period of neglect, is being discussed afresh. This has to do with the institutional nature of industrialism itself. The industrial system imposes its own structure of relationships on managers and workpeople. To maintain and expand the system requires the widespread acceptance of an ordered array of values by which persons in different positions in the system set their aims in life and guide their day-to-day actions, and these values have to be inculcated by a variety of means. For industrial concerns to operate at all there has to be specified a range of roles, each with a set of constraints; there have to be also disciplinary codes or social controls in order to confine admissible conduct within these constraints. In all these senses, the industrial system marks the host society with its own special imprint. The members of such a society are, so to speak, 'processed' by industry into human resources and, as now appears, into conformity with its needs as users of its products (Galbraith, 1959).

The kind of 'processing' effected by the industrial system has changed with its own institutional character. For this has changed as well as the inputs of effort and materials and the outputs of goods and services. It is still changing. The general theme of this first kind of study is the nature of these changes.

Material and Social Technologies in the
Three Phases of Industrialism

Industrialism itself is the product of techniques of social organisation linked with techniques of manufacture. It has developed in spasmodic fashion from the rudimentary forms of the eighteenth century by alternate advances in first one technology and then the other.

The elementary form of industrialism lies in Adam Smith's conjunction of the division of labour traditional in advanced society with the extension of its advantages by 'those machines by which labour is so much facilitated and enlarged' (Smith, 1776). The modern industrial system was founded when the perception by early mechanical scientists that natural events 'obeyed' certain laws became widely diffused in the eighteenth century. The legend that Arkwright was first struck by the feasibility of mechanical spinning 'by accidently observing a hot piece of iron become elongated by passing between iron rollers' (Smiles, 1910, p. 41) may be fiction, but it reflects truly the commonplace terms in which the new habits of scientific thought could be used by craftsmen-inventors, who saw not just an interesting analogy but one process obeying a law which might also apply to a different and entirely new process.

Simultaneously with Adam Smith's observation of the archetypal form of the two technologies, a third step was being taken with the creation of the first successful factory, by Strutt and Arkwright (Fitton and Wadsworth, 1958). By 1835, Ure could discount the basic principles of division of labour as outdated and misleading (1835, p. 19); the industrial system was simply the factory system as developed by Arkwright, the term, 'factory' meaning 'the combined operation of many workpeople, adult and young, in tending with assiduous skill a system of productive machines continuously impelled by a central power' (p. 13). 'It is,' he adds, moreover, 'the constant aim and tendency of every improvement in machinery to supersede human labour altogether' (p. 23).

At the time Ure was writing (1832), only a small fraction of the working population of the United Kingdom was employed in factories, and some of these were central workshops rather than organised factories. Bendix, in his study of industrial management in England during this period (1956, ch. 2), points out that the usual form adopted for comparatively large-scale industrial undertakings was a system of subcontracting – very little different from what Zimmern describes as obtaining in classical Greece (1936, p. 261). Bendix cites evidence that this system prevailed not only in building and engineering, but in clothing, cutlery, iron-founding and even in textiles. 'It was obviously up to these subcontractors to deal with their underhands whom they recruited, employed, trained, supervised, disciplined, paid and fired' (1956, p. 53).

Factory organisation stayed for three generations at the point at which Arkwright had left it, a collection of machines in a building, all driven by one prime mover, and, preferably, of the same type and engaged on the same process. Attending the machines were men and women who themselves were attended by 'feeders', most of them children, who fetched and carried away materials. There was also a 'superior, but numerically unimportant' class of maintenance and repair workers (Marx, Bk I, ch, XV, sect. 4, 'The Factory'). All of these worked under a master, and a few chief workmen or foremen. Where the factory system had gained ground, the subcontractor had been incorporated, along with his 'underhands', into it, first as agent and then as foreman. But he was shorn of many of his functions. Those that were removed from him passed to the master. The primitive social technology of the factory system still confined it, even by the 1850s, largely to the mass production of textiles. Outside this there remained 'domestic' industry and small tradesmen.

Technical developments in transport and communications, the impact of the international exhibitions of London and Paris, freer trade, and the armaments revolution supported by the development of machine tools and of steel and chemical technology, all combined during the 1850s and 1860s to form the springboard, in material technology, of the next advance in the social techniques of industrial organisation.

As yet, there is no account of how that advance took place. All that can be said is that with the extension of the factory system into engineering and chemicals, iron and steel processing, food manufacture and clothing, an organisational development took place which provided for the conduct and control of complex series of production processes within the same plant. The overt sign of this development is the increase in the number of salaried officials employed in industry. According to Bendix (1956, p. 214), quoting unpublished sources, the proportion of 'administrative employees' to 'productive employees' in Britain had risen to 8.6 per cent by 1907, and thereafter to twenty per cent by 1948. Similar increases took place in Western Europe and the United States.

The growth in the numbers of industrial administrators and functionaries or managers reflects the growth of organisational structures. Production department managers, sales managers, accountants, planning engineers, inspectors, training officers, publicity managers, research managers and the rest emerged as specialised parts of the general management function as industrial concerns increased in size. Their jobs were created, in fact, out of the master's either directly, or at one or two removes. This gives them and the whole social structure which contains their newly created roles its hierarchic character. It is indeed – what one would expect to emerge from the spontaneous subcontracting phase of management if history followed set patterns – a quasi-feudal structure. All rights and powers at every level derive from the immediate superior; fealty, or 'responsibility', is owed to him; all benefits are 'as if' dispensed by him. The feudal bond is more easily and more often broken than in feudal polities, but loyalty to the concern, to employers, is regarded not only as proper, but as essential to the preservation of the system.

Chester Barnard makes this point with unusual emphasis: 'The most important single contribution required of the executive, certainly the most universal qualification, is loyalty, domination by the organisation personality' (1938, p. 220). More recently, Gouldner has pointed out that 'Much of W. H. Whyte's recent study of 'organisation man' is a discussion of the efforts by industry to attach managerial loyalty to the corporation' (Gouldner, 1954, p. 216).

The growth of a bureaucratic system of control which made possible the increase in scale of undertakings had other aspects. The divorce of ownership and management (Berle and Means, 1932), although by no means absolute, has gone far enough to render survival of the enterprise (and the survival of the existing management) at least as important a consideration as the maximisation of profit, which, indeed, wears a different aspect for the large-scale corporation (Keirstead, 1948, p. 254). More important, the growth of bureaucracy as the social technology which made possible the second stage of industrialism was only feasible because the development of material technology was held steady. The early years of industry based on major technological advances show a high death-rate among enterprises; growth occurs when the rate of technical advance slows down. Thereafter, consumer demand tends to be standardised, through publicity and price reductions, and the consequent restraint of technical progress enables undertakings to maintain relatively stable conditions, in which large-scale production can be built up through the conversion of manufacturing processes into routine cycles of activity for machines or semi-skilled assembly hands.

Under such conditions not only did concerns grow in size, not only could manufacturing processes be routinised, mechanised and quickened, but the task of co-ordination, of ensuring co-operation and of planning and monitoring could also be broken down into routines and inculcated as specialised management tasks.

It is this second phase of industrialism which is regarded as having dominated the institutional life of Western societies. Between 1870 and 1930, the formal organisation of industrial undertakings along bureaucratic lines, coupled with the concurrent growth of national armies and governmental administrations, suggested to sociologists that 'bureaucratisation' was as intrinsic to the character of modern society as was scientific and technological progress. For Weber, the founder of the study of bureaucracy, it seems to have exhibited the same feature of rational thought applied to the social environment as does technology in the case of the physical environment. Tönnies, earlier (1887), had provided a key to the development of a technology of social organisation by indicating the transformation of the relationships involving the individual which were characteristic of earlier small-scale society ('Gemeinschaft') into 'Gesellschaft' systems.

Bureaucracy, then, stands as the 'formal organisation' of industrial concerns. The formulation given by Weber is a generalised description of the 'ideal type' of bureaucracy – i.e. a synthetic model composed of what are understood in society at large to be the distinguishing features of actual bureaucratic organisations, military, ecclesiastical, governmental, industrial, etc. These distinctive characteristics are:

1. The organisation operates according to a body of laws or rules, which are consistent and have normally been intentionally established.
2. Every official is subject to an impersonal order by which he guides his actions. In turn, his instructions have authority only in so far as they conform with this generally understood body of rules; obedience is due to his office, not to him as an individual.
3. Each incumbent of an office has a specified sphere of competence, with obligations, authority and powers to compel obedience strictly defined.
4. The organisation of office follows the principle of hierarchy; that is, each lower office is under the control and supervision of a higher one.
5. The supreme head of the organisation, and only he, occupies his position by appropriation, by election, or by being designated as successor. Other offices are filled, in principle, by free selection, and candidates are selected on the basis of 'technical' qualifications. They are appointed, not elected.

6. The system also serves as a career ladder. There is promotion according to seniority or achievement. Promotion is dependent on the judgement of superiors.
7. The official, who in principle is excluded from any ownership rights in the concern, or in his position, is subject to discipline and control in the conduct of his office.[1]

It is 'bureaucratised' industry and business which has given advanced industrial societies their distinctive social character. Managers, clerical workers, functionaries, and the professional workers employed by large companies and industrial concerns are regarded as forming a new middle-class, larger in size than, and different in interests and values from, the earlier middle-class of small entrepreneurs, shopkeepers, and professional men (Carr-Saunders et al., 1958; Carr-Saunders and Wilson, 1933; Lockwood, 1951; Marshall, 1939; Mills, 1951). Less attention has been given to the social effects of the ordering of these new men in hierarchies. Most positions in a bureaucratic structure involve these incumbents in the role of both subordinate and superior. The structure also serves as a career ladder, in which co-operation for the success of the organisation goes alongside, or masks, or even expresses, competition for career success.[2] More easily dramatised are the alienating effects (in Freudian terms) of immersion in the occupational roles provided by bureaucratic systems[3] and the alienating effects (in Marxist terms) of the ideologies and institutions created in response to the need to adapt conduct and beliefs to the requirements of effective co-operation and competition.[4]

While the greater part of the industrial system is in the second, bureaucratic phase of the historical development of industrialism (and some older and smaller establishments remain in the first), it is now becoming clear that a third phase has been initiated during the past two or three decades. A new, more insecure, relationship with the consumer has appeared as production has caught up and overtaken spontaneous domestic demand[5] and the propensity to consume has to be stimulated by advertising, by styling, and by marketing promotions guided by consumer research, motivation research, market research. Also, partly as one of the endeavours to maintain expansion, partly because of the stimulus of government spending on the development of new weapons and military equipment, industry has admitted a sizeable influx of new technical developments,[6] and agreed to accept industrial development as a major commitment of its own. So far, the implications of this new phase in the evolution of industrialism have been studied only in so far as they have presented themselves as overt, public, social problems: the shortage of scientific manpower, the new forms of human effort called for by machinery automatically operated and controlled, and the effects of automation on employment.

There are signs that industry organised according to the now traditional principles of bureaucracy is no longer able to accommodate the new elements introduced by large-scale industrial development and by the new relationship with the markets which industry serves. Both demand a much greater degree of flexibility in internal organisation, much higher levels of commitment to the commercial aims of the concern from all its members, and an even higher proportion of administrators, controllers and monitors to operatives.[7]

Industrial Relations

Some of the firms most exposed to the new situation are, in sporadic and tentative fashion, developing organisational techniques which will equip them for living with rapid technological development and unstable markets. But these moves are masked by the much more widespread – though by no means universal – change in the norms governing the relationships between persons and categories of persons within industry. In particular, there is a distinct shift in the relationship between management and labour, reflecting but also generating a concurrent shift in the distribution of income, power and social standing between the two.

There are, as Lutz has pointed out (1960), two elements of the relationship. 'As it is part of a class society, an industrial undertaking is an instrument of domination. The power exercised over the workers also derives, however, from the element of constraint which seems essential to any system for the division of work.' It is the *responses* to these two elements which have for the most part been the object of study. Trade unionism and cognate forms of organisation outside the workshop, and restrictive practices of an institutionalised kind within it, have been extensively examined and reported on as responses to the power exercised over the lives of workers by employers and managers as a class. Absenteeism, labour turnover, and sickness and accident rates have been studied as indicators of pathological response to the adverse psychological as well as physical conditions attaching to industrial labour.

It is the first of these subdivisions to which the title 'industrial relations' has been appropriated for textbooks, and indeed, official government publications. Normally, it is reserved for all aspects of collective bargaining between employers and labour, whether the issues are national or local, apply to single concerns or many, and whether they involve trade unions and employers' associations or *ad hoc* organisations (such as unofficial strike committees). Description of the historical development of labour organisation, of the kinds of procedure employed in bargaining, and of types of trade union represents the bulk of the literature on the subject. During the past decade, studies at the level of wages, of the criteria which are used when wage-claims are discussed (e.g. Wootton, 1955), case-studies and statistical analyses of strikes (Knowles, 1952), and descriptions of the vicissitudes encountered during the post-war years by the joint management-labour production committees forced on industrial concerns during the Second World War (Scott, 1952), have reflected to some extent the shift in the fundamental relationship of management and labour, without attempting to explain it.

Of particular interest and relevance in this context is the new direction taken by the study of Trade Unionism. The increased standing and power of workers has been demonstrated quite explicitly in the increased political and industrial influence exerted by trade union leaders. At the same time, trade union consensus about objectives and about attitudes to the often divergent, sometimes opposed, objectives of both industrialists and government has broken down. Third, trade unions, which grew up during the phase of bureaucratic expansion, have, like industrial undertakings themselves, carried into the new situation structural forms shaped according to the needs and circumstances which prevailed then. So far, British studies have not advanced beyond the stage of posing questions or debating the democratic or undemocratic nature of trade union organisation. In America, a series of studies by Tannenbaum (1956a; 1956b; with Kahn, 1957) of the nature and the distribution within unions of control over policy and decisions introduces a reconsideration of the distribution of power between the different levels within a hierarchy – hitherto treated as a single invariant form – similar to that which has occurred in the case of management structures.

Both the obsolescence of bureaucratic forms and the changed nature of industrial relations are arguably the outcome of the same features of industrialism's third phase, which I have already sketched.[8] Unfortunately, no aspect of industrialism is so little explored in Britain and America as the link between its internal evolution and the sequence of roles, commitments and changes in power open to working members of society. The dramatic change in management-worker relations which has occurred in every Western country during the past twenty years has still no more profound interpretation in English than the road-to-Damascus revelation of the business virtues of good relationships[9] and the premise of a Social Ethic replacing the Protestant Ethic (W. H. Whyte Jr, 1956). In Britain, attempts at interpretation of the change have stopped short at any convenient point at which the task could be handed over to the economists – where one could invoke, for example, the change from mass unemployment to full employment, or inflationary pressures catching wage-levels up in a rising spiral of claims, or the increased importance of export markets, or the replacement of a surplus-dominated international situation by one of chronic shortages.

The Sociology of Work

Developments in the study of the second aspect of the worker's situation – his experience, as 'an appendage to the machine', of an extreme form of the constraints of the factory system – have taken a rather different path. What began, in the first post-war flush of enthusiasm for raising productivity, as a series of investigations into local managerial problems of labour turnover, low productivity and absenteeism has turned into interpretations of these and similar kinds of behaviour as 'alternative methods of withdrawal' from the work situation, and as symptomatic of a malaise engendered by the alienating pressures of industrialism. Such analytical studies reveal a growing interest in the interaction between work and the rest of life, which is also apparent in some recent and current observational studies of dock workers (Liverpool University, 1954), steel workers (Scott *et al*, 1956), fishing communities[10] and labour groups in large civil engineering schemes (Sykes). This interest is still tentative as far as Britain is concerned, but may lead in the direction of the sociology of industrial work which is the necessary complement to a sociology of industrialism.

The most relevant work in this connection is largely French, beginning with Naville's 'occupational demography' – studies of the duration and age-structure of different occupations and the distribution through the working population of different skills and vocations (Naville, 1954).[11] Intimations of a new kind of interaction between work and the rest of life are contained in the work of Dumazedier (1957) on the influence of leisure-time pursuits, interests and obligations on the structure of occupational careers and choices.

Finally, the development of a new work situation for the industrial worker has been a major theme of French industrial sociologists. The growing complexity of industrial processes, especially in engineering, is seen not only as constantly destroying or reducing or modifying the skills and knowledge on which both the comparative standards of living and the self-regard of the worker depend, but also as changing the social context of work. The autonomy that used to invest work, once orders were received from superiors, is now replaced by enclosure in a network of requirements and expectations from an increasing number of specialist functionaries (Friedmann and Reynaud, 1958; Touraine, 1955). For Touraine, this new work situation involves a new working-class situation, and underlies the enstrangement of the worker from traditional working-class movements and ideologies which were rooted in values derived from the former proletarian situation of subjection and poverty (Touraine, n.d.).

THE INTERNAL RELATIONSHIPS OF INDUSTRY:
INDUSTRIAL SOCIOLOGY

As in the case of educational institutions, central and local government departments, prisons, military units, trade unions, hospitals and other closed establishments, access to industrial undertakings for research purposes is only granted by the controlling authorities when they are assured that the research will further the interests the establishment exists to serve; and most controlling authorities reserve the right to make their own appraisal of these interests and of the pertinence to them of the research proposed. The great majority of industrial studies, therefore, have had as their ostensible purpose the improvement of work methods, the control of industrial delinquency, the extension of understanding and control of workers' conduct, the development of a technical understanding of organisation and of management roles, and the elimination of frictional waste caused by inadequate co-operation and communication.

It is as well to recognise the consequent 'ideological bias against business' and against 'internal' studies of industrial undertakings that Lazarsfeld has recently discussed (1959). 'Aiding the doctor, promoting justice, or supporting the agencies of the law – all these are in accordance with accepted norms; helping the businessman make money is not.' While this last aim may not be present in the researcher's mind, he is unlikely to obtain licence to enter and study industrial or other closed establishments unless the possibility of his realising such an aim is entertained by the head of the undertaking. The moral issue may not be different in essence from that present in any study which may result in increasing the power of controllers and manipulators and the subjugation of the controlled and manipulated; Lazarsfeld implies as much. But it presents itself more blatantly and unavoidably. It is certainly not avoided by rotating the axis of moral values and applying terms like pathology and therapy to business concerns; the one still finds its only effective expression in less earning capacity and the other in more. It cannot be glossed over by professing sympathy with the underdog or squaring trade union officials.

There are considerations which blunt the dilemma somewhat; we may also regard money-making by businessmen as proper or necessary. Eventually, however, one has to decide whether the existence of the moral issue puts an embargo on one's studying the internal affairs of industrial undertakings (other than in disguise) or whether other considerations override it. These other considerations are, first, that industrial undertakings, industrial work and industrial milieux are of central importance in our society, and it is becoming rather more difficult to equate ignorance with objectivity in studying the nature and more immediate consequences of industrialism. Secondly, the institutional forms which work has assumed, the organisation of individual and co-operative work, the beliefs about its nature and about related motives and aims, and the systems of values associated with different kinds of work together represent a sizeable section of the fields of study appropriated by the social sciences. Thirdly, business and industrial undertakings exist as communities, or sub-communities, in which a wide variety of forms of behaviour are far more accessible to study than in any other milieu. They exist as enclosed, separate, social establishments, in which people are obliged to deal with each other and to do so observably. Lastly, such communities have many other aspects than those related to work; they are social structures with their own systems of stratification, with different rights and duties, privileges and obligations attached to positions in each level, their own criteria of esteem and marks of prestige, and with their own internal politics. And in both these last respects, because there is a constant pressure towards rationalisation, towards making the whole structure of roles and relationships more explicit and understandable to the members of the community, the detailed study of social structures and of institutionalised conduct is in many ways more easily and more fruitfully pursued in such milieux than in most others.[12]

Such inducements, and some rather more mundane, have been enough to maintain growth in industrial studies, especially in the last decade. Yet it remains true that for every twenty studies of the lowest ranks of manual operatives there is perhaps one of managing directors, whose work and occupational situation are of possibly equal interest and significance; that demarcation disputes and absenteeism among workers attract attention, and identical conduct equally prevalent among managers never does; that there are scores of diagnostic studies of such delinquencies as shirking, or of 'lightning' and unofficial strikes, and none of such offences as pilfering and expense-account swindling, which are possibly more prevalent, more costly, and more damaging to industrial efficiency, but are either condoned or are cloaked under a conspiracy of silence which involves the highest and lowest ranks in industry.

Human Engineering

The earliest studies reveal their alignment with managerial interests very clearly. The tradition of industrial studies as now established begins in America, at the beginning of the century, with Frederick Taylor (1903 etc.). 'Taylorism' was based on the principle, which its founder constantly reaffirmed, that there is ordinarily a large margin between the potential and the actual amount of work done by workers. The task of management was to reduce this margin.

The Health of Munition Workers Committee (1915–17; 1917; 1918), with whose investigations the continuous tradition of industrial studies begins in Britain, was created in 1915 out of a similar though less evangelistic enthusiasm for making better use, in the engineering sense, of human resources. Disappointed in the expectation that women could fill twice as many shells in sixteen hours as they did in eight, doubting whether – as so many members had asserted in the House of Commons – shipyard men working a seventy-hour week absented themselves for one or two days at a time entirely because of incorrigible drunkenness, the Ministry of Munitions set afoot a series of inquiries into the nature of industrial fatigue and the causes for absenteeism.

The experimental and observational studies carried out in Britain during the First World War added the merits and prestige of scientific study to the more dramatic attractions of Taylorism, which had made themselves felt in Europe before 1914. These circumstances seem to have determined the line of development in Britain between the wars. The study of human problems internal to industry was conducted almost exclusively under the auspices of the National Institute of Industrial Psychology and the Industrial Health Research Board, the lineal descendant of the Health of Munition Workers Committee. Their studies were usually directly to do with operatives and the efficiency (in engineering terms) of their labour. Methods were developed for guiding them into, or selecting them for, jobs which matched the resources, fixed, limited and measurable, of intelligence or manual dexterity or physical capacity they brought into industry. Other sequences of studies dealt with the effect of conditions of work and environment on their efficiency, and with methods of economising their work movements, time and effort.[13]

The assumption of the role not only of human resources engineer but of management consultant and aide, which was implicit in Taylorism, was reinforced by the psychologist's bent for – in Friedmann's words – individualising the task and always considering the workers as separate individuals (1955). This set of conditions still applies to a large part of the contribution now being made by psychology; but since 1939 the growth of interest and activity among other social scientists has set rather better defined limits to the aspects of work behaviour to which their assumptions and methods apply. The scope of studies now comprehended by workers in this tradition are, briefly, vocational selection and guidance, techniques of training, and ergonomics, i.e. the design of working conditions, machinery and other equipment in the light of what is known about human capacities and limitations. Since 1939 also, in response partly to the development of methods of selecting officers for the armed forces, and partly to the development of other interests by social scientists, studies related to vocational selection and guidance have reached upwards in the industrial hierarchy to include foremen and managers.

Hawthorne and After

The general movement away from exclusive preoccupation with the individual – as resource, machine or response system – has taken place since 1939. While the Second World War, like the first, provided the operating cause of this development, it would be a mistake to ascribe its theoretical origins to wartime activities in industry and the armed forces of teams of psychologists, psychiatrists, and other social scientists – although undoubtedly it was their work which changed the whole scope of industrial social studies during the 1940s. So far as one can discern now, it is the successive impact of ideas imported from Freudian psychology and social anthropology before the war, social psychology and the classical sociology of Weber and Durkheim during the 1940s, and, after 1950, communication engineering and biology[14] that has widened the scope of the social study of industrial undertakings.

Without using too procrustean a method of simplifying, one can arrange the kinds of studies now current under three heads, each of them corresponding to one of these three successive expansions of the theoretical horizon.

Observational Studies of Working Groups

The psychological holism of the psychoanalytic school bears a distinct resemblance to the sociological holism of social anthropology, as developed by Malinowski and Radcliffe-Brown. The concurrence of these two during the 1930s in one or two American academic milieux bore issue: the theories of the culture-personality school, with which we are not here concerned, and the painstaking exploration of the forms of interaction between social roles and social norms in the behaviour observable among small groups of people.

Not surprisingly, the groups of people most easily accessible for such study have been either employed in industrial activity, or have been convened for some semblance of the same purpose; they are given a task to perform or a problem to solve.

In the first kind of study, the usual procedure has been that of the direct observation of behaviour and the wide-ranging interviews with amenable informants practised by social anthropologists. From the accumulated records of such experiences the observer compiles a detailed description of the relationships prevailing between members of the group, predicates a system of beliefs which might be expected to uphold such relationships, or which have in fact been expressed about them, and goes on to suggest the function, or implicit purpose, which the structure of relationships and the system of beliefs serves for the group and its members. There are variants of the role of observer. He may, as in the Bank-Wiring Observation Room at Hawthorne (Roethlisberger and Dickson, 1939, Part iv), be present without disguise as an observer of the group, a procedure which has obvious disadvantages even when, as we are assured was the case in this classic instance, he gained acceptance as an observer, and enough time was allowed for the group to learn to ignore his presence. These disadvantages are avoided, albeit at some risk of injury or embarrassment, by assuming the guise of a *bona fide* member of the group, and thus becoming a participant observer. The liveliest account of the procedures and hazards involved here is Dalton's (1959). Thirdly, a student may assume some role for which society already provides – of the interested outsider, offering for information some return in receptive listening and informed discussion. The expectation attached to this role may be raised to the point at which the student becomes a consultant and technical assistance is looked for in specific instances, or still further to the assumption of a therapeutic relationship which may require diagnostic exploration of the whole system, psychological, social, technical or economic, of the undertaking or of any of its parts.

If one compares the work undertaken from each point in this range of strategies, the underlying theoretical and methodological unity becomes discernible. Anthropological studies of mining communities in Yorkshire (Dennis *et al.*, 1956) and Fife (Patterson and Willett, 1951), carried out with no heavier disguise than – presumably – an ingratiating demeanour, are directed towards the unveiling of the autonomous systems of beliefs and of social relationships existing in them; the reflections of larger systems which bespeak their membership of a total British society are only very lightly suggested, and then mainly to stress the incompatibilities between the larger society's norms and expectations and those obtaining in the communities studied. That there are losses as well as gains from the blinkered intensiveness of these methods when practised in complex societies has been well known since their first application in the Hawthorne studies of workpeople, in which very little mention of unemployment, and none of Trade Unions, occurs, although the period covered was that of the Great Depression and was also one of the most disturbed in the history of management-labour relations in America. Participant observer studies such as those of J. Sykes in Glasgow and T. Lupton in Manchester tend to avoid this kind of oversight in that the working-man role they assume for lengthy periods brings a more comprehensive appreciation of their associates' ideas, the constraints on their conduct, their interests, and the means adopted to pursue them; on the other hand, they are, like their workfellows, locked into one compartment of the social system they are studying. Dalton appears to have avoided at least the awareness of this effect by moving out from firm to firm during his study (1959). Nevertheless, the research aim is very similar: to characterise the systems of relationships and beliefs existing among the groups of which they are temporary members, and to indicate their incompatibility with the overt aims and beliefs of management as well as their compatibility with the covert aims of the managed.

The clear advantages in the amount of information open to access and the insights gained by close and continuous association with the group to be studied, or by actually playing an assumed part in it, are lost to the observer who stays inside his role of academic observer; the compensatory gains lie in his freedom to move between all groups in the total system of the undertaking, a freedom which is entirely dependent on his remaining, and appearing to remain, detached from the interests of one group which are in conflict with those of other groups. This can most easily be ensured by withholding responses other than non-committal ones to the information asked for in interviews, and this detachment is won most effectively by formalising the situations in which information is obtained by using questionnaires or other standardised interview procedures. However, the point of studying groups of people is at least to collect information, and while standardised procedures and carefully prepared questionnaires may give the wished-for appearance of detachment, it would be presuming too much to reckon on the information collected in this way being equally standardised. Whatever the merits of survey techniques in collecting information from a population when the members of it are fully aware of both their anonymity and their own disengagement, and when the purpose of the inquiry is remote from their interests or generally approved, they are not to be looked for in closed social systems, where beliefs, commitments, attitudes, facts and observations of fact may all bear closely on the perceived self-interest of each member. Discrepancies between the accounts of the self-same incidents, between facts and between views, unfailingly appear in interviews with different people in the system. It is these discrepancies, indeed, which provide the starting-point for inquiry proper in observational studies of the kind[15] in which the student declares, accepts and enacts his role of social scientist, and is prepared to interpret as he goes the information he collects and to discuss his interpretations with his informants.

Such procedures require the exercise of restraint and care in avoiding breaches of confidence. This need arises in all studies of industrial situations. It becomes peculiarly awkward, however, when the student is also confessedly active as a management consultant. While senior managers themselves may feel more disposed to facilitate inquiries, they are also possibly less ready to regard the student differently from all the other resources at their disposal, and so less willing to see themselves as equally under observation (except for form's sake, to encourage the others); the student exposes himself to any resistance or hostility to management from those who feel their interests opposed to management's, and although he may circumvent this, the dilemma of breaking either confidence or the terms of his contract with management is sharpened. Last, and perhaps most seriously, his inquiries must be pursued with the primary aim of improving efficiency. These are the terms on which he must necessarily be engaged, and they govern not only the criteria by which the outcome of the study will be judged but also the terms in which it must be planned and carried out. All these limitations are visible even in work which has nevertheless produced findings of the greatest interest.[16]

The Sociology of Organisations

In reciting the methods and approaches which have developed since the intrusion of ideas from Freudian psychology and social anthropology, we have included some which are applicable to the second kind of studies, those which can be said to have originated in a specifically sociological interest in organisational forms and processes. What we have termed the methods of detached observation and of consultancy have been those most widely used in studies of the operation of bureaucratic hierarchies, of differences in the structure of business and industrial organisations, and of the working relationships of their members. In the first half of this chapter, it was suggested that the second phase of industrialism was giving place to a third, characterised by a new unstable relationship between manufacturing industry and the consumer and the importation on a large scale of scientific techniques as a major, and continuing, industrial resource. Changes in the social technology of industrial organisation which would adapt the undertaking to this new situation were also, it was said, visibly in progress, or at least were being attempted or resisted.

This general disturbance in the industrial system underlies the recrudescence of interest in organisation, some two generations after the accounts of the bureaucratic organisation

developed in industrialism's second phase had been sketched
by Weber, Veblen and others. During the 1930s, when industrial
sociology became an established branch of the study of society,
the bureaucratic structure of business enterprises seems to have
been accepted as given, and attention focused on the deviant
and pathological aspects of human condust and relationships
which prevented the bureaucratic system from achieving the
full effectiveness properly belonging to it. The hierarchy of
management as illustrated by an organisation chart and the
description in an organisation manual of the specialist functional roles attached to each position on the chart were together
regarded as the 'formal organisation': an ideal system of control, information and authority aimed at the most efficient use
of physical and human resources. Over against the 'formal
organisation' was set the 'informal organisation' – the behaviour,
the relationships, the sentiments and beliefs, the commitments
and self-identifications of workers which are irrelevant to the
'formal organisation', or even incompatible with it and its
purposes.[17]

By the early 1950s, this dualism had become an accepted
dogma of industrial sociology. 'Although formal organisation
is designed to subject production to logical planning, things
never seem to go "according to plan", This is evidenced by the
many "problems" managers encounter. They find that no matter
how carefully they organise, despite the concern in anticipating
problems, unanticipated ones always arise. For these eventuali-
ties formal organisation offers little guidance because it is
created as a guidepost for the routine, the typical, and the
unforeseeable' (Miller and Form, 1951, p. 160).[18] For an explanation of these unanticipated consequences, the authors prescribe
a study of the 'informal organisation', and this, indeed, is what
represents the object of study in the observation of work groups
discussed in the previous section.

There are three fairly distinct stages in the subsequent
attempt to resolve this dualism. The first accepted the 'pathological view' and attempted a 'cure' by treating the informal
organisation as if it were the Freudian unconscious of the system, using observation, attitude surveys, and open interview
programmes to explore it, bringing its hidden activities and
commitments and conflicts into the open (i.e. to the knowledge
of management) and enabling its misdirected efforts to be

checked or harnessed to ends consonant with those of the enterprise. The complement to this pragmatic exercise (seriously and expensively undertaken by many companies in America and, latterly, in the UK) was the widening of the conception of management beyond the limits of the functions defined by formal organisation to comprise a range of training activities, of welfare provisions, and of attempts, tagged generically 'human relations', to remove hostilities and improve working relationships.

The second phase is one in which the formal organisation is treated simply as part of the institutional environment of a community at work (Selznick, 1948). This line of interest has led directly into studies of the third type, dealt with in the next section, in which the industrial undertaking is examined as a sub-community, i.e. with its commercial purposes treated as only one of its many institutional aspects, all of which form an interconnected social system.

Thirdly, there has been a dawning realisation that the 'formal organisation' itself is not a management machine which social scientists may safely ignore as they do other technical apparatus like accounts and production technology, but an institutional system which can repay study in the same way as the informal organisation. Gouldner (1956) has described how managers and workers can devise a variety of systems by which they mutually sustain each other's beliefs, expectations, status and self-regard in face of an imposed organisational structure. 'Organisation theory' is the name given to a new pre-occupation with the way in which co-operative systems work, whether in business, manufacturing, government, service industries or the armed forces. While the subject of study is the structure of organisations and their efficiency, attention is focused on what had previously been assumed as axiomatic – the rationality of formal organisation. It is, as Eisenstadt (1958, p. 106) says, 'concerned with the conditions which make for maximum rational behaviour, calculations, and performance within a given structural organisational setting, or, conversely, the extent to which various structures and organisational factors limit rational calculations and efficiency'.

Turning the picture face upwards in this way has been as revelatory as the oddly similar discovery that educational performance might be related to the organisation and institutional character of schools, as well as to the structure and the material and social circumstances of families.

There are three fairly distinct levels of research, each with its own methodology. Studies of whole structures are normally pursued by observation and open-ended interviews. They are aimed at eliciting the rationale of the distribution of functions throughout an organisation and the way in which the total task is thereafter discharged by the co-operation of functionaries through the means provided for them, and the means devised by them. Such studies as Gouldner (1956), Woodward (1958), Crozier (1955; with Guetta, 1956) and Burns and Stalker (1961) are more or less taxonomic in intention: it is now fairly well established that there is no one system of 'bureaucracy' rationally appropriate to any of the kinds of tasks which confront working organisations. The central problem of this kind of study, therefore, has shifted away from exploration of the nature and progress of 'bureaucratisation', founded on the notion of the perpetually denser ramification of bureaucratic order in every aspect of social organisation, as well as of the increase in scale and in complexity of existing bureaucratic structure. There is now more concern with the types of organisational structure which exist, and the reasons for their existence.

It is below this level of the total organisational structure that the focus of study becomes the scrutiny and comparative analysis of the institutionalised procedures of which an organisation is made up. It is here also that one or two significant extensions of empirical methods of study have occurred. Simon and others have painstakingly recorded the discussions, transactions by correspondence, journeys and meetings involved in the course of a management decision to instal new kinds of business machinery (Cyert et al. 1956). Sune Carlson obtained the co-operation of several managing directors in recording, on standard diary schedules, the way in which their working time was distributed among activities, places and people (1951). The present writer extended the self-recording method to comprehend the simultaneous activities of top management groups in some ten manufacturing concerns over periods of three to five weeks (Burns, 1957). Guest trained observers to accompany foremen and record their conversations verbatim and their actions from minute to minute during a single working day

(1956). Mechanical devices have also been used for recording the frequency and direction of the traffic of oral information as well as written information and signals.

The effect of a good deal of this work has been to destroy the image of the formal management structure as a rational system applying known techniques to the mastery of known problems. Even the most complicated, or the most successful, or the largest organisations reveal themselves as meaningful largely in terms of ritual and traditional beliefs, of unconscious adaptations to the requirements of the situation, of codes of management practice thought to be strictly standardised, and of the use of such codes of practice to justify or to advance interests divorced from, and even opposed to, those of the undertaking. What we have called the social technology of industrialism, in fact, is a primitive and rather heterogeneous collection of skills and crafts practised for the most part without much regard to the ends they are supposed to serve, and without much knowledge of the extent to which they serve them.[19] The first apprehensions of this situation have prompted the exploitation of operational research methods in fields other than the accepted one of the better control of manufacturing processes. In particular, it is thought possible, or at least worth the attempt, to improve control and understanding of working organisations, especially business enterprises, by treating them as response systems, with material technology, the market and the sources of supply of financial, material and human resources as the external conditions to which they respond. It is in this connection that some of the elementary concepts and analytical procedures of cybernetics and communication engineering in general have been brought into use.

Doubts about the assumption of rationality in working organisations have also helped to generate, and later been generated by, the study of artificially constituted work groups. There is by now large body of experimental studies by social psychologists in America and Europe. Some are designed to test out hypotheses about the effectiveness of different organisational structures in different situations. Others enable close observations to be made under controlled conditions of the way in which simple co-operative systems work. A third group is concerned with how decisions are made in competitive or co-operative situations.

144   *Description, Explanation and Understanding*

The Study of Working Communities

During the 1930s, students of the roles and conduct of industrial operatives had to forego the simple engineering conceptions of the economic or wasteful use of a fixed flow of human effort, and of workers' time being spent either in working or in shirking. Similarly, the distinction between the rational formal organisation, uniformly bureaucratic in structure, and the largely irrational informal organisation partly or wholly at odds with it has been discarded. The relics of the distinction remain in that still drawn between the studies described in the previous section, which start from a critical analysis of the overt tasks of the organisation and the means believed to be used in carrying them out, and those others which start from a consideration of the community at work as a social system, with a large number of inter-related institutions and a generalised, organic function of keeping itself in being on the best possible terms.

Theoretically, and empirically, in the kind of problems attacked and the methods employed, these two approaches seem to be merging. During the years immediately after the Second World War, Selznick, in the United States, could write:

> All formal organizations are moulded by forces tangential to their rationally ordered structure and stated goals. Every formal organization – trade union, political party, army, corporation, etc. – attempts to mobilize human and technical resources as means for the achievement of its ends. However, the individuals within the system tend to resist being treated as means. They interact as wholes, bringing to bear their own special problems and purposes . . . It follows that there will develop an informal structure within the organisation which will reflect the spontaneous efforts of individuals and sub-groups to control the conditions of their existence . . . It is to these informal relations and structures that the attention of the sociologist will be primarily directed. He will look upon the formal structure, e.g. the official chain of command, as the special environment within and in relation to which the informal structure is built. (1948, pp. 250–1)

Such a statement would be fairly applicable to the general theoretical orientation of the research team of the Tavistock Institute of Human Relations at the beginning of its work in Glacier Metals (Jaques, 1951). Both Selznick (1957) and the

Tavistock researchers have moved substantially towards treating the social techniques of management – the formal structure itself – as an intrinsic part of the total system of institutions by which the members of a working community achieve their own ends. The Tavistock Institute, indeed, has been evolving a unitary conception of the 'socio-technical system' existing in any industrial milieu; this envisages the total material circumstances (including machinery and technical processes) and working behaviour observable in any workplace as a complex organic system by which individuals achieve, through various combinations and tensions, some balance between the explicit and implicit psychological, cultural and physical demands of the work situation and their own goals. A parallel development appears in the work of Argyris over the past decade.[20]

Working from the other end, so to speak, Simon has expanded his earlier concern with such formal elements of management structure and technique as composite decision-making and planning to an examination of the total institutional setting to which individuals' actions have to be referred, and a wide-ranging critique of the 'rationality' of management systems and even the aims of business enterprise.[21] This particular course has been followed empirically by the writer's own research. The study which began as an attempt to observe the organisational adjustments made by established firms which were entering the field of electronics development and production, and moving from a stable market and technical situation into one of rapid change, had to develop into an inquiry into the reasons why no such organisational adjustments were in fact made. As a consequence, the internal politics of firms, the manoeuvres of groups and individuals in order to advance or defend their status, the different limits put to commitment to the interests of the firm, the significance for the whole organisation of the social isolation of the managing director at the top of a hierarchy, all had to be considered in the light of their bearing on the capacity of the working organisation to adapt itself to its actual tasks and circumstances (Burns and Stalker, 1961). The development of such interests, and their conjunction with those emerging from the tradition of studies of informal organisation and 'human relations', gives added significance to inquiries into the internal politics of organisations on such lines as

Crozier's analysis of the power structure of a large office (1960), and Tannenbaum's comparative study of the distribution of control over decisions in trade unions (1956b; with Kahn, 1957).

The present situation in the very wide field of research subsumed here under the title of 'Studies of Working Communities', is one in which there is a growing connection, in empirical as well as theoretical terms, between studies of the internal structure and institutions of industrial undertakings, those of the way in which the industrial system is evolving, and those, again, of the way in which industrialism processes society and its members. There is, in fact, an explicit seeking after a synthetic view of the institutional patterns in modern society which derive from and contribute to its essentially industrial character.

Method

Some remarks have already been made on the 'techniques' of field inquiries carried on inside industrial undertakings. Little need be added here; apart from the specialised techniques of psychometric tests, and the traditional procedures of attitude surveys, both developed within the established discipline of industrial psychology on the one hand, and experimental closed-room studies of small groups on the other, there are very few technical methods specific to industrial studies beyond those of Guest and Carlson, mentioned above. What do apply to industrial studies with particular force, however, are certain general methodological considerations which may do something to explain the procedure normally followed by researchers.

This review of studies has to some extent, and inevitably, given a false coherence to the paths of development they have followed. Like any other kind of enquiry which has a history and an establishment, industrial studies seem at the time to be pursuing not so much the right kind of knowledge, as the right kind of questions, not definitive information, but fresh hypotheses; not exploring and mapping new territory, but staking claims and prospecting.

R. K. Merton has recently (1959, p. x) quoted Aubrey, Darwin and Agnes Arber to remind us, that, as the last of these has said, 'the difficulty in most scientific work lies in framing the questions rather than in finding the answers'. But questions do not suggest themselves; they arise from doubt. Doubt, in turn, arises from a discrepancy between facts, or between facts and the way in which they are usually interpreted or between different interpretations of the same facts. A stricter system of management raised doubts about the inevitability of 'bureaucratisation' and suggested to A. W. Gouldner the possibility of alternative sub-types of bureaucratic system (1956). More prosaically, the present writer started a lengthy and elaborate study in nine firms of the structure and functions of senior management because individual managers in one firm were unable, when asked, to describe their present jobs. They recited instead the main episodes of their careers in the firm and explained, equally lucidly, what they would be doing when the 'current panic' was over or an overdue reorganisation completed, and they could settle down to the work their department was now planned to do. After a succession of interviews, it became impossible not to suspect that all such descriptions, including those given by other managers in more stable firms, were interpretations of history or of an ideal working programme, rather than reports of actuality.[23]

Incompatibilities in the information given by members of the same milieu about facts, situations and purposes are, in the writer's experience, always present. The student's own misconstructions, and the errors of chance or the casualness or sheer ignorance of informants have to be distinguished from incompatibilities inherent in the fact that people speak from different situations and roles; this can be done in the interview itself, but is an essential part of 'reporting back'.

This last is an intrinsic part of social research in industrial milieux, and constitutes a peculiar advantage (or perhaps disadvantage, in certain circumstances) of industrial sociology. Research reports are usually, and properly, heard or read and criticised in the first instance by the people to whom they most directly refer and who supplied the information on which they are based. When information has been winnowed in ensuing discussion, the question presented by internal inconsistencies is not 'Which version is right?' but 'How do these differences arise? How is it that these different versions of the same set of circumstances have arisen in the minds of people who have to co-operate in the very circumstances they view so differently?' The need to account for these differences marks the first stage beyond description. Many studies are wholly concerned with the definition and explanation of different accounts by managers and factory operatives of the same circumstances. Latterly, for example, R. M. McKenzie has examined the incompatible beliefs and statements of fact expressed by production workers and managers and inspection staff about each other's work. This study has provided evidence of the manner in which the social situation of individuals prescribe their appraisal of measure and quantity and has some connection with the more general hypotheses of Friedmann and of Touraine (see p. 131 above) concerning the development of functionally specialised management systems as a way of substituting impersonal authority for personal command, a relationship increasingly rejected by both sides, and perhaps increasingly irrelevant.

The significance for the social scientist of these differences and incompatibilities of viewpoint and fact lies in the help they provide in ascertaining what for him are the essential elements in the structure of the institution: viz., those elements which vary with variations in the external or internal situation of the concern, and those elements which, by contrast, appear to remain unaffected. Thus, Woodward (1958), from a study of the organisation of 100 firms in Essex, found that the number of ranks in the management hierarchy was less in process industries than among large-lot engineering manufacturers. In the writer's study of 100 managers in nine firms previously cited, it was found that the amount of time they spent in conversation with each other grew, and subordination to seniors was increasingly rejected, the greater the rate of technical development in which the firm was involved.

There is also a method, perhaps resembling that of comparative anatomy, in which the social character of an institution is matched with that of some other socially remote institution. Engelhardt (1958) has presented the latest of a series of reconstructions of organisational in efficiency in terms of the adjustment of a patient to sickness or disability. Bradney (1957a; 1957b) and Sykes (in an unpublished paper) have explored the social significance of 'joking' and 'quasi-familial' relationships, both part of the familiar currency of concepts used in investigating primitive societies, in attempts to elucidate the status system of employees in a department store and a large office. The danger when studies are directed to the establishment of such parallels is that they may be regarded as complete when a description has been translated into the technical language of psychiatry, social anthropology – or sociology for that matter – or that the heightening of descriptive writing by an elaborate simile may be taken for explanatory analysis or new information.

Nevertheless, the purpose of comparative social studies is to achieve an understanding of social institutions which is different from that current among the people through whose conduct the institutions exist: different, new and better. The practice of sociology is critcism: to criticise or to raise questions about claims and assumptions concerning the value or meaning of conduct and achievement. It is the business of sociologists to conduct a critical debate, in this sense, with the public about its equipment of social institutions. This purpose is as important in the social study of industry as in any other field.

NOTES AND REFERENCES

1. For Weber's formal statement of bureaucracy as an ideal type, see Weber (1947), pp. 329–34.
2. Some aspects of the ambiguity of the demands of rationalised functional roles and pursuits of promotion are discussed in Bendix (1956), ch. 5. See also Burns (1956), Lewis and Stewart (1958), Warner and Abegglen (1955).
3. These form the theme of D. Riesman's *The Lonely Crowd* (1953) and W. H. Whyte Jr's *The Organization Man* (1956). For general statement of the Freudian thesis, see H. Marcusse (1956).
4. See, for example, Whyte (1952) and Bendix (1956).
5. See the discussion of this relationship in J. K. Galbraith (1952; 1955; 1959).
6. The best available indications of the rate of growth of industrial research and development are provided by the US National Research Council Bulletins, *Industrial Research Laboratories in the United States,* issued from 1921 onwards. For Britain, no comparable figures exist for the period before 1955, the year of the survey (carried out by E. Rudd) (1947), for the Department of Scientific and Industrial Research (1958). G. L. Payne (1960) gives an exhaustive review of published information.
7. For some material differences in the internal situation of firms in stable and changing circumstances, see Burns (1957). For a more general discussion of the current organisational dilemma, see Burns and Stalker (1961).
8. See also Galbraith (1959), ch. 8, 'Economic Security'.
9. Ideally (in the sense of almost too good to be true) presented in the Buchsbaum Case, an autobiographical narrative of the way in which one American employer changed over from the inflexibly tough-with-labour policy of the 1930s to the 'playing-along-with-

the Unions' and 'human relations' strategy of the 1940s (W. F. Whyte, 1949).

10. Studies now in progress in Hull and Aberdeen.

11. As early as 1945, Naville produced a general critique of vocational guidance as claiming to be a straightforward technique capable of pointing the child in the direction best indicated by his aptitudes. The objectives of vocational guidance, according to Naville, are impossible to achieve outside the context of a vast apparatus of organised information about the structure of employment, the economic system, and technical industrial and economic trends (1945).

12. For example, most of the illustrations of 'expressive' behaviour in Goffman (1956) are drawn from studies of occupational milieux.

13. The topics covered during the inter-war period by the research reports of the IHRB have been classified by F. E. Emery (1960).

14. It might be useful to set down here the points at which these fertilising ideas have penetrated industrial studies.

   (a) The interviewing techniques developed as a result of the first Hawthorne experiment were admitted to 'owe something to the methods developed by psychopathology' (Mayo, 1933, p. 86). Mayo himself had practised as a psychiatrist.
       For the much fuller development of the connection, see A, T, Wilson (1947) and other papers contributed by members of the staff of Tavistock Institute of Human Relations to *Social Therapy, Journal of Social Issues*, vol. III, no. 2.

   (b) The second major study at Hawthorne, begun in 1931, was of restriction of output among a team of men employed in wiring and soldering connection in telephone exchange equipment. 'The general methodological concepts employed throughout this study were chiefly derived from Mr. Lloyd Warner . . . at that time Assistant Professor of Social Anthropology at Harvard University' (Roethlisberger and Dickson, 1939, p. 389, footnote).

   (c) The origins of attempts to study the nature of the social norms governing behaviour with *ad hoc* groups, especially with the aim of re-setting the norms (Group Dynamics), lie in Kurt Lewin's wartime projects (1947).

   (d) Weber has been the reference point in American sociological studies of the formal organisation of undertakings, which have developed with great speed and vitality since the publication of Barnard's *Functions of the Executive* in 1939. See Gouldner (1956), Merton et al. (1952), Simon (1945).

   (e) Studies of labour turnover and absenteeism by Rice and Trist and by Baldamus most clearly show Durkheimain influence in the treatment of withdrawal form work as a 'social fact', but the method of the comparative study of institutions, which may be traced to the same source, is central to an increasing body of later work.

   (f) Apart from the appropriation and misappropriation of a number of the more familiar terms, the exploitation of the concepts of communication engineering in the social sciences has come largely through the recent experimental studies of Alex Bavelas and the school founded by him at the Massachusetts Institute of Technology and the observations of Colin Cherry and D. M. Mackay. Much of the experimental

work inspired by Bavelas has to do with the comparative efficiency and economy of different organisation patterns considered as communication networks, and with the kind of
decisions made by individuals when confronted with calls for
action and when in possession of varying amounts of information (Bavelas, 1951). The contributions of Cherry and
Mackay have less empirical reference to industrial contexts,
but are of obvious importance to the study of interaction in
formal organisations. See Cherry (1958).

(g) Many of the statements made some years ago in 'cybernetics'
terms may be – and some have been – rendered into equivalent terms taken from biology; this fashion trend follows
upon the popularising work of J. Z. Young, Konrad Lorenz
and L. von Bertalanffy. Again, apart from this kind of conceptual infection, the notions developed by some biologists
about the interaction between an organism, considered as a
system, and its environment, have been of considerable influence on the work of members of the Tavistock Institute of
Human Relations.

15. See Burns and Stalker (1961), pp. 12–14, for an account of this
observational and interviewing procedure.
16. A demonstration of the possibilities and limitations of the consultant role may be seen in A. K. Rice (1958).
17. Rothlisberger and Dickson (1939), Part IV, 'Social Organization of
Employees', esp. ch. 23, 'Formal *versus* Informal Organization'.
18. See also Roethlisberger (1941), ch. V, 'A Disinterested Observer
Looks at Industry', and Moore (1947), ch. VI, 'Blueprint Organization', and ch. XV, 'Informal Organization of Workers'.
19. Not so much the writing and publication as the striking popularity
of C. Northcote Parkinson's *Parkinson's Law* (1958) has provided
one indication of how widespread are the doubts about the rationality of bureaucratic structure and of traditional features of
bureaucratisation.
20. Compare C. Argyris's early study, reported in *What Budgeting
does to People,* with his recent papers (1957; 1959).
21. Cf. Simon, *Administrative Behaviour* (1945) with *Models of Man*
(1957) and March and Simon (1958), *Organizations.*
22. It should also be said that an important purpose of social studies
has been to raise doubts about current assumptions or traditional
wisdom in the minds of administrators and the public. The earliest 'participant observer' studies were directed towards collecting
facts about wages and conditions in the 'sweated industries' in
order to challenge contemporary apathy (see Booth (1893), esp.
ch. III by Beatrice Potter, 'The Tailoring Trade'. See also Webb
(1898) and Idem (1929), pp. 311–39.) The astonishing feature of
the 'Our Towns' report on the conditions of children evacuated
from city slums in 1940 was not the squalor and unseemliness of
the children but the blank ignorance of all other sections of society about them (Women's Group on Public Welfare 1943).
23. In fact, the subsequent study, carried out in nine firms, revealed a
sizeable discrepancy between the way in which senior managers
spent their time and their ideas, or recollections, of the way in
which they had spent it (Burns, 1957, pp. 45–60).

BIBLIOGRAPHY

Argyris, Chris (1957) 'The Individual and Organization'.
Administrative Science Quarterly., 2.
Argyris, Chris (1959) 'Individual-Organization Actualization'.
Administrative Science Quarterly, 4.
Argyris, Chris. *What Budgeting Does to People.*
Barnard, Chester I. (1938) *The Functions of the Executive.* Cambridge,
Mass: Harvard University Press.
Bavelas, A. (1951) 'Communication Patterns in Problem-Solving
Groups', in von Foerster, H., (ed.), *Cybernetics: Transactions of the
Eighth Conference, March 1951.* New York: Josiah Macy, Jr,
Foundation, 1952.
Bendix, R. (1956) *Work and Authority in Industry.* London: Chapman
and Hall.
Berle, A. A., Jr, and Means, G. C. (1932) *The Modern Corporation and
Private Property.* New York: Macmillan.
Booth, Charles (1893) *Life and Labour of the People in London,* vol. 4.
London: Macmillan.
Bradney, P. (1957a) 'The Joking Relationship in Industry'. *Human
Relations,* 10, 179–87.
Bradney, P. (1957b) 'Quasi-Familial Relationships in Industry'. *Human
Relations,* 10, 271–8.
Burns, Tom (1956) 'The Reference of Conduct in Small Groups;
Cliques and Cabals in Occupational Milieux'. *Human Relations,* 8,
467–86.
Burns, Tom (1957) 'Management in Action'. *Operat. Res. Quart.,* 8 (2).
Burns, Tom, and Stalker, G. M. (1961) *The Management of Innovation.*
London: Tavistock.
Carlson, S. (1951) *Executive Behaviour.* Stockholm: Stroenberg.
Carr-Saunders, A. M., Jones, D. Caradog, and Moser, C. A. (1958)
A Survey of Social Conditions in England and Wales. London: Oxford
University Press, ch. 9.
Carr-Saunders, A. M. and Wilson, P. A. (1933) *The Professions.* London:
Oxford University Press.
Cherry, C. (1958) On Human Communication. New York: Wiley.
Crozier, M. (1955) *Petits Fonctionnaires au Travail – Compte rendu d'une
enquête sociologique effectivée dans une grande administration publique
Parisienne.* Paris: Centre National de la Recherche Scientifique.
Crozier, M., and Guetta, P. (1956) *Une Organisation Administrative au
Travail. Résultat d'une enquête sociologique sur le personnel d'une
compagnie d'assurances.* Paris: de Paris, Université Institute des
Sciences Sociales de Travail.
Crozier, M. (1960) 'Les relations de pouvoir dans un système
d'organisation bureaucratique'. *Sociologie du Travail,* 1, 61–70.
Cyert, R. M., Simon, H. A., and Trow, D. B. (1956) 'Observation of
a Business Decision'. *Journal of Business of the University of Chicago,*
29, 237–48.
Dalton, M. (1959) *Men Who Manage.* London: Chapman and Hall.

Dennis, N., Henriques, F. M. *et al.* (1956) *Coal is Our Life*. London: Eyre and Spottiswoode.

Department of Scientific and Industrial Research (1958) *Estimates of Resources devoted to Scientific and Engineering Research and Development in British Manufacturing Industry. 1955*. London: HMSO.

Dumazedier, J. (1957) 'Loisirs et dynamique socioculturelle'. *Cahiers Int. de Sociologie*, 22, 75–96.

Eisenstadt, S. N. (1958) 'Bureaucracy and Bureaucratization'. *Curr. Sociol.*, 6 (2).

Emery, F. E. (1960) 'Applied Social Science in British Industry', OEEC, *Social Research and Industry in Europe*, pp. 81–2.

Engelhardt, H. N. (1958) 'Medical Comments on the Use of the Word "Disease" in Sociology (Social Pathology)'. Paper presented to Cégos International Conference, Brussels, 1958.

Fitton, R. S., and Wadsworth, A. P. (1958) *The Strutts and the Arkwrights*. Manchester University Press.

Friedmann, Georges (1955) *Industrial Society*. Glencoe, Ill.: Free Press.

Friedmann, G., and Reynaud, J. D. (1958) 'Sociologies: Techniques de Production et du Travail', in Gurvitch, G. (ed.), *Traité de Sociologie. Paris:* Presses Université de France.

Galbraith, J. K. (1952) *American Capitalism*. London: Hamilton.

Galbraith, J. K. (1955) *The Great Crash, 1929*. London: Hamilton.

Galbraith, J. K. (1959) *The Affluent Society*. London: Hamilton.

Goffman, Erving (1956) *The Presentation of Self in Everyday Life*. Edinburgh: Social Sciences Research Centre, University of Edinburgh, Monograph no. 2.

Gouldner, A. W. (1954) *Patterns of Bureaucracy*. Glencoe, Ill.: Free Press.

Gouldner, A. W. (1956) *Patterns of Industrial Bureaucracy*. London: Routledge.

Gouldner, A. W. (1959) 'Organization Analysis', in Merton, R. K., Brown, Leonard, and Cottrell, L. S. (eds), *Sociology To-day*. New York: Basic Books.

Guest, R. H. (1956) 'Of Time and the Foreman'. *Personnel*, pp. 478–86.

Health of Munitions Workers Committee (1915–17) *Memoranda 1–20*.

Health of Munitions Workers Committee (1917) *Interime Report on Industrial Efficiency and Fatigue* (CD 8511). London: HMSO.

Health of Munitions Workers Committee (1918) *An Investigation of the Factors concerned in the Causation of Industrial Accidents: Memorandum no. 21* (By H. M. Vernon). (Cd 9046). London: HMSO.

Jaques, Elliott (1951) *The Changing Culture of a Factory*. London: Tavistock.

Keirstead, B. S. (1948) *The Theory of Economic Change*. London: Macmillan.

Knowles, K. C. J. C. (1952) *Strikes*. Oxford: Blackwell.

Lazarsfeld, Paul F. (1959) 'Reflection on Business'. *Amer. J. Sociol.*, 65, 1–31.

Lewin, K. (1947) 'Group Decision and Social Change', in Newcome,

T. M., and Hartley, E. L., *Readings in Social Psychology*, pp. 330–44. New York: Holt.

Lewis, R., and Stewart, R. (1958) *The Boss*. London: Phoenix House.

Liverpool University Department of Social Science (1954) *The Dock Worker*. Liverpool: Liverpool University Press.

Lockwood, D. (1951) *he Black-Coated Worker*. London: Allen and Unwin.

Lutz, B. (1960) 'Notes on Industrial Sociology in Germany', in *Social Research and Industry in Europe*. (Organisation for European Economic Co-operation.)

March, J. G. and Simon, H. A. (1958) *Organizations*. London: Chapman & Hall.

Marcuse, H. (1956) *Eros and Civilization*. London: Routledge.

Marshall, T. H. (1939) 'The Recent History of Professionalism in Relation to Social Structure and Social Policy'. *Canad. J. Econ. Polit. Sci.*, 5, 325–34.

Marx, Karl. *Capital*.

Mayo, Elton (1933) *The Human Problems of an Industrial Civilization*. New York: Macmillan.

Marton, R. K. (1959) 'Problem-Finding in Sociology', In *Sociology To-day*: see Gouldner (1959).

Merton, R. K., Gray, A. P., Hockey, B., and Selvin, H. C. (1952) *Reader in Bureaucracy*. Glencoe, Ill.: Free Press.

Miller, D. C., and Form, W. H. (1951) *Industrial Sociology*. New York: Harper.

Mills, C. Wright (1951) *White Collar*. New York: Oxford University Press.

Moore, W. G. (1947) *Industrial Relations and the Social Order*. New York: Macmillan.

Naville, Pierre (1945) *Théorie de l'orientation professionelle*. Paris: Gallimard.

Naville, Pierre (1954) *La vie travail et ses problémes*. Paris: Armand Colin.

Parkinson, C. Northcote (1958) *Parkinson's Law*. London: Murray.

Patterson, T. T., Willett, F. J. (1951) 'Unofficial Strike'. *Sociolog. Rev.*, 43 (4).

Payne, G. L. (1960) *Britain's Scientific and Technological Manpower*. London: Oxford University Press.

Rice, A. K. (1958) *Productivity and Social Organization: The Ahmedabad Experiment*. London: Tavistock.

Riesman, David (1953) *The Lonely Crowd*. New York: Doubleday.

Roethlisberger, F. J. (1941) *Management and Morale*. Harvard University Press.

Roethlisberger, F. J., and Dickson, W. J. (1939) *Management and the Worker*. Harvard University Press.

Scott, W. H. (1952) *Industrial Leadership and Joint Consultation*. Liverpool: Liverpool University Press.

Scott, W. H., Banks, J. A., Halsey, A. H., and Lupton, T. (1956) *Technical Change and Industrial Relations*. Liverpool: Liverpool University Press.

Selznick, Philip (1948) *TVA and the Grass Roots*. Berkeley: University of California Press.

Selznick, Philip (1957) *Leadership in Administration*. Evanston, Ill.: Row Peterson.

Simon, H. A. (1945) *Administrative Behavior*. New York: Macmillan.

Simon, H. A. (1957) *Models of Man*. New York: Wiley.

Smiles, Samuel (1859) *Self-Help*. 58th edn. London: Murray, 1910.

Smith, Adam (1776) *The Wealth of Nations*. Book I, ch. 1.

Sykes, J. Unpublished papers.

Tannenbaum, A. S. (1956a) 'The Concept of Organisational Control'. *J. Soc. Issues*, 12.

Tannenbaum, A. S. (1956b) 'Control Structures and Union Functions'. *Amer. J. Sociol.*, 61, 536–45.

Tannenbaum, A. S., and Kahn, R. L. (1957) 'Organizational Control Structure. A General Description Technique as applied to Four Local Unions'. *Hum. Relat.*, 10, 127–39.

Taylor, F. W. *Scientific Management*. New York: Harper. (Includes *Shop Management* [1903], *Principles of Scientific Management* [1911], and Taylor's testimony before the Special House of Representatives Committee to Investigate the Taylor and other Systems of Management [1912].)

Tönnies, E. *Gemeinschaft und Gesellschaft*. Leipzig, 1887. Trans. C. P. Loomis, *Community and Association*. London, Routledge.

Touraine, A. (1955) *L'Evolution du travail ouvrier aux Usines Renault*. Paris, Centre National de la Recherche Scientifique.

Touraine, A. (n.d.) 'Situation du mouvement ouvrier' in *La Classe ouvriére: Mythe et Réalitiés*. Paris (collection published from *Argument* 12–13. Editions de Minuit.

Ure, Andrew (1835) *The Philosophy of Manufactures*. London.

US National Research Council (1921ff.) Bulletins on 'Industrial Research Laboratories in the United States'.

Warner, W. L., and Abegglen, J. G. (1955). *Big Business Leaders in America*. New York.

Webb, Beatrice (1898) 'Diary of an Investigator', in S. and B. Webb, *Problems of Modern Industry*, London: Longmans, ch. 1.

Webb, Beatrice (1929) *My Apprenticeship*. London: Longmans.

Weber, Max (1947) *The Theory of Social and Economic Organization*. Edinburgh: Hodge.

Whyte, William F. (1949) 'Patterns of Interaction in Union-Management Relations'. *Hum. Organiz.*, 8, 13–19.

Whyte, William H., Jr (1952) *Is Anybody Listening?* New York: Simon and Schuster.

Whyte, William H., Jr (1956) *The Organization Man*. New York: Simon and Schuster; Harmondsworth: Penguin Books.

Wilson, A. T. M. (1947) 'Some Implications of Medical Practice and Social Casework for Action Research', *Social Therapy, Journal of Social Issues*, 3 (2).

Women's Group on Public Welfare (1943) *Our Towns: A Close-Up* London: Oxford University Press.

Woodward, J. (1958) *Management and Technology*. London: HMSO.
Wootton, Barbara (1955) *The Social Foundations of Wage Policy*. London: Allen and Unwin.
Zimmern, Alfred (1936) *The Greek Commonwealth*. London: Oxford University Press.

8

Sociological Explanation

This was very much a *piece d'occasion*. The Department of
Sociology had been established in 1964, and I was appointed
to the Chair in the following year, so the *'occasion'* was, for
the three people who made up the dapartment's staff then,
more than usually fraught – or, as I began by saying,
'daunting'. Hence its rather manifesto-like character, and
the sustained argument, mostly by example, that sociology
is properly a critical, assumption-testing, discipline.

Having to give an inaugural lecture is a rather daunting affair
though, I am sure, a salutary one. Luckily, there is always
tradition to sustain one and to afford some guidance. There are,
one finds, models, or types, of inaugural lectures. I cannot claim
to be a connoisseur, but, judging from a small and heavily
biased sample, they seem to fall into three groups. There are
those, to begin with, which announce new departures for a
subject, new horizons, recent territorial acquisitions in teaching
or research, perhaps a reformed constitution: they are, in short,
manifestoes – delivered, of course, modestly, even diffidently
sometimes, and with proper deference to neighbours and previous tenants, but manifestoes nevertheless; muted manifestoes.
The second kind defines itself more precisely. There is hardly a
single field of scholarship or science in which the contribution

First published as Inaugural Lecture, no. 28, University of Edinburgh, February
1966.

of Scotland, of this University itself, has not been extensive and weighty – even, at times, momentous; very few branches of learning in which it is not possible to point to a noble and inspiring tradition of intellectual endeavour. There is special propriety on the occasion of an inaugural lecture, then, in recalling – invoking – the achievements of predecessors, of the giants on whose shoulders we presume to stand; there is a special propriety in setting oneself the aim, not unduly modest, either, of continuing or reviving the traditions they formed. And for those who invest in this kind of inaugural, there is the very large bonus to collect from the rich deposits of portable quotations which lie embedded in so much of Scottish intellectual history, with its unique and rewarding blend of wit and sententiousness, of high thinking and low living. Inaugurals of this kind are known to the trade as Scotch, or Upper Library, jobs.

Third, and last, is the guided tour through the main thoroughfares of a new and unfamilar subject. Less striking in its appeal than the first, less elegant in manner than the second, more pedestrian by definition of course than either, the guided tour runs the twin hazards of losing half one's audience by boring them with what is already distressingly familiar stuff, and the other half by hurrying them through the more complicated or remote precincts.

These risks I have to ask you to face with me, however, because this is the form and pattern I want to adopt for this lecture. I do so not because sociology is new or unfamiliar – for me to think so would be both false and presumptuous – but because it has seemed to me a subject more than usually susceptible to misconception and misconstruction.

There is, I shall argue, a special reason for this. All branches of knowledge, scientific and other, are concerned with description as well as with explanation, have their substantive content as well as their methodology, are fact-finding, diagnostic or taxonomic activities as well as theoretical and model-building activities. It is indeed by their descriptive activities, their substantive area of study, that specialist studies are known to the non-specialist public. Sociology is no exception, and it is because of this, I believe, that the misconceptions have arisen. For the misconceptions, such as they are, relate to what is publicly known about the descriptive activities of sociology.

The title I have chosen for this lecture, therefore, while not deliberately misleading, is rather elliptical. I shall have to deal with sociology in its descriptive aspects, and, moreover, to try to show how both as description and as explanation sociology is always a critical activity. In considering sociological explanation, furthermore, I shall not seek either to present you with a review of the methods of research used in sociology or of customary procedures in analysing research data – which would be very tedious and exceedingly inappropriate. I shall also steer very clear of the ground which has been ploughed so heavily in recent years by British and American philosophers. My references will be to empirical sociology rather than to what is commonly designated by sociologists as social theory. My object is to try to point out by example and to explain as best I can what is distinctive about sociology in its approach to its subject matter. And I shall do this cumulatively, adding items to the account as we go.

Let me begin by taking it as common and undisputed ground that we tend to live more and more in a world of organised, departmentalised, bodies of knowledge; and that this is not a matter merely of the exigencies of university curricula, or of the shortness of life and the accumulation of knowledge which forces increasing specialisation on us. Intellectual life, scholarship and science are subject increasingly to the principles which govern the division of labour in the rest of civilised existence. We have become acutely aware of the cutural divisions which can grow up as consequence, and, in time, as reinforcement, of specialisation, and there is an increasing number of enthusiastic or conscience-stricken attempts to bridge the gaps. But there are other consequences which we are perhaps less conscious of. Among them is the odd tendency for the world in which we live, the environment of physical matter, of natural circumstance, and of events, to shape itself and to become organised after the same pattern of specialisms, and in their terms. History is both the past and the study of the past – of course; more particularly it is the body of ascertainable facts about the past which is regarded by historians as relevant to historical studies. Law has the same familiar and entirely undeceptive ambiguity in common usage; it is both the body of law and the study of law. And it is difficult to think of a time or a possible circumstances in which it might have made sense in either case to regard the subject matter in any different way from the study of it. But it also makes equal sense to talk of chemistry and physics in the same way; and there was certainly a time when even quite civilised people did not. For us there is a chemical world and a physical world: the chemistry of aircraft engines or their physics, the chemistry or the physics of the human body, are terms in general currency. More significantly, during the past few generations new disciplines have acted on the world and on circumstances in the same fashion. Instead of enumerating all the particulars of forms of livelihood, standard of living, division of labour, system of exchange, modes and rates of capital formation, range of products, and so on, it is meaningful, acceptable and common usage to speak of 'the economy'.

There is a specific reference here to those actions, events and objects which are the relevant objects of study to economists. And the reference is really quite specific. It is not uncommon, for instance, to find in accounts and explanations of movements in prices, or of fluctuations in consumption, allusions to 'non-economic' variables, so-called, which nevertheless do effect changes in the 'economy'. Psychology has acted as an organising principle in a similar fashion, so that the special attributes of individual attainment emotional response, mental experience and development which have become appropriate for psychological study mow make up a recognised and recognisable sector of the world as we experience it. We can speak meaningfully of the psychology of a person and mean something different from what we mean when we speak of 'a person'.

In all these instances, a science or a discipline has come to achieve so established a recognition as a map of a segment or a set of elements in the world of common experience that it serves as a handy way of discriminating the world of common experience itself. It is one of the ways in which the world becomes a manageable place to live in. Most of us, after all, do seem to think most easily of the world itself as a map. But the process by which economics maps into 'the economy' or by which chemistry maps into 'the chemistry' of our bodies tends for the most part to be taken for granted or completely elided.

Organising our experience of the world in this fashion, convenient, customary and unexceptionable as it is for the layman, is often unwelcome and embarrassing to the specialist himself.

Every decade produces its fresh crop of new specialisms which transcend the boundaries of disciplines almost as soon as they are firmly established in the public mind. But the point of this excursion into the higher generalities is to underline what I am sure you have run ahead of me to perceive: namely, that there is no segment or set of elements in the world of common experience which is organised in this way by sociology. We cannot speak of the sociology of Scotland as one can of the Scottish economy, nor of the sociology of children as one can of child psychology. Interestingly enough, substantive fields of sociology, many of them at least, go by titles like the sociology of education, the sociology of law, the sociology of politics, the sociology of medicine. In all of these cases, the substantive area of study is defined by another discipline. The mapping has been done by it, not by sociology.

It is for this reason that this guided tour is taking place under the advertised announcement of 'sociological explanation'. For the substantive areas of sociological studies are composed out of the way in which sociology operates upon previously organised bodies of knowledge, not, let me hasten to add, only and merely upon bodies of scientific and academic knowledge but also upon systems of belief, and codes of accepted practice. Sociology operates in and upon these fields in quite specific directions and in quite specific ways. It does so by questioning assumptions which seem to be made by people, and especially by people in authority in education, law, politics and so forth, about the behaviour of people. These assumptions are sometimes explicit in the form of expressed statements, more often implicit in the form of preference orderings or concealed value-judgements, but they are all formulated within what I can best call the territorial boundaries of each system of organised knowledge and practice; they are assumptions to the effect that the human behaviour visible to the educationist, the lawyer, the politician and so on, is ordered sufficiently for their purposes according to the principles and the vocabulary of ideas developed within the educational system, the law, political science and so on. Let me try to make this rather opaque pronouncement clearer by instances of what I mean.

I can begin by what will be very familiar ground. The 1944 Education Act in England and Wales, like the later Scottish Act, was designed to provide for more education at the secondary level, for different kinds of secondary education, and altogether to ensure that opportunities for educational and thus occupational and social advancement would be equally accessible to all children. There is no reason at all to question the sincerity of those who framed and later administered the Act. Indeed, the strength of the point I wish to make lies in the very genuineness of the attempt to reduce to vanishing point the inequities which had been built into the educational system maintained by the state. Within the perfectly valid frame of reference adopted by legislators, administrators and their advisers, the system of selection for secondary education was as psychologically sophisticated and as fair as we could possibly expect. Certainly, so far as I know, no fairer system of selection has since been devised. Yet a series of studies carried out by Professor Himmelweit and her colleagues during the 1950s demonstrated conclusively that equality of opportunity had certainly not been achieved. These studies were not of course concerned in the least with the techniques of selection themselves, the apparatus of tests, their administration, the impartiality of teachers and educationists – anything but. The enquiries were directed towards bringing to light considerations and factors affecting educational performance which, familiar as they are to all of us now, had simply not been taken into account in the design of the new educational system; it is not that the structure of families and their material and social circumstances were thought of as not affecting the school life and career of the child – of course they were. But those factors had not been treated as affecting attainment in the ways and to the extent they were now shown to do.

During the 1960s the considerations or assumptions treated as external to the frame of reference of education, or disregarded entirely, have been added to by educational sociologists. Educational performance is now being related to organisational features of the school system, to the institutional character of the class-room situation, to the particular difficulties and anomalies of the teacher's role, and the structure of the teaching profession. Those later researches, like the earlier, are directed towards eliciting considerations and determining factors which, previously lying outside the technical scope of the educational system, are nevertheless relevant to the educational process and should henceforward to be taken into account.

There is an important sense, therefore, in which educational sociology is tributary to the theory and practice of education.

I suggested that the clear definition of the boundary of a field of scholarship or science and the coherence and homogeneity of the kind of facts regarded as lying within it – the fact that we can talk about education as a body of knowledge, and as an administrative system, and as a developmental process of a special kind – that all this comes from the existence of a publicly accepted frame of reference and a particular coinage of ideas and beliefs which is in good currency. The frame of reference changes, of course, and so does the body of ideas, aspirations and values accepted as good currency. The main tradition of sociological writings in the field of education – a tradition which stretches through the work of Durkheim (himself, incidentally, a Professor of Education) Weber, and Mannheim (who also, when he came to this country, occupied a chair of Education) – this main tradition bears on the way in which ideas and beliefs about the purpose, the appropriate administration, and the nature of education have changed in response to changing and emerging needs in society. The actual causes of changes, as Mannheim said, are motivated acts, but the motives themselves are shaped by changes in social conditions. And these changes occur at an accelerating pace under industrialism, which throws new burdens on educational institutions – the progressive burdens of mass instruction, promotion of scientific and technological progress, occupational recruitment and now, it seems, social selection – for, in the case of the great majority of people in this country, the place they are going to occupy in the social system and the class structure is settled before they are twenty years old.

'Under conditions of advanced industrialism' as Mrs Floud and Dr Halsey have said, 'the economy becomes increasingly dominated by the institutions of research and technological innovation . . . So that the educational system comes to occupy a strategic place as a central determinant of the economic, political, social and cultural character of society'.[1] On this larger scale, as well as in the study of educational opportunity and educability, the role of educational sociology is to examine, to question, to raise doubts about, to criticise the assumptions on which current policy, current theory and current practice are based.

The essentially critical function of sociology at this level is just as clearly present in political sociology. I have to insist on this critical function in the case of this field of studies, because the rendering of the purpose of sociological explanation in this context that I want to put forward is not widely current. In particular, it is very different from that advanced by Martin Lipset and Reinhard Bendix, who are individually two of the most distinguished contributors to this field of sociology, and who, in combination, carry a very formidable – a papal – weight of authority. They write: 'Like political science, political sociology is concerned with the distribution and exercise of power in society. Unlike political science, it is not concerned with the institutional provisions for that distribution and exercise, but takes these as given. Thus political science starts with the state and examines how it affects society, while political sociology starts with society and examines how it affects the state: i.e. the formal institutions for the distribution and exercise of power.'[2]

We all, as academic teachers and students, deal in over-simplifications and learn to live with those of other people. But this attempt to dichotomise the study of political science and political sociology by polarising them, so to speak, on different points of origin is more than a pardonable over-simplification. It seems to me false as to the facts – possibly with regard to political science, certainly with regard to political sociology, which began with the attempt to measure the extent to which political institutions of a particular kind – namely, political party machines – can and do influence the behaviour of people in society. It is categorically false; the two kinds of study do not occupy two halves of the same football pitch or defend two goals, one labelled 'state' and the other labelled 'society', and advance towards the other; they are different kinds of game, played on different pitches. And the statement is, I believe, false as to the relationship between the two studies. Political sociology is not just the study of the same substantive field as political science but from a different angle of approach. It is tributary to – or, if you like, parasitic upon – political science, in the same way as educational sociology is upon education – parasitic, in the sense in which criticism is parasitic.

There are several fairly distinct divisions of activity in political sociology. The best known is the study of voting behaviour which effectively begins, despite Andre Siegfried's notable work completed before the First World War, with Lazarsfeld, Berelson and Gaudet's panel study of the American presidential election of 1940.[3] What Lazarsfeld and his research team did was to interview a sample of 3,000 electors in a part of Ohio at the beginning of the election campaign, and to interview sections of the main sample at regular intervals up to the presidential election in November. The research design was concerned specifically with estimating the actual influence exerted on voting by the campaigns of the two parties throughout the whole six months preceding the election. From this, and subsequent studies in America, Britain and elsewhere, we have gained an increasingly vivid and detailed picture of how much voting is a matter of habit, how little rational choice seems to enter in, how far political allegiances are formed virtually in childhood, how few voters change that allegiance in normal election circumstances. We are getting to know more about the influence of demographic factors and about the curiously overlooked part played by religious affiliation in certain countries. None of this work, or of other work on party organisation or pressure groups, on the nature and social function of ideology contributes anything to the solution of the major issues of political principle or of political organisation. It is not an approach to the field of study of political science from another point of departure. But it does affect very much the terms in which these issues are to be debated, and the limits of the considerations which must henceforward be regarded as pertinent to political studies. W. G. Runciman has remarked that 'Lazarsfeld's work has placed an important limit on the scope of *a priori* theorising about democracy; and it has done so by producing sociological evidence directly relevant to the tenets of political theory. It is not evidence which necessarily supports a left-wing or a right-wing view; but it is important precisely because any theory of democracy, whether left or right, must take account of it.'[4] I would, while supporting this, also say that the importance of the sociological work in this field lies not in its limiting the scope of *a priori* theorising but in extending it – of pointing to considerations which political studies must take into account beyond those which were previously seen as 'politically relevant'.

There are two corollaries to which I think I can now point as proceeding from what I have said so far. The first I have already suggested – which is that the relationship of sociology to these and other fields of substantive study is tributary. Sociologists, more than most scientists perhaps, admit the force of the injunction to forget their past, since much of what of value there is in it has been incorporated and has taken root in other disciplines. Secondly, while the direction and purpose of sociological kinds of explanation has been to amend and supplement the kinds of evidence and consideration lying within substantive areas of organised knowledge mapped by other established disciplines, the outlines of what might turn out to be a substantive area peculiar to sociology are perhaps becoming perceptible. In the cases I have mentioned, sociology has not only pointed to uniformities and variations in performance and in choice which are inexplicable in terms of the existing rationale of education or of politics, but has identified the external factors in terms of unwitting regularities among groups and categories of individuals, of latent controls and limitations of action, of conventions and observances which hardly can be said to rise to the surface of articulate expression. We are, in fact, dealing with the institutional framework of social behaviour, the implicit, unthinking and unarticulated code of norms which govern or influence individual conduct. Vilhelm Aubert's study of the judiciary in Norway,[5] when it was first published, evoked violent reactions among the legal profession precisely because it pointed to the fact that, in giving sentence, judges appeared to be following a tacit code which contravened the explicit code of equality before the law. We are, in this country, aware of the embarrassing variations in the practices followed in different magistrates courts in giving sentence – the large discrepancies in the penalties exacted for indentical infringements of the law in apparently very similar circumstances. These variations have been the subject of a good deal of discussion and criticism in recent years, and, indeed, investigations have been undertaken to establish just how far the inconsistencies range. But the presumption in this connection, so far as this country is concerned is, I believe, that the inconsistencies are just that – that the natural range of variation which must occur because of differences in temperament, idiosyncratic interpretation of the law, uncontrollable prejudice against persons, and so on, is perhaps wider than it should be. What Aubert did was to scrutinise and compare the sentences and the utterances of

judges (senior as well as junior) in giving sentence, relate those
to the recorded circumstances of the cases on which sentence
was pronounced, and demonstrate that the variation in senten-
sing behaviour correlated extremely closely with the social
class of the accused person. Not an astonishing conclusion,
perhaps, but interesting. Interesting, because the correlation
bespeaks a rule, a normative principle influencing the sentences given, which is certainly external to the principles which
overtly apply to the behaviour of judges, and even contravenes
those principles. Other studies, notably the Chicago studies of
the conduct of arbitration cases by lawyers, point to the existence of rather more complicated normative principles which
seem, in the same latent, unwitting fashion, to distort or contra-
vene the principles of action which prevail, and which are – I
must emphasise – honestly maintained, within the system of
law itself.

I have, so far, kept to what I have thought might be more
familiar ground for this explanation of sociological explanation,
largely because I hoped in doing so to make clear the way in
which sociological explanation is shaped by its special purposes.
I want now to discuss rather more closely the essentially critical,
assumption-testing nature of sociological investigation. I can, I
think, bring most light to bear by recounting some research
experience of my own in industrial organisations.

Most empirical studies of organisations depend a good deal
on interviews with managers. One begins these interviews
conventionally with questions about the particular job one's
respondent does, and how it fits in with other people's and with
other departments. The next step is to examine the discrepancies between the picture one gets from different respondents of
the organisation in which they all work. There always are
discrepancies, of course. But the question presented by these
inconsistencies is not 'Which version is right?' but 'How do
these differences arise? How is it that these different versions of
the same set of circumstances and actions have arisen in the
minds of people who have to co-operate with each other in the
very circumstances they view so differently?' The need to
account for these differences marks the first stage beyond
narrative description.

Some years ago, at the outset of one such enquiry, I encountered a major difficulty even before reaching this first stage,

when comparison becomes feasible. The firm was in a very
rapidly expanding and technologically advanced industry. A
whole series of interviews with managers followed a rather disconcerting pattern. After listening to my account of myself and
of what I was interested in finding out, they would say, in
answer to my first question, 'Well, to make all this clear, I'd
better start from the beginning', and then proceed to give me
an account of their careers in the firm. This account would be
lucid, well-organised, and informative, but would stop short at
some time beforehand – when, in fact, they had arrived at their
present position. I would then ask again what they were in fact
doing now, what the different functions were that they carried
out, whom they saw in connection with them, and so on. After
a pause, they would then go on to explain, equally lucidly, how
they and their department would operate when the present crisis was past, or the very big job they were rushing through was
completed or when the re-organisation I had doubtless heard
about had been carried through, and they could all settle down
to work to a plan. After a succession of such interviews I was
fairly certain that I had encountered the sociologist's poor substitute for the natural scientist's 'discovery' – the feeling that
what had looked like good, common sense ground (and what
could be more common sense than that managers know what
jobs they are supposed to be doing?) was turning into rather
liquid assumptions.

Luckily, the managers who had provided me with this experience found my reaction, when I was sure enough of myself to
tell them, as interesting as I did, and agreed, four of them in
one department, to carry out an experiment. This consisted
merely in each keeping a detailed record over a period of five
weeks of how he spent his working time, whom he met, what
problems he was concerned with, whether he issued instructions, whether he gave, exchanged, or received information,
and so on.

I should like to dwell on this account of the genesis of a particular piece of research a little. Like any other kind of enquiry
which has a history and an establishment, sociology seems at
any one time to be pursuing not so much the right kind of
knowledge as the right kind of questions, not definitive information but fresh hypotheses. Anyone who has done research in

any field will testify to the truth of Agnes Arber's remark that the difficulty in most scientific work lies in framing the questions rather than in finding the answers. What is not so often insisted upon is that questions do not suggest themselves or rise at the bidding of the specialist student with a little time on his hands. They arise from doubt. Doubt, in turn, arises from the existence of an alternative where none was previously suggested; it arises from a discrepancy between facts, or between accepted interpretations, or between intended and achieved results. In this particular case, it arose from doubt as to whether what everybody regarded as an abnormal departure from the pattern of activities as they should be was not in fact the normal condition of things.

Let me go on to say a little more about the research project which followed. The four people who carried this through did so in quite exemplary manner, swamped me with thousands of record forms and launched a research project which kept me, and a hundred other managers in a number of different industrial concerns, fully occupied at intervals over the next two years. There is one aspect of the results of this first, pilot, study which I want to mention here. I extracted all the record forms on which the departmental manager and one or other of his subordinates had recorded meeting each other. There were 240 of these. In 165 of them, the departmental manager had noted that he was giving a subordinate instructions or decisions; when one turned to the records made by the subordinates of the same episodes, only 84 of them indicated that they were receiving instructions or decisions. In fact, then, half the time, what the manager thought he was giving as instructions or decisions was being treated as advice or simply information.

This result, which I talked over at some length with the people who had done the recording, is open to a number of interpretations, all of them throwing some light, I think, not only on what we may call the pathology of the systems of bureaucratic authority on which so much of organised life in society depends, but on the way in which people living in a world in which equality is their prescriptive right as citizens yet accommodate themselves to the working necessities of subordination and inferior status. But for my present purpose, what I want to underline is the way in which the rules of the

170 *Description, Explanation and Understanding*

game which was actually being played between these four people – all of them young, intelligent, hard-working, ambitious – were in fact unrecognised by them. There were many other ways in which the same suggestion made itself felt – that organisations are made to work very often by the unwitting observance by their members of rules of the game which are not only different from the formal articulated body of rules but are not realised in anything like explicit form by the players themselves. The management of this department, for example, when they were asked at the end of this five-week period– when they had been composing almost minute-by-minute records of their activities – how much of their time was spent on all matters directly related to production, gave roughly well over half of their combined time as the answer. And in this they were, they thought, being conservative; after all, they *were* running a production department. In fact, they spent less than a third. In other companies, estimates of how the whole management group's time was spent – given after each individual member had spent several weeks in unusually close attention to just this – were even more wildly out. These results, incidentally, have inclined me to attach rather less than full objective validity to the figures published in one of the appendices to the Robbins Report (which are based on an enquiry conducted by postal questionnaire) into the way in which university staff distribute their time among their various activities.

I have used a miniature, perhaps trivial, illustration to demonstrate the widespread and pervasive tendency for human action to proceed in a *context* of thought and belief and intention very largely at variance with the manifest import of the actions themselves. In his 1961 Trevelyan lectures, E. H. Carr argues that what the historian is called upon to do is to investigate what lies behind the act. It was, he went on to suggest, a serious error to assume, as Collingwood had, that this meant the investigation of the thought and purposes of the individual actor. These may, said Carr, be quite irrelevant. 'The relations of individuals to one another in society and the social forces which act through them produce from the actions of individuals results often at variance with, and sometimes opposite to, the results they themselves intended.'[6]

Sociology also has been described – by Karl Popper among

others – as concerned, in the way E. H. Carr suggests, with the unanticipated consequences of human action. There are innumerable examples of this in the field of administrative action and planning. I can take one from near home. In 1954, a group of professional people working in Pilton, a large Edinburgh ward which is almost wholly made up of municipal housing estates, asked the Department of Social Study to carry out a survey which would help clarify some of what they saw as the social problems of the area. Most of these, at the time, had to do with juvenile delinquency and with a whole series of related difficulties to do with the unruliness of children and adolescents and their hostility to ordinary controls. As part of the preliminaries to the survey, which was carried out by graduate students in the department, I looked at the make-up of the population of the ward – which, even at that time, numbered some 28,000 people – about the same size population as Stirling. There were three noteworthy features. First, there was a marked preponderance of young people. Virtually one in four of the population was between ten and twenty years old; this compared with one in eight for Edinburgh as a whole, and one in eleven for the Central wards. In some parts of Pilton, this disproportionate number of children was even higher – in one section, over half the population was composed of school children and older teenagers. There was also a corresponding numerical deficiency of people between twenty-five and thirty-five years old – the most active section of the mature adult population, and there were very few old people.

Now it seemed to me then, and I still believe, that the implications of this state of affairs are quite obvious. The social control and social education of children is immeasurably more difficult in a population with mature adults so heavily outnumbered. The mere thickness on the ground of young children and adolescents will tend to make them a much more powerful force in any community than normally, will reinforce any resistance to adult control from inside or outside a community, and will tend to make adults look for their own entertainment and recreation away from the area. The incidence of unacceptable forms of individual and group activity among children and adolescents will appear to be much higher than in other districts of the City. The forms of activity at any given time, and the choice of companionships open to the individual child, will be much more diverse than usual. Child and adolescent society will tend, therefore, to be more self-sufficient.

I think it is reasonable to conclude that the 'youth problem' of Pilton at the time was largely demographic in character. And the population structure which produced a kind of dislocation in the normal system of relationships between adults and children and in the behaviour of children, was the direct consequence of a housing policy which, in Edinburgh as everywhere else, filled large housing estates built in the 1930s with young families. From ten to fifteen years later, the population of course consisted largely of the middle-aged and the adolescent, and there appeared the sudden growth of delinquency rates in suburban areas which was a notable feature of so many English and Scottish cities. It is as though society played confidence tricks on itself.

On a larger scale, society seems to play not confidence tricks so much as self-confidence tricks on itself. These are a familiar element in social history. It took an immense amount of painstaking effort over many years to prove that a third of the working-class population of London was living in poverty; more years of work still, by Rowntree, to prove that the vast majority of families able to afford less food, clothing and warmth than on the most spartan of reckonings constituted bare subsistence level, had not been plunged into distress through some moral obliquity or defect of character, but through pressure of circumstances which they had no possible means of controlling. The astonishing feature of the *Our Towns* report on the condition of children evacuated from city slums in 1940 was not the squalor and unseemliness of the children but the blank ignorance of all other sections of society about them and the circumstances of urban life which had produced them. Within the last few weeks, Professor Townsend's survey of the millions of families in Britain living at or below the subsistence level represented by national assistance has come, again, as a shock. The results of Harrington's survey of the incidence of poverty in the United States three years ago came as a shock. Now, they are the stock-in-trade of the weekend political speaker.

The traditional role of descriptive sociology, in the UK and elsewhere, has largely been to point out what is immediately obvious to everybody as soon as the task of collecting and presenting the facts has been done. In this, sociology performs its familiar tributary function, this time in the formation and development of public opinion and common knowledge. In its other, more specialised, task of searching for explanations of behaviour, sociology often seems even more directly concerned with the obvious. A little while ago, I said that if one could point to a substantive area which constituted the field of study for sociology, it would be the institutional norms which seem to govern action in the sense of providing navigational rules for decision and action, or limits and constants which the behaviour of people seems to observe. But there exists already an enormous fund of knowledge – common knowledge based on common experience and common sense – about the characteristic patterns of behaviour which can be observed among different groups of people and in different kinds of situation. Many years ago, Paul Lazarsfeld wrote a lengthy review of the first two volumes to be published on the studies conducted during the Second World War into the morale of American troops and the reactions of conscripted men to army life. He lists a number of conclusions, and suggests that most people would dismiss them as familiar, or as so obvious that there was no point at all in examining them. For example: better educated men show more psycho-neurotic symptoms during training than those with less education – (the mental instability of the intellectual compared with the psychological resilience or impassivity of the ordinary man has often been commented upon). Second, men from rural backgrounds were usually in better spirits during their army life than men brought up in the city. Third, troops from the southern states were better able to stand up to the climate in the hot Pacific Islands than northerners. Fourth, white privates were more eager for promotion than Negroes. One can add a fifth, equally obvious: officers and men in units where promotion was most frequent and rapid were more satisfied with their present positions and prospects than were people in units where there were least chances of promotion.

Lazarsfeld remarks: We have in these examples a sample list of the simplest kind of interrelationships which provide the bricks from which an empirical social science can be built. But why, since they are so obvious, is so much money and energy given to establish such findings? Would it not be wiser to take them for granted and proceed directly to a more sophisticated type of analysis? This might be so except for one interesting point about the list. Every one of these statements is the direct opposite of what was actually found. Poorly educated soldiers were more neurotic than those with higher education; southerners showed no greater ability than northerners to adjust to a tropical climate; Negroes were more eager for promotion than whites; and so on.

In this last instance, as in all the others, sociology defines itself as a critical activity. The purpose of sociology is to achieve an understanding of social behaviour and social institutions which is different from that current among the people through whose conduct the institutions exist; an understanding which is not merely different but new and better. The practice of sociology is criticism. It exists to criticise claims about the value of achievement and to question assumptions about the meaning of conduct. It is the business of sociologists to conduct a critical debate with the public about its equipment of social institutions.

This purpose of critical understanding is more important now than it has ever been. Sociology, like other social sciences, is the creature of the new human situation which industrialism has brought about. It emerged, tentatively at first, as the need grew to understand, mitigate and possibly even control the transformation which individual lives and the social order continually undergo. As it has developed, it has become clothed with more and more of the objectivity and methodology of the natural sciences, and has become infused with more of their spirit of enquiry and discovery as ends in themselves; but like other social sciences, its character has nevertheless remained basically ideographic. All the social sciences are, I believe, governed by the need to understand and to represent in adequate terms the nature of individual personality and mental experience, or the relationship of individuals to each other, or the varieties of economic and political institutions and relationships, or the social order itself.

The new impetus which has been given in our generation to the pace of scientific and technological development and to industrial and economic change all over the world gives a new urgency to these studies.

In many ways, the pressing need to know more about human behaviour in all its context – a need which has found increasingly popular expression during this century – is a manifestation of the disparity between man's understanding and control of nature and his insight into and command over his own conduct and his own affairs. Traditional wisdom, the oversight of the 'intelligent amateur', and the accumulation of experience over a lifetime, which served earlier generations are now insufficient when we are so promptly confronted with the direct and the indirect, the projected and the unanticipated, consequences of discoveries and decisions. Earlier generations, however fast they saw their world changing, were at least persuaded that certain traditional institutions and values were immutable, and even that the passage of time alone might solve major difficulties and problems.

Time, indeed, was seen in the nineteenth century as on the side of man. Now, it seems, time is against us. More accurately, perhaps, if more prosaically, the difference lies in the sheer multiplicity and technical difficulty of the factors entering into the decision-making process. The point here is that we are in a fundamentally different situation from that obtaining when piecemeal changes could be made in social, economic or political systems as and when it seemed best, and when institutions could be discarded or replaced without much regard being paid to the social fabric of which they formed part. Decisions, planning and action in scientific, educational, economic and social affairs must now take cognisance of an ever-increasing span of considerations if they are both to be effective and not do more harm than good. Similar circumstances obtain for public and private corporations; and the concurrent growth of studies of decision-making in economics, sociology and psychology is again a manifestation of the way in which development in the social sciences reflects the emergent needs of society.

It is not fortuitous that all societies, whatever their political character or stage of economic development, have realised the need for some form of planning. 'Planning', in fact, is a word of dubious relevance to what is happening, if it is read in its traditional sense of producing a design which future actions, at set times, will convert into a finished construction in complete accordance with it. It is much more a matter of deciding the direction and the goals of activity, or setting the upper and lower constraints to the amounts and to the kinds of activity which are pertinent to the achievement of the goals. This new connotation places much more emphasis on selecting the sets of relevant variables and on understanding and controlling them and the factors which affect them. Planning, in short, has become a complicated process of social cybernetics, into which psychological, social, geographic, economic and educational factors enter, and a process which has to be implemented in terms of organisational and administrative expertise compared with which our existing procedures are but primitive craft skills.

The demands which present social needs are putting on the social sciences are already enormous. I am convinced that a far greater volume of demands and needs are present in latent form, or are building up. They are being expressed in a bewildering variety of forms. These demands are altogether out of proportion to the present capabilities and resources of the social sciences. If they are to come within measurable distance of an adequate response to the need which society has to them, positive and substantial efforts must be made to foster their development. These efforts are now, I believe, visible in a number of countries in Europe. They appear to be imminent in Britain.

I began this lecture by observing that sociology was not a new discipline. This is true, but it is, in one sense at least, new to this University. It has been born at a time when the demands on it, as on other social sciences, are growing, and at a time also when the character of the discipline itself is changing out of recognition. Sociology in Edinburgh looks forward to a strenuous but, I hope, an adventurous and lusty infancy.

NOTES AND REFERENCES

1. Jean Floud and A. H. Halsey, 'The Sociology of Education', *Current Sociology*, vol. VII, no. 3, 1958, p. 169.
2. Reinhard Bendix and Seymore M. Lipset, 'Political Sociology', *Current Sociology*, vol. VI, no. 2, 1957, p. 87.
3. Paul F. Lazarsfeld, B. Berelson and H. Gaudet, *The People's Choice*, Columbia University Press, 2nd ed. 1948.
4. W. G. Runciman, 'Sociological Evidence and Political Theory', in Peter Laslett and W. G. Runciman (eds), *Philosophy, Politics and Society*, Basil Blackwell, 1962, pp. 42–3.

5. Vilhelm Aubert, *Sociology of Law* (Chapter 6, 'Law Courts and the Class Structure'), Institute for Social Research, Oslo, 1964 (mimeographic).

6. E. H. Carr, *What is History?*, Penguin Books, 1964, p. 52.

7. Paul F. Lazarsfeld, 'The American Soldier – An Expository Review', *Public Opinion Quarterly*, 1949, p. 380.

9

Consumer Behaviour

This article began life as a paper read to a joint seminar on consumer behaviour arranged with the Economics Department at Edinburgh – hence the original sub-title, 'a sociological view'. Its subject-matter was something of a new departure. For one thing, now that I was responsible for a university department I had lost a good deal of the freedom required to engage in empirical research of the kind I had practised hitherto. But it was also undertaken in acknowledgement of a need to expand my interests beyond the study of organisations to other major sectors of social conduct and relationships.

There is in the social sciences a common assumption which has led, I think, to a great many false research strategies and to some noble but futile endeavours of scholarship. This assumption is to the effect that all social sciences are concerned with the same common field of study. Economics, politics, psychology, sociology, anthropology and the rest all have their own body of systematically ordered information, their own procedures, their own terminology perhaps, but properly – i.e., broadly – viewed, they are all single aspects of the one study of human behaviour; singly, they are partial and therefore imperfect branches of the one science of human behaviour.

Despite the common-sense appeal of this assumption, it is

First published as 'The Study of Consumer Behaviour: A Sociological View', in *European Journal of Sociology*, vol. 7, 1966, pp. 313–29.

based on a peculiar fallacy to which we as social scientists ought to be the least susceptible. It is that, as R. W. Ackoff phrased it at a recent conference, there is a social reality, ontologically prior to our perception of it. Yet, as the uncompromising holism of psychoanalysis and social anthropology demonstrates, to presume the connectedness of everything with everything else is just as specifically an intellectual framework as that which we commonly see in psychological behaviourism or Marxist economics.

I have begun on this tack because it seems to me that the subject matter of this seminar should properly be read as somewhat ambiguous. For, in discussing consumer behaviour, we are concerned not only with what economists and sociologists make of the subject, but also with economics and sociology. If we took the view which I have said is implicit in the commonsense assumption of a common social reality, then obviously economists and sociologists have been asked to carve up between them a single area of study called consumer behaviour, or at least to give their perhaps differing views of a single area of study. I should like to propose that, instead of this orthodox view, we regard the two disciplines as occupied with different kinds of 'social reality', with their own systems of ideas, with their own ways and their own criteria for developing ideas. Academic disciplines in this sense are, so to speak, media in which concepts may be grown as living cultures and may develop their own organisation, their own paradigms. Of course they share the same *common-sense* reality, as biophysicists, psychologists and ethologists may be said to study the constitution and behaviour of living objects. Of course there are useful and sometimes fertile analogies, and transfers of concepts. What I want to point out the danger of is the encapsulation of one in the other, of regarding both as (very unequal) competitors in the same intellectual endeavour, as engaged in a sort of academic lifemanship, with each side trying to pre-empt the other's bids for providing the intellectual substructure to consumer behaviour, leaving the other, or hoping to leave the other, the job of topping off the upper stories, or merely decorating them.

The relationship between the two disciplines is itself one of exchange. In the case of consumer behaviour, where economists' interests have been dominant almost throughout, this relationship has been very one-sided. The literature of consumer studies has been written almost entirely by economists, with sociological contributions either derived by economists from the currency of ideas put into circulation by sociologists, or supplied *ad hoc* by survey research. In either case consumer behaviour studies are directed towards testing economic hypotheses, amending economic theory, or filling in information needed to establish the limits of variables or the existence of constants.

It is not surprising, for example, to find that it is Duesenberry, of Harvard, putting forward an emendation of the 'absolute income' hypothesis associated with Keynes.[1] Whether or not the phrase 'keeping up with the Joneses' originated in Harvard at the time of Lloyd Warner's work, it is clear that Warner's Yankee City studies, conducted from Harvard, were of crucial importance to Duesenberry's thesis, published in 1949 (and quoting Warner's books). Warner's researches had drastically altered the traditional image of American society, and had added ideas of class structure and of 'status-seeking' to the currency of accepted ideas. At the same time Keynes' absolute income hypothesis, which held that 'men are disposed, as a rule and on the average, to increase their consumption as their income increases but not by as much as the increase in their income' had shown itself increasingly leaky. In particular, a number of studies had shown that the aggregate saving ratio had remained fairly constant since the 1870s, even though incomes had risen enormously during the same period. Duesenberry's emendation of the hypothesis contained the assumption that the saving rate depended not on the level of income but on the relative position of the individual on the income scale; and this was founded on the sociological thesis – accepted as datum – that a strong tendency exists in the American social system for people to emulate their neighbours and, at the same time, to strive constantly towards a higher standard of living.

> In a fundamental sense the basic source of the drive towards higher consumption is to be found in the character of our culture. A rising standard of living is one of the major goals of our society [...] People do not expect to live as their parents did, but more comfortably and conveniently. The consumption pattern of the moment is conceived not as a part of a way of life, but as a temporary adjustment to circumstances

[. . .] What kind of reaction is produced by looking at a friend's new car, or looking at houses or apartments better than one's own? The response is likely to be a feeling of dissatisfaction with one's own house or car. If this feeling is produced often enough it will lead to action which eliminates it, that is, to an increase in expenditure.[2]

There are three points of interest in this pronouncement, based, as I have said, on sociological ideas very much in the air at the time. The first is the missing middle term: Why did the *friends* get *their* new car or superior house? The second it that it underlies the *'embourgeoisement* of the working classes' fallacy, of which more later. The third is that the set of sociological hypotheses on which it rests were themselves drastically revised by Katz and Lazarsfeld[3] a few years later with no apparent effect on the theory – perhaps because Katz and Lazarsfeld were at Columbia, not Harvard.

The same levy on sociological ideas in good, i.e. fashionable, currency, is observable in the later emendation of 'Engel's Law'. This is to the effect that the proportion of household expenditure spent on food declines as household income rises. 'This has now been verified literally hundreds of times.'[4] But, as Nelson Foote pointed out as long ago as 1954:

It now appears that many of our 'middle-incomers' have increased the proportion they spend on food. This suggests that the social rituals of cooking and eating are being elaborated into an art of boundless proportions; not only is cooking becoming more efficient, it is becoming an end in itself. It consumes increasing time, attention and energy; attracts more and more critical audience; requires improved techniques for achieving aesthetic ends.[5]

This kind of development also disturbs any theory of consumer behaviour related to price elasticity, since price changes can only be measured over time. It is furthermore manifest that consumers do not decide on spending patterns once and for all. And when this kind of question is raised, other assumptions come under suspicion too. It is said, for example, that the classical theory of preference ordering

pays insufficient attention to uncertainty. With much justice, it is pointed out that consumers are often in the dark about the properties of the commodities they buy and that they may not even be very sure about the prices they pay or about the

> income they have [. . .] it is hard to imagine that people's
> minds should be equipped with anything so elaborate as an
> all-embracing scale of preferences.[6]

These difficulties have led some economists into social research
either as sponsors or as researchers themselves, like Katona
and James Morgan at Michigan. Katona himself engaged in this
research as an exercise in reductionism. As his preface to *The
Psychological Analysis of Economic Behaviour* announced:

> This book is based on the thesis that economic processes stem
> directly from human behaviour, and that this simple but
> important fact has not received its due in modern economic
> analysis.[7]

A decade later, the author was a good deal more cautious:

> Psychological variables, such as motives, attitudes, expecta-
> tions and group belonging, are interesting variables operating
> between the stimuli of market conditions and the responses to
> them in the form of economic decisions. The psychological
> factors do not alone determine the final decisions.[8]

In fact, instead of committing himself to the task of translating
economics into terms of individual psychology (on the lines of
the sociological effort discussed earlier) Katona, working in the
Survey Research Center, has devoted himself to studying the
influence of variables other than income on consumer behaviour,
an endeavour which has prompted a great deal of research
elsewhere, not least among governments, many of which now
undertake regular household budget surveys. Chief among
these variables are age, family size, and the different ages of
the family's own lifecycle. The pattern revealed in the table
opposite[9] is closely paralleled by Abram's figures for British
households.[10]

Katona's special contribution to the study of 'non-economic'
variables, as Houthakker calls them, is the elevation of consumer attitudes (of 'plans to buy') to predictive force. Regular
surveys by the Survey Research Center show that changes in
consumer attitudes anticipate changes in sales of durable
goods – about a year ahead in the case of the big downturn in
American spending in 1957 – and that sales were in fact much
more sensitive to attitude changes than to income changes, in
the short run.

We have, it is apparent, come at some distance from the
purely economic models of consumer behaviour with which

TABLE 9.1 Differences in durable goods purchased during the life cycle (1956).

Lifecycle Stage	Distributive spending units	New cars	Used cars	Furniture	Refrigerator	Washing machine	TV	Proportion of families carrying instalment debt (%)
Bachelor	10	6	9	5	3	3	5	40
Newly married no children	8	8	11	13	10	9	11	56
Young married with children	35	44	49	50	51	56	47	65
Older married with children	12	14	15	11	11	12	12	53
Older married no dependents	21	23	10	16	18	16	17	23
Older single people	24	5	6	5	7	4	8	16
	100	100	100	100	100	100	100	100

SOURCE: G. Katona, 1960.[11]

we started. The number of variables which have been declared relevant to consumer behaviour as such has increased considerably, but, at the same time, their use has become more and more specific. The role of intentions, expectations and attitudes, as revealed in survey research, has lain more and more exclusively in their capacity to predict purchases of durable goods. The 'keeping up with the Joneses' thesis lost some of its universality in the 1957 recession and the later vicissitudes of the American automobile industry. Thirdly, 'the vital assumption that the individual can rank the alternatives open to him according to his preferences'[12] remains true only within a number of constraints introduced as 'non-economic variables'. These are commonly listed as age, size of family, stage of family life cycle, with, more dubiously, regional and class differences, and the climate of opinion about the economic and political future; even the sputnik was involved as an explanation of the fall in American spending in 1957. The doubt attached to the second group of variables means more than the relegation of such general factors to a second-order component. As Morgan says:

The economist is likely to think of group behaviour as a mere
summation of individual behaviour, responding to the same
forces, and with little sociological reinforcement. The individual is seen as influenced by what goes on around him, but it is
individual behaviour or its sum which is analysed and
explained. Even if the statistical analysis is of grouped data,
the basic theory is of individual behaviour.[13]

The reviews of the literature of consumer behaviour written in
recent years suggest that the resort to psychological and social-
psychological studies in an attempt to resolve discrepancies
between theory and empirical fact has committed students to a
sorcerer's apprentice situation. But if there is a problem about
incorporating these non-economic variables in the classical
models of spending, or saving, behaviour, it is one for the economists. None of these developments alters the primary concern
of economics with the behaviour of commodities rather than
with the behaviour of man, with the mutual adjustment of
means and ends rather than with the nature of the means or
ends as such.

The sociologist *is*, of course, concerned with the nature of
means and ends. This is only another way of saying that he is
concerned with the patterned distribution of rights and privileges, duties and obligations in society, and the particular definition given to them. This patterned distribution constitutes
the social structure of a society, and the sociologist is above all
concerned with the identification of the contemporary social
structure and with those elements or principles of the social
structure which have changed, or are in the process of changing.

It is now a sociological commonplace to speak of the individual's position in Western societies as defined more and more
by his role as consumer as against the part he plays in the
productive system. Those 'non-economic variables' which were
mentioned earlier (see p. 182 above) are themselves indications
of this change. If income is fixed by an individual's place in the
productive system, then those factors which have to be incorporated in the model of consumer behaviour to increase its
empirical usefulness relate to other aspects of the individual's
social situation than his productive role – his job. Duesenberry's
'keeping up with the Joneses' syndrome was brought in to
account for discrepancies between the 'absolute income'
hypothesis and the actual balance between spending and saving, in which getting into debt (dis-saving) is also involved.

This new hypothesis was also an indication that there were regular discrepancies between income and consumption, at least in the short run. More generally, the tendency for the consumer side of living to grow in importance is revealed by the expansion since the 1870s of expenditure with income as against the constancy of the proportion of incomes saved. In concrete detail, the very large difference between the disposable income of young families and their purchases of consumer durables indicate the social pressure towards conformity with certain specific social norms of consumption, and a surprising degree of independence of income (in the short run, of course).

The most popular interpretation of this change relates it both to the shrinking of disparities in income characteristic of this century and the general and continuous rise in the standard of living. All three trends combine to swell the ranks of the middle-income groups, and to incorporate more and more members of society into the ranks of the middle class not only as regards living standards but in terms of aspirations, values, political ideology and leisure and leisure pursuits. In Ferdinand Zweig's words:

> The factory worker has a relatively high security of employment. The bitter memories of the past are fading away. The worker has an established routine, both in working and living. His continuity of employment does not fall very much behind that of the office worker. He has a recognised niche and social position, he is attached to his work-place by many institutional arrangements such as pension rights or seniority rights and other fringe benefits which are constantly increasing [. . .] Every threat to his standard of living, which has been raised so considerably, he views with great concern [. . .] Next comes what is often called 'the revolution of rising expectations'. His appetite is whetted, he wants more [. . .] He wants his own car, more gadgets, often his own house. When asked about his possessions, he would often use the term 'Next on my list is . . .' .[14]

Traditional sociological theory since Weber defines class position in terms of three variables: role in the productive system as determined by forces operating in the labour market; affiliations and associations which tend to be supported by consensus and loyalty; and style of life: the second two variables being largely, though not entirely, dependent on labour market position. Zweig's thesis about the *embourgeoisement* of the working class has been criticised on the grounds that he has ignored the first two variables, and has generalised too freely from his observations of the higher standard of living enjoyed by the more highly paid grades of factory workers.[15] Without defending Zweig, it could be argued that style of life has in fact assumed rather more significance in recent decades, certainly in individual terms and, necessarily but more obscurely, in terms of social structure.

The term 'style of life' has itself undergone some change in usage since Weber. In the passage of *Wirtschaft und Gesellschaft* in which he introduced the term, Weber makes it the determining feature of stratification in terms of status groups (*Stände*) as against social classes

> In contrast to classes, status groups are normally communities. They are often, however, of an amorphous kind. In contrast to the purely economically determined 'class situation' we wish to designate as 'status situation' every typical component of the life fate of men that is determined by a specific social estimation of honour, positive or negative.

Nevertheless, Weber goes on:

> This honour may be connected with any quality shared by a plurality, and, of course, it can be knit into a class situation: Class distinctions are linked in the most varied ways with status distinctions [. . .] Status honour is normally expressed by the fact that a special style of life can be expected from all who wish to belong to the circle.[16]

At the hands of Veblen, and still more of Warner and his colleagues, style of life was developed into virtually a self-sufficient rationale of invidious distinctions in society. The major assumption written into this conception, which was regarded as the basis of the status-ordering in society, was that all members of society held unanimous views about the desirable goals and even possessions in life. One can sympathise with the need which social scientists seem to have felt to elucidate some organising principle employed by members of society themselves when geographical and social mobility appeared to have broken down traditional patterns of association and the consensus and loyalty that went with them. But, as Willmott and Young in this country, and W. H. Whyte in America have shown,[17] there have nevertheless survived, or emerged, institutional forms – church groups, women's institutions, sports organisations, community activities, parent-teacher associations, party-giving, pubs and clubs – which are entirely appropriate to communities of families whose members need social support and friendship and affiliations quickly when they move in, but who, when they move out, will not feel too deep a sense of loss. Age-grading has also emerged as a distinct element in social structure – again visible in geographical terms. Most families found in suburbs live there only during a certain period of their careers. The very rate of mobility helps to account for 'the internal homogeneity, the external distinctiveness of such suburbs. Birds of a feather can more readily flock together than before'.[18] The acquisition and demonstration of a style of life to which a family has moved is a prerequisite of membership – of social acceptance, of the discounting of any suspicion, to itself as much as to others, that it may be unacceptable.

One of the distinctive features of contemporary urban society is the principle of segregation which is more and more strictly followed. The social areas map which the people of any sizeable town carry in their heads is more clearly defined and socially specific than earlier generations needed to fill in. The names of Islington, Camberwell, Willesden, Fulham, Golders Green, Twickenham, Highgate, Hampstead and Belgravia all have their special significance for Londoners, each representing important expressive aspects not only of the income but of the occupations, social proclivities, educational background and social pretensions of the people who live in them – or rather, of the *kind* of people who are *supposed* to live in them. And we persuade ourselves that we can read in the demeanour of streets and frontages and in the interior presentations deliberately, cunningly or rudely offered for view, the values and aspirations of the dwellers within; as easily, for example, as we 'place' people by their accent and dress, as we place looped window-curtains as against straight hanging ones, a living-room with a flight of chain ducks as against African masks, or an assortment of reading lamps instead of a central ceiling fixture.

Further, in larger cities, as Nelson Foote says:

> As we look around, we find suburbs, neighbourhoods, even single apartment buildings that consist homogeneously of young married couples, young parents, middle-aged people,

188   *Description, Explanation and Understanding*

bachelor girls and boys, 'empty-nesters', and the retired. It is
easier to move than rebuild, and thus people in metropolitan
areas tend to segregate themselves voluntarily among their
peers. Among peers the old way of selecting friends on the
basis of propinquity can once more operate without demean-
ing one's autonomy.[19]

It is important, I think, to grasp the precise significance of this
process of finding the right place to live, of matching one's
home, one's furniture, pictures, records, wallpaper and friends
to each other and to one's own essential personal identity. To
write it off as conformism, other-directedness or status-seeking
is to reduce sociology to the primitive state of, say, Locke's psychology, in which the mind was represented as a *tabula rasa* on
which sense impressions accumulated over a lifetime and constituted experience, wisdom, foresight and calculation. People
do not receive their social identities by being pressed into and
shaped by a social matrix. Of course, there are uniformities; it is
a necessary consequence of there being a finite number of
styles. There is display; it is a necessary consequence of having
to declare to others the sort of reaction one looks for, of having
to lay claim to *some* position in the social order. But the teenager
whose designation is written out so explicitly in his shoes, jeans,
sweater and haircut has also himself chosen that designation.
The young couples who spend their Saturday afternoons
searching through the albums of wallpaper patterns are looking not for something that will necessarily match the Joneses',
or even go one better, but for something which will 'suit' – i.e.
will fit the existing style into which they have been organising
their lives.

The general thesis suggested by the sociological study of
consumer behaviour is that consumption is the expressive
aspect of style of life, and that style of life has developed a
much greater significance as a mode of organising individual
behaviour and leisure, careers and, therefore, as a form of
social structure. It is possibly, as some writers suggest, a
response to the growing constraints evident in the occupational
side of life; the organising effort put into consumption matches
the development of more and more control over the individual
as producer.

Dumazedier has suggested that this kind of organising principle extends beyond consumption itself.[20] Occupational choices

are made not so much to provide the income which will support the highest standard of living as to consort with a preferred style of living. It imposes constraints in terms of hours of work, opportunities for occasional supplementary earnings, and the social milieu of the working-place and of fellow workers. In addition, of course, it affects location. Skilled craftsmen, technicians, industrial scientists and highly qualified industrial managers are difficult to tempt away from London and the south of England. When the United States spending on defence and space research flattened off there appeared, and remains, a sizeable 'pool' of unemployed Ph.Ds in California, despite the continued demand for industrial scientists in the eastern states.

We can take as reasonably well established first the fact that individuals do organise their lives in terms of a preferred style of life which is expressed concretely in terms of a pattern of consumption ranging from houses, and other consumer durables, to clothing, holidays, entertainment, food and drink; second, that this organisation of his life by the individual is reflected in the social structure; and thirdly, that this represents a change in the situation of the individual and in the social structure from what obtained before, although there has been no revolutionary or sudden change – rather a gradual conversion from a production-oriented to a consumption-oriented society.

All these circumstances can be related to quantitative increases in incomes and in the range of consumer goods available, the increases in both being a function of developments in both physical and social technologies. But economic and technological development does not enable us to define the ways in which the new opportunities for consumption and the ways in which they are organised in terms of individual behaviour or of social structure. The sociological problem here can be put in simple terms as, 'Who are the Joneses whom everybody has to keep up with?' As Alberoni[21] has remarked, this conception of the diffusion of consumer goods and the determination of styles of life presupposes a one-dimensional view of social differentiation, and a unanimity about the value of having more goods for use and display than others. If this were so, one can imagine that consumption patterns would be adopted only and merely to indicate position on a continuous gradient of status differences. Without denying that this might be valid for sectors of American society, Alberoni declares that it cannot apply to a society still bound to traditional values or even to one in which traditional values and structural ordering are breaking up.

The current view, reflected by Zweig, of what happens when traditional orientations to other values are eroded by mobility and rapid rises in living standards, is that such values are slowly replaced by those directed towards emulation and invidious imitation of the better-off. In Alberoni's view, the radical change is one in the frame of reference. On the one hand, the traditional leisure-class loses its definition as a '*Stand*' and lower-class families look beyond the local community as a 'reference style of life' and adopt what they see as that of the national society's. The 'community' of the nation differs from the local community in that it possesses two élites: one a power élite, political, economic and, in Italy, religious; the other an élite without power, made up of all those personages who are the object of imitation, admiration and collective attachment – the '*divi*', who are the protagonists of the mass media, and who suggest ways of behaviour and influence popular values without making decisions about them. The *divi* in modern society take the place of the better-off members of traditional small-scale communities, in that they become the collective objects of gossip, now a conversational traffic involving millions of people. They are the exemplary protagonists of communal verbal behaviour, and although they are few and privileged, they are not at the summit of the social system, neither do they constitute a social group or class. As such – and this is of critical importance – they are not the object of envy or class resentment. Any person, rich or poor, can 'adopt', or become identified with, one or another individual in one or other category, which means that they act as a kind of structural solvent: in face of the *divi*, the members of society become a populace, a 'mass'.

In adopting styles of life and patterns of consumption and individual purchasable terms from the powerless élite, people are not involved in emulating them or each other. The social significance to be attached to individual instances of these actions varies, but what is common to them is that they transcend the scheme of reference consensually supported by the traditional community. 'The girl who dresses like Elizabeth Taylor is not trying to display wealth or to testify to her membership of the leisure classes. She is expressing her membership, along with that of innumerable other girls all over the country, of a world to which Elizabeth Taylor belongs.' Hence, Alberoni goes on, the familiar preference of television sets to sewing machines, and to the other more mundane and useful consumer durables among those confronted for the first time with the actual possibility of choice between them. The television set is an escape hatch from the local community, and an entrance to the larger world in which one can now participate, and in which one can, in a new, oblique, but meaningful sense, consort with the *divi*. This process of participation is of course particularly effective when it involves new articles, in which there is virtually no connotation of status aspirations within the confines of a community of neighbours, and which constitute the basis of new kinds of experience. Also, the membership of the new world imposes its new obligations; there are the specific norms of behaviour in terms of consumption which attach to the claim to be 'modern', 'with it' or merely urban, norms which apply most lucidly and explicitly to women's toilet articles and dress.

The sociological view of consumer behaviour is thus one which endows action with significance, in Weber's terms, a significance which is shared. The unit of study is not individual behaviour, that is, but the collective activities which involve individuals in one or other of their social identities. The fact that individuals do select these ways of acting rather than any of the other possibilities open to them which may serve their interests, the fact that there is compatibility in social behaviour, suggest that there are normative – i.e. moral – considerations entering into preferences. There is, as Alberoni points out, a feeling that one *ought* to invest in certain purchases and modes of living, and this kind of consideration is one which transcends the expediential calculus of interests.

The sociological study of consumer behaviour, therefore, is directly related to the study of structural changes in society which have to do ultimately with the same processes of population growth, technological progress, industrial development and urbanisation as underlie those changes which have hitherto seemed to be logically prior to changes in style of life and to have served as the substructure.

In other words, the presumption is that the study of

consumer behaviour is the most likely means of developing both a classificatory system and an understanding of the social significance of styles of life, and the understanding and classification of styles of life bears directly on the *most* significant structural changes in contemporary society. This, in turn, presupposes that there have been fundamental changes in the terms in which society is organised. But we have long accepted the fact, at least by implication, that fundamental changes have occurred in the way in which the members of society construe and construct their institutional equipment.

In most general terms, the characteristic social form of society in Britain and the West has changed from small rural community to large industrial society. The development has been from a society in which individuals, typically, lived – as child, parent, worker, buyer, churchgoer, companion, enemy or neighbour – in the context of the same group of people. Each social position had both to be distinguished from all other aspects of conduct and reconciled with them; for the people who dealt with them in one capacity – as husbandman say, or housewife – were those who dealt with them as neighbours or relatives. Each kind of social occasion, therefore, which involved one rather than another position carried with it an appropriate code of observance, styles of behaviour, address, demeanour and even clothing – its own species of tact. An elaborate social order could be maintained within each community because of the universal regard within it for the specific etiquette which attached to the specific occasion and which governed the relationships assumed to resumed in it – a regard which could be exercised through shared knowledge of how one should behave at any time, and shared recognition of the specific role and the specific relationship with others which any one occasion called for. Each and every individual learned this all-important fund of knowledge from parents, older kin, the pastors and masters of all kinds who formed the adult world into which they grew, and of which they would form part; the parts they played, moreover, might be composed from the models as well as from the instruction the adult world provided.

The central and distinguishing fact about social behaviour in such a society was that the whole set of rules and relationships available to an individual born into one particular status in it was visible and could be learned as he or she grew up in that status.

The central and distinguishing fact about social behaviour in modern industrial society is that all the different social positions occupied by a person can be – and usually are – acted out in different social milieux, often geographically distinct, and usually with totally different membership.[22]

The need has gone for ceremonies, ritual and etiquette to mark off one role, or set of relationships, or social occasion from another. The division of one role – one *persona* – of the self from others has become physical in the sense that the social setting for each aspect of the social self is segregated from others. There is no need to indicate the passage from one role to another by special phrases, changes of dress and demeanour, and so forth, at the boundary. There is no need, either, for one role to cohere with another, since the audiences and other actors tend to be different for each setting. Children happily learn different vocabularies and even accents, different standards of behaviour and moral codes for home, street and school. First employment and new jobs invite the cultivation of new social identities, as do new acquaintances and new houses. Individuals now have a variety of distinct status positions, each with roles which they play out in a style, and according to moral and behavioural norms, distinct from what obtains in other capacities – distinct, and even incompatible; the unlucky intrusion of people familiar with one role into the setting appropriated for another role presents embarrassing dilemmas. And, lastly, it is quite impossible for the individuals to acquire the social knowledge and skills necessary for an adequate performance in so many different novel settings from parents and the adults who relate to them in their own birthright social position.

There are two corollaries which have become manifest in recent decades. First, in contemporary society, the values, sentiments and attitudes of the individual are increasingly nobody else's affair. If relationships are mostly those in which others are regarded and treated as means to personal ends, if people behave towards some in ways which are at variance with the way they act with others, then there is clearly an element of increasing dissociation between the individual and the primary group.[23] The acquisition of standards of behaviour, values and beliefs from the people among whom they grow up is less important. The self-image – that conception of oneself into which is projected the normative elements to which one's behaviour is inclined – becomes both a more important element in conduct and more divorced from the traffic of activity with parents, older kin, teachers and familiar adults through which the important aspects for mature membership of society were learned. The first corollary, then, is that the individual has become more self-concerned, more socially detached.

The second corollary is that in their self-regarding relationships, and in acting out each distinct status, individuals will adapt their conduct not merely to what is approved by or acceptable to the other people with whom they are involved; too many encounters are transient, too many require apt conduct from the outset. They must have regard to what they can learn as approved or acceptable behaviour in circumstances and milieux which may well be at some remove from anything previously encountered. They must, that is, be concerned not with the conduct and standards learned and validated by contact over time with familiar others but with effective conduct and values in situations which are unfamiliar to them but are treated as standard – normal – in the larger society. And knowledge about effective conduct and values – 'cultivated behaviour' – is derived not from immediate ('primary') groups but from élites.

There is, of course, nothing absolute about these characteristics. What is under discussion are tendencies, now apparent and marked, but emerging over lengthy periods of time, and a balance in our social existence of pressures, appetites, chances and resources which is different from what obtained for earlier generations, and different in the way I have suggested. In principle the primary characteristics of the mass society (a term which has nothing to do with totalitarian propensities) are the gradual sealing of the individual from consensus through immediate relationships into a more self-regarding, autistic, form of living; and the derivation of cultural norms from élite groups. By élite is meant not an aristocracy, or Wright Mills' oligarchic power élite, or even the minority of leaders of thought, values and behaviour – Bagehot's ten thousand. The word is used here much more in its literal sense of the chosen, chosen in the way that pin-ups are chosen. Alberoni's term, 'the powerless élite', is admirably appropriate.

For this process of continuous social learning to be effective *en masse*, there has to exist a means of disseminating the cultural norms displayed by élite groups to large and otherwise unorganised bodies of people. This is done by the mass communication industries – popular newspapers, popular fiction and magazines, radio, cinema, television and, especially, advertising.

These institutions exert their influence not so much by the offer of packaged codes of conduct or sets of values for direct acquisition or imitation but indirectly. Certain kinds of goals, or appurtenances and possessions, pursuits, styles of living, manner, dress, and personal appearances are registered as appropriate to those parts of the social world one encounters or is likely to enter, or to which one aspires; they become incorporated in a self-image, a process of absorption or modelling which is only rarely pushed to the limit of simple identification – with consequences which the BBC is more aware of than most whenever it carelessly disposes of a Grace Archer, or re-casts Mrs Dale's Diary – and which is only beginning to be exploited in the development of brand-image selling. More pervasively, they form the elements from which people compose half their conception of themselves, the upper frequencies of an oscillating self-consciousness forever rebounding between self-doubt and aspiration. In so far as conduct and thought is directed to avoiding the one and approximating to the other, lives are directed along lines laid down by the images presented by the institutions of mass communication.

I take mass communications, then, to be a necessary equipment for handling social and psychological realities no less than political and economic. Mass communications, that is, serve as a technical extension of the personal equipment we have for interpreting our environment and our situation in it, and for coming to the best terms with it, just as there is now a complex social, economic and political technology, in bureaucratic and other organisational forms, which has taken us beyond the limits of face-to-face control, competition and co-operation.

However, as the major American study in this field has shown, mass communications do not operate entirely outside the context of traditional face-to-face social intercourse. The values, the codes of behaviour, the appropriate equipment, the styling of one's children and one's home are formed according to models and instruction derived ultimately through mass communications from élite sources, but there are intermediaries. Katz and Lazarsfeld's study of the parts played by mass communications and by personal influence in different social – fashion, film-going, public affairs and consumption – showed that there exists a flow of information and advice from opinion leaders to opinion followers in every social *milieu*.

Opinion leadership, in this context, is not simply a matter of being more interested than others; it is a matter of being interested when others are interested too. The structural effects of the mass dissemination of norms and the existence of interpersonal networks, in which selection and organisation of styles occurs, are specified as linked in a two-stage flow of communication. Formulated first in *The People's Choice*[24] this suggests that ideas flow from radio, television, journals, advertising and so forth to opinion leaders and from then to the less active sections of the population. It is not that the less active sections do not watch television or read magazines, although they may read significantly fewer magazine then opinion leaders. It is that the organising ideas around which the lifestyle and individual preferences in consumption and activities are formulated among cliques, neighbours and age sets are clearly defined for each individual group by this process of consultation and advice. Opinion leaders are created by the organisational needs of the opinion followers in each milieu.

The two-stage process involving élites, mass communications, opinion leaders and relatively homogeneous groups provides only the most elementary features of the structure we are concerned with. Obviously, the cultural and cognitive character of the group varies enormously. Qualitative differences in knowledgeability and sophistication can be presented, as Moscovici's work[25] suggests, in quantitative terms, as varying spans of socially, occupationally, or culturally acceptable skills and information. Some of these *domaines d'apprentissage* are broad, others narrow, and there is a hierarchic structure apparent. After all, to be in the London set which makes a point of deliberately avoiding Design Centre goods, one has to know the articles – or know about the kind of article – selected by the Design Centre. This means that the world of cultural information, style of life and patterns of consumption form a kind of asymmetrical pyramid, a system of stratification organised in much the same way as the more familiar system of multibonded stratification which relates the individual to the productive system of society, but following different principles, and involving individuals in different ways. Broadly speaking, it is a social structure based on information content, and reflecting the internal organisation of the plural culture which modern Western societies contain. This structure is given substance, so to speak, and built into the more durable and visible organisation of society, through geographical clustering and through association with others in terms of compatibility of age or occupation and through consumption.

The study of consumer behaviour, for the sociologist, is of central importance for the understanding and definition of major social and cultural changes. The actual purchase of goods and services represents preferences in a specific measurable and comparable way. Patterns of consumption can reasonably be taken as representative of styles of life. In their own kind of studies, sociologists will have to make what use their limited knowledge of economics permits of the theoretical and empirical results of economic studies. It is for this reason, to achieve greater facility in the exchange of ideas of a relatively finished, approved and appropriate kind, that one wants the two disciplines brought into touch; not, I have argued, in order to bring about some abstract and intellectually sterile merger, or in order that one should be tributary to the other.

NOTES AND REFERENCES

1. J. M. Keynes, *General Theory of Employment, Interest and Money* (London, Macmillan, 1936).
2. J. S. Duesenberry, *Income, Saving and the Theory of Consumer Behaviour* (Cambridge, Harvard University Press, 1949).
3. E. Katz and P. F. Lazarsfeld, *Personal Influence* (Glencoe, Free Press, 1954).
4. R. Ferber, 'Research on household behaviour', *American Economic Review*, LII (1962), pp. 19–63.
5. N. Foote, 'The Autonomy of the Consumer', in L. H. Clark (ed.), *Consumer Behaviour* (New York, New York University Press, 1955).
6. H. S. Houthakker, 'An economist's approach to the study of spending', in N. Foote (ed.), *Household decision-making* (New York, New York University Press, 1961).

7. G. Katona, *Psychological Analysis of Economic Behaviour* (New York, McEwan-Hill, 1951).
8. G. Katona, *The Powerful Consumer* (New York, McEwan-Hill, 1960).
9. From the 'Survey of consumer finances', *Federal Reserve Bulletin* (Washington, 1956).
10. M. Abrams, 'How and why we spend our money', *Twentieth Century*, CLXXII (1963), pp. 130–8.
11. G. Katona, op. cit.
12. H. S. Houthakker, op. cit., p. 127.
13. J. N. Morgan, *The Economic View point in Family Research* (Ann Arbor, The University of Michigan Press [Survey Research Center], 1964), p. 5.
14. F. Zweig, *The Affluent Worker in an Affluent Society* (London, Heinemann, 1961), pp. 205–8.
15. D. Lockwood and J. Goldthorpe, 'Affluence and the Class Structure', *Sociological Review*, XI (1963), 133–63.
16. H. Gerth and C. W. Mille, *From Max Weber*, Essays (New York, Oxford U. P., 1946), pp. 186–7.
17. P. Willmott and M. Young, *Family and Class in a London Suburb* (London, Routledge and Kegan Paul, 1958); W. H. Whyte, *The Organisation Man* (London, Cape, 1957).
18. N. Foote, op. cit.
19. Ibid.
20. J. Dumazedier, 'Loisirs at dynamique socioculturelle', *Cahiers internationaux de sociologie*, XXII (1957), pp. 75–96.
21. F. Alberoni, *Consumi e società* (Bologna, II Mulino, 1946). I am indebted to my colleague, Dr G. Poggi, for introducing me to the work of F. Alberoni, whose *Consumi e società* represents a considerable and fertile contribution to the sociology of consumer behaviour. The following four paragraphs are based on a number of comments by Dr Poggi, as well as incorporating his rendering of passages from Alberoni's book.
22. Cf. M. Gluckman, 'Les rites de passage', in M. Gluckman (ed.), *Essays on the Ritual of Social Relations* (Manchester, Manchester U. P., 1962).
23. Tom Burns, 'Systems, commitment and identity'. Paper read at Annual conference of British Sociology Association (1965).
24. P. Lazarsfeld, B. Berelson and H. Gaudet, *The People's Choice* (New York, Columbia U. P., 1948).
25. S. Moscovici, personal communication (1965).

10

The Revolt of the Privileged

This article began life as a paper presented to a conference
convened by the Social Science Research Council at the
University of Sussex to discuss student unrest and, in particular, the kind of research strategy which might provide
some answers to the questions it posed to social scientists.
The opening paragraphs review the kind of questions that
were uppermost at the time. They were real enough, but
could hardly be regarded as carrying the same sensational,
even momentous, message as did the *evenements* of May
1968 in Paris, or the irruptions that broke out in so many
American universities.

It is included in this collection as a kind of memorial to
an almost forgotten and still unexplained episode in the
social history of Britain.

There is a dramatic – perhaps even satiric – richness about the
challenge to sociology presented by the happenings in British
universities during the past year. For the problem of explaining
the origins and interpreting the nature of student unrest is, one
would say, peculiarly and uncompromisingly, sociological.

The student population of 1968 has much the same social
characteristics as that of two or three years ago. Universities
have hardly changed at all. The material circumstances of both
haven't altered for the better or worse, except marginally. And

From *Social Science Information*, vol. 7, no. 4, 1969, pp. 137–49.

so far as expectations are concerned, although forebodings have been expressed about the 'cut-back' in expenditure, the effects haven't really been felt yet, certainly can hardly have penetrated anywhere near the point at which they are felt by students, and in any case are commonly regarded as a temporary recession from a long-term expansionist trend.

Secondly, we have a social problem of some seriousness which has all the appearance of demanding a purely sociological mode of enquiry manifesting itself just at the time when sociology as an academic discipline has just established itself in a majority of British universities (the number of graduates in sociology this year has, I believe, risen more steeply than ever before) – established itself to the point when it can be attacked in a recent article, along with economics, as the 'traditionally privileged' social science.

Thirdly, there is a view, widely held in universities and finding its appropriate expression in *The Times*, that these two developments are causally connected – that, in fact, it is either sociologists or sociology itself which must somehow be responsible for the sit-ins, the Grosvenor Square demonstration, the examination leaks, and so on (a rather pleasing invocation of the conspiracy theory of society by the Establishment itself!).

So that, fourthly and finally, being members of universities, seeing our own students caught up in these events, professing a discipline which claims not to have, indeed, but to be especially equipped to *find* the answers, we are directly involved, whether we like it or not. We are morally obliged to participate; I would rather our participation took the form of empirical analysis than polemics.

There are dangers in acting out our involvement, at least in part, as researchers, but the biggest danger which surely beset us in the past – that we should simply make fools of ourselves by claiming a special prerogative as social scientists to investigate and pronounce upon social problems – has lost much of its threat. I believe, with Etzioni, that 'our efforts are starting to pay off' (although perhaps not 'handsomely') and that 'we are more ready than ever we were to apply our theories and methods to major social problems and to be systematically concerned with the problems such application raises'.[1] Nevertheless, we are still creatures of our society and our generations, and in so far as we are concerned with current social problems.

Sociologists must necessarily reflect current perceptions of the total situation of their society and culture. What we have eventually to come to grips with is the particular perceptions and interpretations of the student situation which obtain among certain sections of the middle classes – our own section included.

This requirement, that we try to grasp and explore and articulate the perceptions and values we share with others, and the inevitable constraints this process lays upon us, are not always clearly admitted. It is because of this that sociology sometimes seems to exist as a kind of fashion centre for current ideologies. But it is only by transcending this necessary preoccupation with contemporary value systems and the cathectic relationships we necessarily have with them that sociology can hope if not to become *wertfrei*, than at least to justify its existence. We have an obligation to try to do this, and not merely define our positions and let the whole question slide.

To begin with therefore, one must review the kinds of perceptions and evaluations which have gained some currency for the same reason that one explores attitudes and perceptions in organisational and community studies – in order to determine and interpret the *discrepancies* between them; for, as I have said perhaps too often, it is at this point that one move from sociography to sociology.

As a small sample let me offer the following ten:

1. Student unrest is the work, basically, of a hard core of activists. They are of middle-class professional liberal-minded parents, mostly, and enjoy good, supportive relationships with them. The implication is that such students are re-enacting the social and political role which their parents have either abandoned or have allowed other pressures and commitments to erode.[2]

2. Not very far removed is the identification of the hard-core as intelligent but shiftless drop-outs. They are, or become, academic deviants attacking a system which impersonally and ceremonially degrades them from the élite status they achieved merely by gaining a university place.

3. With the third view, we shift, at least at first sight, to a rather more sympathetic view; it is certainly more widely held, and may be taken as an instance of the popular, Marxist-by-hearsay, interpretation. Some students are in protest because they are the alienated victims of a society in which the

educational system is becoming almost wholly the servant of industrialism, bureaucracy and technological progress. Government and University Grants Committee policy for the universities has become more and more undisguisedly the instrument of manpower policy ('the national interest').

In fact, this interpretation shares the pathological connotations of the first two, but takes what might be called the classic Mertonian stance of attributing deviance to a major discrepancy between two sets of values which are nevertheless integral to the social order. Students are reared in a system which rewards merit by restricting continued membership of the system to those who achieve success in terms of traditional values of humanistic learning – not so much science for science's sake, or learning for learning's sake, but learning as a way to personal salvation. Yet it is this very system, they find, which processes, packages and labels them, apparently for life, as human resources for the world of industry, with its very different values, demands and criteria. Matters are not improved when students discover that a number of labels are not very easily marketable.

Protest takes the form of attacking university authorities partly because they have leant themselves to this fraud, or malversation of the true destiny of academic existence, partly because it is the part of the system nearest to hand which has proved vulnerable to attack, and partly because it is manifestly a highly illuminated scene for counter-action.

4. Predictably, the next line of interpretation is organised around the theme of anomie, arising from the abrupt liberation from the strictly controlled and regulated life of school and home – the control coming, of course, not so much from authoritarian schoolteachers and Victorian parents as from the four or five years of intensive, directed, planned school work which leads up to A-level examinations. This particular pressure has increased substantially in recent years with increased competition for places; at the same time, control of university studies has relaxed; cafeteria curricula force more decisions on them, ignorant as they are, especially of the new branches of study into which they are attracted;[3] rising numbers remove students even further from any but the most formal contacts with teachers and what they feel to be the substance of university life. The whole situation is aggravated by the strong

likelihood that a proportion of students work for their places in response not to their own need for achievement but to that of their parents, which carries them into universities and then ebbs from them; having failed to internalise the norms of their parents, they are hardly likely to pass satisfactorily through the process of secondary socialisation into the role of committed student in the circumstances which now obtain.

5. A variant of this last interpretation is one which regards student unrest as only the latest expression, in articulate, publicly visible and militant form, of the generation gap. The sheer distance between the middle-aged and the young in terms of cognitive worlds and values has now produced dissatisfaction among the young with the present social order and their place in it – a role previously played (again more violently on the continent and in the US than in Britain) by teds, mods and rockers, provos – but all within the context of a youth culture aggressively running counter to the established order of the adult, middle-class world. In this, interestingly, youth culture is usurping – or succeeding to – the role of working-class culture, and, like it, and for the same reasons, is cultivated and supported by the Orwellian, dissident, section of the world of intellectual journalism.

6. Lastly, among these universalistic interpretations, is the 'bankruptcy of the left' thesis. Intellectuals in the West have produced nothing more than reiterative exegesis of nineteenth-century ideas, most of which is irrelevant to the contemporary situation. Since it is the middle class, especially the highly-educated middle class, which is now under direct pressure to conform to the exigencies of bureaucratised industry, the computer revolution, the new technology, and the apparatus of social and economic planning, it is they who are driven to protest. But, in the absence of any coherent body of social and political ideas or of any explanatory analysis relevant to their situation, they are reduced to incoherent militancy and the rejection of any kind of order. The basic slogan (and slogans have become extraordinarily prevalent as a substitute for ideas) is that painted in large letters on a building in Leeds University: 'If the system stinks, disrupt it'.

This almost nihilistic stance is not the end of it. One of the paradoxes which needs exploring is the coexistence of this apparently impassioned advocacy of disruption with a belief present among some students in their special capacity (including new knowledge and new skills) for comprehending the essential structure and significance of contemporary society, an understanding beyond the grasp of the mass of people, and accordingly of their special vocation, and moral authority, for leading society and controlling its development along the right lines. What we may have, it seems, is the emergence of a meritocratic élite which is nevertheless not prepared to accept the present system.

7. There are several particularistic interpretations on the market. Perhaps the simplest is that the frustration or the seeming ineffectiveness of the para-political activities of CND and the anti-Vietnam War movement – or their sheer momentum – has flooded over into action against university authorities and within the university system at the slightest sign of any defaulting by the university administration or staff from an attitude of sympathetic alliance with such protests. The major disturbances at the London School of Economics, Leeds, Essex and elsewhere were all set off by protests and demonstrations with a specific political point. The crux here is the assumption by students that the universities have a political and moral role in society, and that this is in danger of being betrayed by the academic establishment.

8. In contrast with this is the perception of the movement as essentially a-political. Without imputing any consciously planned, conspiratorial, endeavour to cloak seditious or malicious enterprises, it is suggested that the initial outburst or demonstration commonly has a political character because it *legitimises* militant action. At bottom, however, the movement's drive comes from unfocussed dissatisfaction and disappointment with the apparent arbitrariness of the university system – with the curriculum as well as with disciplinary rules – and a long overdue reaction against paternalistic authority which, long extinct in middle-class families, is still the norm in universities, and is exercised through a body of rules and through powers which constitute, in fact, a private body of law outside the legal system which binds them as citizens.

There are, it seems, four levels at which this kind of movement may be seen to operate. At the lowest level, students merely seek to call the bluff of the paper-liberalism professed by many universities, especially the new ones, and to seek to limit the arbitrary powers which may almost always be invoked by vice-chancellors when faced with what they feel to be indisciplined, aggressive, immoral or violent behaviour which is not 'sanctioned by tradition' (i.e. condoned as not threatening either the system or authority).

9. The slogan of 'no victimisation' attached to the first level of challenge to authority also serves to connect it – in practice as well as notionally – with the second. At this point, challenge is translated into a demand for power. If there is anything which the protest movements in European universities have ideologically in common, it is an insistence on the autonomy of individuals, the separate and particular quality of their physical cultural and intellectual attainments and needs, and on their right to participate in the government of the institutional order which controls so much of their present life and future prospects. The articulation of this demand into specific goals, however, seems to pose a dilemma. In some cases, but certainly not as clearly anywhere in this country as in France, the university comes to be regarded as a base from which the political, social and moral order of contemporary society can be challenged, and, ideally, could be reconstructed into a feasible model of a new institutional order to replace that of a bureaucratised world. In the majority of cases in Britain, however, the vision of the university as a structure of power and authority seems to have materialised (at this point of goal-formulation) into an image of the university as an industrial organisation. Thus the university can be seen to comprise a *patronat, cadres* and *contingent,* with the first two composed of relatively permanent members, and high rewards and security of tenure, and the *contingent,* the lower orders, temporary, picked and recruited in impersonal and highly bureaucratised ways, subject to separate norms and codes of discipline, monitored in performance by the cadres, liable to dismissal, arbitrary decisions about expansion or shrinkage of numbers, clearly subordinate to all members of the *patronat* and *cadres* alike, and poorly paid. Simply, the university becomes equated with 'the employers' and the university staff with 'the management', and the students with 'the workers'. Hence the preoccupation with negotiating machinery, union organisation, representation on Senate and Faculty, and the pressure for committees of staff and students

to assume control of teaching methods, and syllabus and the curriculum, of staff recruitment – the whole apparatus of *Mitbestimmung,* joint consultation and works councils.

But experience of representation and committees may lead on to the next stage, which is dominated by the 'politics of mistrust'. The inevitable surrender in negotiation and in committees of points at issue which, whether major or minor, are always regarded by the body of students as points of principle, leads to a rejection of negotiation and representation altogether – 'to negotiate is to surrender'. Hence the demand for total involvement of all students in all decisions which has dominated student movements abroad, and which has made itself felt here, with all matters to be decided in the Assembly of students and staff – a position based not so much on a Rousseauist innocence as on a refusal to trust anybody except those present and subject to the overriding control of a mass meeting.

10. And, finally, there is the level of challenge to authority at which it is discovered that violence – or merely the public embarrassment of university authorities – pays. Again, this is not meant to impute sheer malevolence or cynicism, but to point to the fact that orderly demonstrations and formal protests manifestly achieve nothing, but that disorder and uproar directed to the same ends do call immediate attention to grievances, do claim public attention, and do sometimes provoke reprisals or police action which, being of itself usually indiscriminate and sometimes (even in this country and certainly in France, Germany and America), tough to the point of brutality, at least gains immediate sympathy for the victims and perhaps their cause. The role of the press and television in all this is familiar, although by no means clearly analysed.

It will be apparent that there are affinities and connections between these interpretations. These are also discrepancies and antitheses (as well, of course, as omissions). But the purpose of this rather improvised review is to point to the first of three major considerations which, I suggest, should affect research strategy in this area.

The first relates to the way in which the kind of interpretations in good currency determine the basic formulation of the research. The 'What is the problem?' question that one puts to oneself at the outset of any research can be answered in the present instance in a variety of ways. Clearly, if one adopt the line suggested by the last group, concerned with the direct and internal challenge to university authority and the claim for participation, one almost of necessity adopt a framework derived from industrial sociology. If the university is being equated with industrial organisation, then student unrest is visible as akin to industrial unrest.

There are several model 'frameworks' available from industrial sociology – that of the neo-human relations movement, for example, concerned to lubricate the passage of individuals and organisations to a more satisfactory, productive and adaptive work-system, and with the design of roles and relationships which will promote participation and therefore commitment; a second might be that of organisational analysis, with student unrest treated as symptomatic of the organisational deficiencies of universities, and research aimed at identifying divergent goals, the vagaries of the decision-making system, the formal and informal processes of communication, segmentation and the like. And I am quite sure that the results of either kind of study would be interesting and probably valuable. They would, of course, be utterly different from the findings of studies which took off from any of the first three kinds of current interpretations, all variants on the aetiology of student unrest seen as deviant behaviour. And lastly, if what is happening in universities is only explicable in terms of ideological bankruptcy, or the appearance of structural divisions based on generational differences or the like, then the only point in studying students is that their behaviour and attitudes might serve as a politico-social, or a social-psychological, indicator of social change.

The second strategic consideration arises out of the impossibility, if we are to be honest, of merely choosing, for reasons of circumstance or discretion or personal preference, one of these kinds of answer to the question, 'what is the problem?' It is impossible because we are, I believe, as sociologists, committed to procedures which accept different analytical approaches precisely because we are studying not simply action but action into which people read meanings – the kind of meanings I have been rehearsing. Action, in addition to being deeds, 'stands for' intentions, feelings, expectations, beliefs – significances which are attached to action by the actors and by others. And in attaching meanings, and *these* meanings rather than *those*, people demonstrate both their common membership of specific collectivities and their exclusion from others. Sociology exists as a study because the shared significance of the same kind of social action can alter between groups and collectivities; not only between agents and patients and audience, but between sections of each of them.

The answer, then, to the basic question 'What is the problem?' is not to adopt some or other of the interpretations available, to construct what one rather embarrassingly calls a theoretical framework and derive testable hypotheses from it. The answer lies in the very variety of interpretations itself. What has been happening – among students and within universities and *to* society – to give rise to these interpretations and render *all of them*, in some measure, plausible?

Having said that, it is also clear that to reach any kind of solution to this central question requires the antecedent exploration of the social context – in particular 1) the attitudes and aspirations of students themselves; 2) the institutional and organisational structure of universities; and 3) the elementary participation of university people, staff and students alike, in the structure of society – in which that particular question has arisen. I mean by this that the array of interpretations which I have said represents the necessary *logical* starting point of enquiry itself exists intellectually as an open system – just as we have learned, albeit rather slowly, to treat any collectivity of persons or structural form of society as an open system.

A SOCIOGRAPHY OF STUDENT UNREST

I hope I shall not be thought perverse if I include the sociography of student unrest as part of the *context* of the main problem. What is relevant here is basically the process of articulation and institutionalisation – from what might be called the *casus tumultus* onwards to tactics, the movement from protest to demand, the emergence of leadership, organisation and publicity; the use or avoidance of the formal apparatus of classroom, department, administration and student organisation; the increase of sensitivity to action by university authorities; the adoption of a particular institutional model (industrial relations or other); the involvement of junior staff. This kind of study, of course, requires first-hand observation and interviewing, of the kind which Erving Goffman and Alfred Willener have been developing.

If behaviour is meaningful in the way sociologists claim, then the conduct of people in these episodes should reflect two normative complexes: first, the kind of variegated value-connotation already described; second, the more familiar stuff of attitude surveys. In this latter, I suggest, we would be concerned largely with the definitions of which students are the object: as the work in progress of an organisation which 'processes people' (as one definition has put it); as clients of the professional body of academic teachers; as fellow-members of an academic community; as the group for whom the university exists and therefore its most powerful section; as the 'workers' in an institution more and more closely modelled on the world of industry for which they are being prepared, and in which the university staff are equated with 'the management' and the university as a whole with 'employers'; as refugees from parental pressure or the exigencies of the occupational world; as a privileged élite; as the alienated victims of a society in which the educational system has become almost wholly the servant of industrialism, bureaucracy and technological progress.

An enquiry into student attitudes, affiliations and objectives has therefore to be much wider in scope than one directed towards establishing the social characteristics, political affiliations and the 'image of society' of active members of the radical student movement. In addition to the need to provide some description of the variety of student attitudes, needs and aspirations, and relating these to the demographic and social characteristics of the student population and secondly to the nature and variety of their participation in university life, and so on, there are three other dimensions which need examination. 1) The expectations and attitudes of staff, and the way in which these are perceived by students; 2) antecedent expectations of parents and school teachers, and the way in which these are perceived by students; 3) the public (and especially the press) image of students and of the university itself.

UNIVERSITY CONSTITUTION AND MANAGEMENT

The student movement can be seen as currently only the more articulate, publicly visible and militant aspect of current dissatisfactions among the young with the present social order and values, and of their rejection of some of the more blatantly materialistic orientations, and injustice, of the educational system as a whole. Yet, plainly, student unrest is also symptomatic of the inadequacies, ineffectiveness or misdirected efforts of universities themselves. Indeed, the comparatively mild uproar which students in a number of British universities have created during the past year has generated a spirit of self-criticism and a preparedness for radical reform unthinkable a few years ago, when the only problems were those of how to encompass the moderate expansion of student numbers envisaged in the Robbins Report without endangering the traditional ethos of the small universities of this country, the quality of the undergraduate population, and the structure of the curriculum.

On their side, the universities have rather less room for manoeuvre than students seem to believe. They operate under fairly strict financial and legal constraints and, more importantly perhaps, are bound by traditional expectations and by demands from government and the rest of society; they are the prisoners as well as the beneficiaries of the high value placed on them by society at large; and their autonomy, already reduced and under threat of greater governmental control, may be seriously jeopardised either if reform from within is regarded as too radical or if they fail to establish a reasonable degree of control over the behaviour of their members.

The Robbins Committee identified four objectives of 'any properly balanced system' of higher education (§ 22–9):

1. Instruction in skills suitable to play a part in the general division of labour [...] In our own times, progress – and particularly the maintenance of a competitive position – depends to a much greater extent than ever before on skills demanding special training.
2. The aim should be to produce not mere specialists but rather cultivated men and women.
3. The advancement of learning.
4. The transmission of a common culture and common standards of citizenship.

The report emphasised that these aims are not necessarily incompatible, eclecticism being 'imposed by the circumstances of the case'. Nevertheless, it seems evident that while all these objectives may be compatible in the sense of being visibly pursued within the same university, the balance of emphasis varies between different sectors of the same university, and the considerations which are brought to bear in judging between the claims of these different sectors for attention and support have regard to values *other than those of maintaining an existing balance*. It is the pressure exerted in support of one objective against the others (not necessarily to their actual exclusion) which converts debate about aims into conflict about the allocation of resources and time. For some, universities exist as an enclave, a minority world, which is both far more varied in terms of intellectual and cultural interest, moral values, political belief, ethnic and social origins, and far more tolerant of such pluralism than any other habitable social world. For others, especially among the young, it represents a base from which the political, social and moral order of contemporary society can be criticised and challenged, rather than perpetuated.

There are also, certainly, other objectives for which a place is claimed, alongside – or even over and above – these four. Furthermore, all objectives can be, and are, rephrased in depreciatory and unflattering terms by different sections of a university, according to a particular interpretation of its current changes in balance between those objectives, and of a particular set of interests and aspirations.

We have, therefore, to examine the variety of interpretations which exist of the university's role in society and of its purposes and functions, the characteristics of the sectional and of the individual proponents of these interpretations, and the influences such interpretations have on the distribution of resources, rewards and power: in short, the particular definitions of the university, their relation to particular interests, and the ways in which this relationships is expressed and makes itself felt.

Organisational and constitutional problems may be subsumed under the following headings:

Decision-making

The university presents in an acute form the general organisational dilemma between:

a) those decision-making processes which are analytical (and can be conducted by experts on the basis of either straight problem-solving or of persuading others who share the same view about objectives) and

b) those processes which involve bargaining or conflict, because there are discrepant views about objectives.

Like other organisations (but in a more extreme and arbitrary way) the university attempts to solve the organisational dilemma by:

1. Creating an administrative hierarchy which reduces the number of groups and individuals involved in decisions as they become more critical

2. Reducing the amount and altering the nature (e.g. from requirements for new developments in research, teaching, equipment, etc., to requests for money) of decisions as the decision-process moves up the hierarchy

3. Abrogating interaction between the levels of the hierarchy (confidentiality, etc.)

4. Treating bargaining and conflict-type processes as if they were analytical and therefore legitimate.

Communication

Study of the decision-making processes clearly requires concurrent study of the communications network – formal and informal.

Management

Like other professionally-based organisations, the university has created an inner managerial core – 'the Administration' – which is there to conduct the day-to-day affairs of the university as a 'business' – i.e. to manage its duties as employer, to administer and monitor its investment and expenditure on capital and current accounts, to control relations with other bodies and the outside world at large, to record and transmit information. The relationships of this management system with whom – or for whom – it manages are uneasy and changeable, and tend to give rise to classic conflict situations.

Commitments of Staff

More than most organisations, the university relies on a commitment of its members to its purposes over and above the performance of duties according to any definable terms of engagement. There are signs that this commitment has in fact changed its nature and its object; but how far commitment is now to the discipline rather than to the institution, to personal career rather than to the educational welfare of students or to the advancement of learning, or how far to some supposed freedom from a devalued occupational and industrial system, it is impossible to guess. But an analysis of this aspect of academic life is an essential prerequisite to any consideration of reform, especially in curricula, teaching methods, involvement in university affairs and administration, and in attention to student needs.

Segmentation

Until the last generation, the university was probably more accurately regarded as a federation of departments than as a single institution. The rationale of this was to be found in the notion of a 'science' or a 'discipline' or a 'branch of learning', and its manifestation in the syllabus and its text-book. The general system of values that bears on this aspect of the university has already been touched on. Here, the concern is more with the extent to which the university comprises a sizeable range of distinct milieux, each with its own criteria for evaluating needs and performance, organisational procedures, group interests and academic ideology.

Internal Politics and Careerism

Whatever the finding under the previous headings, it will remain to some extent true that individuals by and large will be at least as interested in their own present status and future prospects as they are in the promotion of the interests of the university, their students and the discipline they serve. To this end, they will presumably engage in activities which serve private ends at least as much as they serve the university's. There is in all organisations a system of internal politics, with its own 'rules of the game'. There is also similarly a career system, with *its* own 'rules of the game', according to which an individual may advance or protect his position. An important part of any organisational study is the elucidation of these 'rules of the game', and of the kind of occasion when they are transgressed, and 'illegitimate' political gain or personal advancement is achieved.

Ultimately, we have to come back to the social problem itself. Why this kind of disturbance among students, *of all people*? It is at this point that any enquiry into student unrest must relate itself to the social order which is not merely the context of university life but its 'culture', in the biological sense of the medium in which universities are kept alive. Why should the most cherished and valued section of society be in revolt against it, to the point of declaring revolution?

Even if, as some suppose, we have really passed the crisis of student unrest, and the whole movement washes out in interminable committee meetings, consultations, a few time-wasting but unimportant concessions to the demand for participation and two hundred Ph.D. theses, the problem posed by the past year's events remains.

Let me finish by deserting the line I have followed throughout this paper and 1) give one citation from the literature and 2) advance a general hypothesis.

> The universal and chief cause of [. . .] revolutionary feeling [. . .] [is] the desire of equality, when men think that they are equal to others who have more than themselves; or again the desire of inequality and superiority, when conceiving themselves to be superior they think that they have not more but the same or less than their inferiors.
>
> Aristotle, *Politics*

Relative deprivation, then, is not a novel concept. What is new about it is that it has become untied from the institutional forms through which it found organised, political, expression. This, it seems to me, is the fundamental social fact which underlay the situations which became apparent during the 1950s and were discussed in a number of debates which enlivened conferences and filled number after turgid number of journals: 'the end of ideology'; 'embourgeoisement'; 'the fading of revolutionary feelings from the European working class'; and the most famous and fatuous one – 'the disappearance of social class and of the class struggle'. I suggest that the fundamental *political* fact is the differentiation of roles and the segmentation of social milieux under advanced industrialism. Commitment of the kind needed to change the rules of the game comes from individuals committed wholly to their role as worker, or aristocrat, or bourgeois. Total roles of this kind have faded out, except in a very few instances: soldiers, the Catholic hierarchy, the top stratum of industrialists and business men – and students: all of them on occasion have shown themselves as dedicated and sometimes potent political activists. Only with these incumbents of total roles does consciousness of relative deprivation lead to collective and political, rather than egoistic and instrumental, action.

NOTES AND REFERENCES

1. A. Etzioni, 'Social analysis as a sociological vocation', *American Journal of Sociology* 70, March 1965, pp. 613–25.
2. It would be quite impossible to give the provenance of all these evaluations; most of them – recognisably, I hope – summarises or render explicit the tone of British or French press commentaries. But the first is in fact based on a statement by Professor Erwin Scheuch of the results of studies already completed among German students.
3. The growth in numbers of students reading social sciences remains an unexplained mystery. Fashion; the devaluation of natural sciences as a result of 'space-age' publicity; the search for a solution to personal mystifications about society and their own position in it; and, of course, the fact that social science places are far cheaper for the government to provide in a period of 'university expansion', have all played their part.

11

Public Service and Private World

This is a paper based on passages extracted and recomposed from the report I wrote on a study of the organisation of the BBC carried out in 1963, and which the BBC refused to allow me to publish (see Introduction, p. 000). Publication of this particular paper was, of course, 'cleared' with the BBC's Department of Administration.

*

The question of what the purpose or goal of a group is, and, consequently, what things will help or hinder the achievement of the purpose, is very often a political question. Factions within the group disagree, and manoeuvre to have their own definition of the group's function accepted. The function of the group or organisation, then, is decided in political conflict, not given in the nature of the organisation.[1]

It is difficult to think of any institution, public or private, with a more explicit and precise definition of its purpose than the BBC's, which is to operate a broadcasting service as a means of information, education and entertainment. Yet the same definition could be, and has been, claimed for the services provided by commercial television companies; and public controversy about the aims of the BBC's service is one of the stand-bys of press and publicists since its foundation.

From P. Halmos (ed.), 'The Sociology of Mass Media Communicators', *The Sociological Review Monograph*, no. 13, January 1969, pp. 53–73.

The definition of its primary task given by society and voiced by Parliament in the BBC's Charter therefore, is only a first step, essential perhaps, but no more so than the injunction laid on a commercial company by its shareholders that it should make a profit, or on the State itself that it should promote the welfare of its citizens and protect them and their interests. The prescription itself immediately poses a number of questions about the nature of the information, education and entertainment, about their quantity and quality, and about the proportion which each should represent as well as about what will promote and what will prevent their successful presentation. Indeed, these questions have formed the matter of the national debates, inside and outside Parliament, and of the committees of enquiry which have preceded the review and renewal of the BBC's Charter. The Corporation itself contributes to these debates, and in so doing claims the right to have a voice in the framing of the Government's prescription. The debates are inevitably reflected within the Corporation itself.

Dispute about current interpretations of the task of radio and television broadcasting seems to have mounted within the Corporation itself in recent years.

Three distinct views made themselves apparent. For many people, the 'pragmatists', the three purposes of informing, educating and entertaining the public seemed to be quite distinct but nevertheless compatible because there was in fact an explicit and general public demand for all three things. Others – the 'platonist' school – saw the BBC as an institution with a specific and now inalienable historic part to play in the life of the nation. Whether this role had been deliberately chosen and achieved or was the consequence of social forces which had operated through historical circumstances, the BBC's relationship with the nation was now normative. In international or national crises, it spoke in a real and important sense for the nation as well as to it. For the majority of people, the measure of the significance of any public issue was the weight the BBC gave to it. Moreover, while nobody is naïve or presumptuous enough to see the BBC as prescribing some national code of morals, it is believed that the normative function which it undoubtedly has discharged in politics is also attached to its observance of moral standards, in entertainment principally, but also in comment and criticism; so the programmes broadcast carry a special sanction in that they are what the BBC, the national broadcasting authority, sees as fit and proper to offer the nation. A third section of opinion – whose reported slogan 'television for television's sake' underrates the Aristotelian authority of their position – seems to regard this normative role either as undesirably arrogant, or played out, or as imposing irrelevant constraints on the development of broadcasting forms so as to mirror contemporary events, society and culture swiftly and forcibly.

While I believe that the only injustice done in this account to these three views lies in its brevity, it should be said that they are in fact inferences from the interviews and conversations rather than summaries of statements explicitly made; the most explicit statements tended to be about opinions imputed to others which were in conflict with the stand which could be assumed to be the speaker's.

There may, of course, be other views of the BBC's function, or purpose, or mission in society. All I have done is to present, in capsulated form, the three which made themselves evident to me in interviews with some 200 members of the Corporation's staff in the middle and higher ranks. The form and length of the present paper prohibit any discussion of the public debate itself. Indeed, the whole report of which this forms part, while it is about the BBC, is not about the BBC as a public institution. Varieties of policy and changes of policy, the extent and exercise of public control, the content and merit of programmes, the competence of producers and performers and the inevitable speculation and public interest aroused by an organisation which probably absorbs more of the time of the people of the country than any other single institution – all these familiar and proper matters of discussion enter in only in so far as they represent the outer environment of the situations which have been the object of study.

But it would be wrong to omit any reference here to the case which has been argued from time to time in lectures, speeches and articles by the Director-General and other official and unofficial spokesmen of the Board of Governors and the Board of Management of the BBC. In fact, the best statement of this viewpoint has been made not by any of these, but by a former

Controller of Programmes, Television, Mr Stuart Hood. He writes:

> The BBC functions on a system of devolution. A producer is given full powers in making a programme or series of programmes. On him rests the final judgement of what is right and seemly to present to his audience. His decisions may range over a wide field. They may concern a theme, a topic for discussion or debate; the choice of a film-clip; a dramatic situation; a camera-angle; the words of a song; a single word. If he is doubtful on any point he may refer his problem to his superior, who will either make a decision or refer the matter higher. The ultimate instance is the Director-General, who – before giving his ruling – may consult with the producer himself or with senior members of the staff. Judgements are not based on written laws – although there is a code of practice governing violence in children's television or 'that area of adult time when children are known to be viewing in substantial numbers'. In part, they are based on precedent and tradition; but precedents can be ignored and traditions questioned and modified. What they are based on can best be described as a programme ethos – a general view of what is fitting and seemly, of what is admissible and not admissible, which is gradually absorbed by those persons involved in programme-making. It is intangible, undefined and baffling to newcomers and freelance producers or directors. One of the best definitions of it was provided by Sir Hugh Greene in an address delivered in Rome to the International Catholic Association for Radio and Television. One element in what he called 'the in-grained code' was 'the proper sensitivity of production staff to the world around them, so that they are concerned with a relationship to the audience which cannot exist if the language in which they are talking, and the assumptions they are making, seem to be too remote from the language and assumptions of the audience and of the times in which they are communicating'. This formula is both liberal and flexible.[2]

It will be noted that this prescription, liberal and flexible as it may be, is nevertheless concerned with negative sanctions – with the exercise of censorship, rather than with a positive formulation of purpose or function. If anything, it seems to square with the third view I have presented above, of 'broadcasting as a mirror of contemporary life' subject only to the two constraints of 'public opinion' (overwhelming pressure from outside organisations or articulate sections of the public) and 'programme ethos' (the individual producer's interpretation of both the function of broadcasting and of the constraints of 'public opinion'). But, in fact, it represents much more clearly the present stage of the 'liberal dissolution' of the Corporation ethos itself as it was created by Reith's generation.

The great merit of the conception of the role of radio broad-casting, developed in the formative decades when Sir John Reith was Director-General, was that it had a clear view of the matter,[3] if a limited interpretation of the task which this imposed. If the function of broadcasting in society is construed as the provision of political, social and cultural navigation charts, the job Reith chose for the BBC to carry out was that of maintaining a kind of pilot service. Or, to shift the line of vision a little, the BBC developed as a kind of internal diplomatic ser-vice for the nation, representing the British – the best of the British – to the British. 'BBC culture', like the BBC's standard English vocabulary and pronounciation, was not peculiar to itself but an intellectual ambience composed of the values, stan-dards and beliefs of the professional middle class. Sports, music and entertainments which appealed to the lower classes, were, of course, included in large measure in programmes, but the manner in which they were purveyed – the context of pre-sentation – remained indomitably upper middle class; and there was, too, the point that they were only on the menu as ground bait.

But – and this is crucial – the pattern was deliberately worked out. Reith, in short, knew what he was doing. There is no sense in which a public broadcasting service for the nation can become a 'value-free', or neutral administration. 'It is an outstanding characteristic of the European liberal *idea* of the state that it is neutral, that it adopts a *neutral* position in inter-nal values, such as the problem of what truth and justice are; it leaves the choice and judgement of all values of this sort to special social groups (for instance, to the Church) or to the con-science of the individual. The real basis of national sovereignty is a purely "formal" legal structure, divorced form all questions of internal value.'[4] But neutrality of this kind, even nationally, can even so only attach to the State. The rationale of the creation of a Broadcasting Corporation separate from the Government is that neutrality cannot be assumed in these regards. There is no culturally or morally neutral position to assume.

The monolithic structure of the Reithian ethos broke up during the 1950s. Oversimplifying, as one has to, we can point to three principal factors contributing to the change. The advent of television itself probably did most. Broadcasting was no longer *sui generis*. The cinema, television's model as well as competitor, had its own conventions, standards and mythology, and, more important, an entirely different relationship with its audience (i.e. it put a different construction on the social task of providing a navigation chart of the social and physical world.) Commercial television, when it came, destroyed not only the monopoly of the BBC in the economic sense but also its special relationship with the nation of universal representation and total responsibility.

The breaking of the uniqueness and the unity of the link between broadcasting and the nation which first television itself, and then commercial television, accomplished, meant the intrusion of other renderings of Britishness and of rightmindedness and the consequent shrinking of BBC values to something sectional and questionable. So that while the social function of commercial television was, as before, to provide interpretations and models with the greatest acceptability (but this time obviously and admittedly to provide ground bait, and for a very different kind of fishing), one considerable side-effect has been to put the whole BBC operation and policy into the framework of 'brand-image' making.

It is also arguable, thirdly, that changes in Britain's social structure which occurred, or became manifest, during the 1950s brought into question the authority of the whole hierarchy of values on which the Reithian system depended. But arguments of this global sort quickly become circular; after all, the collapse of the old BBC ethos played no small part in the change in orientation of British society.

The BBC has not by any means turned its back on the Reithian ethos and purpose; many, indeed most, of its activities still faithfully reflect the traditional image. But there has been change, and it is change which is significant, as it is change of which we are most conscious. The breaking of the BBC monopoly was achieved by political manoeuvres within one party; and however nobly the BBC strives to retain its reputation for political neutrality, it has been brought down from the heights of supra-political, almost supra-national, authority it enjoyed during the sound broadcasting monopoly.

A consciously 'circulation-building' element has entered into the handling of news and comment on news; successful presentation is related more and more to exclusive, sometimes sensational, interviews and reporting. Many programmes have appeared to make bids for popularity by disregarding the cautious (or responsible) standards associated with the earlier days of monopoly. The hauteur which governed Corporation attitudes and behaviour towards commercial television at first has given way to a more or less open acknowledgement of rivalry on the same terms, a rivalry which admits of the interchange or common employment of popular performers and producers and of the growth of a policy of short-term contracts – both of which must dilute any distinctively BBC style or approach, and reduce the public appreciation of differences of ethos and purpose between the Corporation and commercial television companies.

The Corporation has felt itself compelled to fight on two fronts; the old certainty of purpose has gone; and the clear challenge and opportunity has been replaced by a dilemma.

There is nothing particularly novel or distinctive about the three 'insider' views with which we began; they echo major sections of opinion outside the Corporation. But while the content of all the utterances which bore on this matter was what is vaguely called the relationship of the BBC to the public, the debate was carried out as an internal affair. The principals in the debate whose rehearsals were quoted by adherents and opponents were in strategic positions within the Corporation. The three kinds of interpretation of the BBC's task were identified with them.

This is natural enough, since the main issues in the debate about interpretation have to be settled within the Corporation and as the result of the interplay of discussion and argument among its officials. Equally naturally, each view squared with the interest of such sections in either keeping its present standing or influence, or bettering it.

Thus the catholicity of the pragmatists was not illogically related to the suspicions of the staff in Light Entertainment and Schools Broadcasting, and of others who felt some affinity with them, that their contribution to the BBC's output was tolerated as an 'unfortunate necessity'. The slogan most frequently

encountered was 'a balanced programme' – i.e. a total output
in which Light Entertainment would have a rightful share.

> There's some disquiet here because we see the top places in
> the top places in the Corporation all being filled by journal-
> ists. You see, when you had a few showmen up there, they'd
> take the view 'I didn't like this but it's popular and – in the
> interests of a balanced programme – I'll put it in.' The journal-
> ists now will quite likely take the view that if they don't like a
> show and if it's not getting a *very* big audience, they can scrap
> it.

A 'balanced programme' policy would, in fact, serve as an
insurance policy – something which would quieten the unexpectedly widespread feelings of insecurity about the future
which turned up in many interviews in Light Entertainment
and in Schools Broadcasting. Thus:

> One has the feeling that the Corporation could well do with-
> out Light Entertainment. It has Light Entertainment because it
> has to – that although it did many good things even prior to
> the advent of commercial television, that if they could do
> without us they would. That is the feeling. It's only very
> recently, when things became competitive, let's face it – that
> audiences are wanted to keep the Corporation alive – that
> they really acknowledge that they had to have Light Enter-
> tainment, and there was no way out of it. Although, of course,
> there's always the feeling that if you can develop the big audi-
> ence puller with *Your Life in Their Hands* then probably they'd
> junk it. They'd let Light Entertainment go.
> You're here as ground bait. All right, so stick to your job as
> ground bait, and don't think of Light Entertainment being a
> viable television commodity in its own right.

and again:

> It's an unsafe world ... If we're talking of allies – which is the
> point you made – I don't think there are any allies. I think
> they're a bunch of hostile critics.
>
> *Has this feeling of it being an unsafe world grown in the last year or
> so?*
>
> Yes. Oh yes. Prior to Pilkington, there wasn't the feeling of
> quite so much insecurity as there's been since.

Obviously, there is no active, present, fear that the Corporation
will 'junk' Light Entertainment, or even that it wants to, but
there remains the uncertain feeling that Light Entertainment is
there to act as ground bait for the mass audience, that its first

and only job is to attach the audience to the BBC channels, and
that its existence depends on keeping mass audiences in a way
that other output departments' existence does not. There is,
beyond this, an awareness that over the past few years a critical
ideological campaign has been fought and won in BBC television, the outcome of which has been to place Talks Department
in the centre of the programmers' picture of television, with
News and Current Affairs and Outside Broadcasts within the
main frame. All these three departments observe the same
canons of life immediacy, of the television screen acting as
reflector of the 'real world' of people, happenings, things and
ideas – a world which is real in so far as it is topical. Drama
remains a datum of existence for television in its 'home cinema'
function. Light Entertainment, equally, remains an 'unfortunate
necessity', its marginal character inescapably perpetuated in
the adjective tagged on to its very title. So:

> It is very difficult, no matter what kind of prestige one attains
> in a good Light Entertainment show, to realise that prestige in
> comparison with other parts of our output. The cachet isn't
> there.

The visible direction of these observations shows that the belief
that BBC policy should be guided by the actual and actively
expressed public demand for a balanced variety of kinds of
programmes rests on apprehensions about the unwilling acceptance by 'The BBC' of the very existence of whole departments.
The insecurity engendered by such apprehensions and the suspicion felt in such departments that they are victims of tacit
demarcation rules about status or, at least, esteem within the
Corporation both find a rational basis in the sweeping successes
of people from Talks Department is gaining the dominant
position in Television Service, and the striking contrast of the
shrinking of influence or representation of other kinds of
production experience in the higher ranks.

In both the television programme departments included in
this study, there was a great deal of discussion of the paradoxi-
cal situation of there being far more insecurity prevailing in the
Service now the BBC had entered on a new lease of secure
existence.

As in other contexts, the goal of political conflict is to have
the leaders of one or other party gain positions of power;
thereafter, of course, they will administer in the interests of the

community as a whole, and with strict justice and equity, but it is at this point of succession to positions of power that the political system and the careers system of organisations meet. The success of people from one section of the organisation rather than others must be seen as reflecting on the general level of ability and initiative in that section. The kind of talents and experience which that section requires and rewards is shown to be demonstrably relevant to the kind of talents and experience required by the organisation as a whole. The success of individual members from a section suggests that the cases it has argued have been well argued by them in the past; more particularly, that their view of the Corporation's task and of the best way of discharging it has won over other views – that the career victory is also an ideological victory. The structure of working relationships and functions in the section from which they came, and the jobs of people who operate within it, are less likely to be adversely affected than those in other sections by the changes instituted by the new men who have appeared from that section, have gained by its existing structure and may perhaps have modelled it. While the experiences, expertise and viewpoints the section now has in common with the man at the top may not be an unmixed advantage in the eyes of the members of the section, it seems to be so to others. And there is, lastly, the immediate benefit of the current of promotions set going by any displacement from the top positions in the section.

The outcome of competition for succession to senior posts in an organisation tends therefore, to have repercussive effects throughout its membership, affecting far more, and far more people, than the small group of contestants for the positions.

You used to have big names (from your side of things) around the Corporation at one time?

Oh well, you've got the journalists in now. When——was here you felt you had the ear of the bosses. But now he's gone, and because——(his successor), I suppose, is a BBC man, let's put it, from way back – he's probably looked upon as such by the top brass – we've become much more of a 'department' than we used to be, just another limb of the Corporation, and feeling just a bit more remote.

I see. So far from having your people fed up to the top, you're having people fed into your top.

> Yes. And I think this will probably go on. For instance what future is there for a producer here? I'm personally quite interested in administrative jobs and have done them in the past . . . but I don't really reckon there's a great deal of opportunity, unless I managed to get the ear of somebody somewhere, to make the jump from production to administration. You see, and there's this feeling – as was definitely stated when——addressed us. One of the chaps said 'You don't want to finish up with a lot of producers who are fifty-five or sixty' and the answer was 'That's quite right'. So you see immediately one feels a little more remote, and cut off and wondering about the future.

It is this repercussive effect which links the legitimate self-interests of the members of a department or section in an organisation to the actual and possible changes which occur in the occupancy of the senior posts at the top. The kind of consequences which are to be looked for from such changes are, for the general run of staff, legible in the attitudes taken in the general debate about policy by the new occupants. At the very outset of this study, the new appointments to the highest posts in the Engineering Division were discussed largely in terms of their meaning for career prospects, and the kind of qualifications or personal qualities or Corporation experience which might be most favoured; there was no apparent concern in other kinds of policy change the new men might institute. More generally, such attitudes are related to alternative lines of action which are actually or possibly pursued by different sections.

> Individual programmes now have greater freedom. People think in terms of this or that programme rather than of the BBC as a whole. The amount of control exercised over them centrally has slightly diminished. Individual programmes have more autonomy.
>
> *This applies to matters of content – journalistic content, perhaps. Is there any other sense in which this greater freedom, or autonomy, is exercised?*
>
> Yes, I think in its attitude to its audience. This applies much more to television – a feeling not so much that a programme is only justified by the audience that it gets but that, bearing in mind the cost of the service, and the physical limitations of it, you have to think very very hard before you put on a programme that is only of interest, say, to one million as against six million. I think there is a difference between this

and saying 'Oh, this is a programme which will bring in an audience of thirteen million and therefore we can charge a lot for the advertising.' I'm not sure, though, that the distinction is always made in that form. Sometimes the BBC attitude to justification by figures is just as blatant as the commercial companies'. It can be very honest and very democratic, this feeling, but it can be used as a stick to beat everything that doesn't command a large audience.

There is a patchiness, then, partly because of the nature of television?

And partly because of history. I mean, Reith lives on at Broadcasting House and not at Television Centre.

The growth of the Television Service within the BBC, its success in the battle for audiences with commercial television, and the more recent emergence of a group of young and vigorous people into controlling positions within the service have all contributed to a greater autonomy in the administration of Television. The internal politics of this change are complicated, but nevertheless clear enough in the practical issues involved.

If you are right in saying that the BBC is becoming more 'plural' – culturally, administratively, and in terms of policy aims – than it was, obviously the resistance must come from the Administration, which is going to be much more comfortable with a monolithic corporation than with a lot of groups who want to go their own sweet way.

I must say this had not occurred to me. It is very easy to talk, isn't it, of 'The Administration' as an external body, without bothering to separate it into its various categories. Frankly, of some sections of the Administration that one comes into contact with – you know perfectly well that they would never have anything to do with deciding the character of the output . . . But may be if one looks at it from the point of view of Television Centre, one certainly gets the impression that in one respect, that is in staffing and recruitment – and I think it is a very widely held impression – that recruiting and staffing in Television is done far more according to the whim, or decision, of the heads – than elsewhere. Appointments Boards, and things like that have less meaning in Television Centre than they do at Broadcasting House.

On the programme side?

Yes – on the programme side. I think it is felt that it is quite clear who will get the job because the man who runs the

programme and his superiors have decided that they want
him on the job. Now this may be a naked geographical thing.
As you say, the Administration is at Broadcasting House. It is
not there.

The broad division of opinion about the way in which the
Corporation should interpret the definition of its primary task
which has been imposed on it as a public institution represents
more than a natural but impotent interest in issues which are
really for the governing body to settle. The debate is ideological, in the sense in which a coherent system of ideas and principles may nevertheless be consonant with the self-interests of a
group of people. This is not to say either that the ideas themselves are thereby invalidated or suspect, or indeed that people
hold those opinions which will tend to their own advantage
– for ideas and actions do *not* simply follow from the social
positions of the individual'.[5] They do, however, strengthen that
particular position which he regards as important for his present and future hopes or chances in life. The kind of views
about policy expressed by individuals, and imputed to others,
are allied to their fears and interests, and serve also to codify
and rationalise courses of action which protect or advance
them.

There is nothing peculiar to the BBC in the development of a
closed system of internal politics out of the variety of interpretations of its task which are publicly available. What was
surprising, in so exceptionally articulate a working community,
was the absence of discussion about the social functions or
social consequences of broadcasting – outside, that is, the context of the issues of 'responsibility' which have already been
touched on, and which are discussed below at greater length.

This may have been merely an aspect of what is supposedly
a traditional British distaste for speculative discussion. Possibly
it derives from a perception of the futility of the efforts made to
trace direct causal connections between broadcasts and the conduct, attitudes, fears or aspirations of the public, adult or child.
It could, again, spring from a reluctance to disturb a complex of
assumptions about the relationships of the BBC to its functions
and to the public.

I am inclined to attach some importance to the last consideration. The lack of interest in the audience which was so evident
can hardly be construed as a kind of schizoid withdrawal,

which was the first construction I placed on it. Certainly, the functional relationship between the views of how the BBC should perform its institutional task, and interest-groups within the Corporation implies that the ideological systems so developed should be autonomous, and thus to some extent shielded from reality. Certainly, also, one encounters something of the 'insider' feeling characteristic of the cultural enclaves inhabited by the highly committed – such as professional musicians, scientific researchers, artists and cult teenagers – although both the egalitarian principles within the enclave and the rejection of the totality of outsiders as 'square' lack the moral fervour of the archetypes.

There is a further general consideration.

Occupations which exist to provide direct services to customers, an audience or a clientele require an organisation of effort or skill directed towards pleasing individuals. This carries with it a connotation of interest, attention or deference which, outside the context of paid or feed employment, would imply that one attached a special value to them and to their well-being. Service occupations therefore tend to carry with them a countervailing, and ordinarily concealed, posture of invidious hostility. This 'latent reversed role' manifests itself at times when the public is not present but is under discussion: in servants, waiters and the occupants of those manifold positions which are needed to lubricate the passage of a public into, through and out of shops, aeroplanes, ships, trains and buses, hotels, restaurants and theatres. There are also episodes when over-exigent demands for attention or deference or some transgression by members of the public licence retribution. More important, in the more highly esteemed reaches of the service occupations, there is the evidence of the traditionally rigorous and irrelevant disciplinary codes prevailing for patients in hospitals and pupils in schools. In the occupations that serve a large and absent public – journalism, advertising and films – the compensatory reaction against the service relationship appears to waver between a cultivated indifference and contemptuous dismissal. It was a television dramatist who pictured the 'typical television audience' as 'mum sitting in the best armchair drinking cocoa with a teenage son on the sofa trying to get his hand up his girl's skirts'. And a public of millions must, it seems, be envisaged as 'moronic'.

It would be easy to multiply quotations voicing the same sentiments as these last, but it would also be absurd to suggest that they are representative of opinion within the Corporation. What is significant about them is that they can be publicly uttered by anyone at all inside the Corporation. That they have been said is, I believe, partly because of the three defensive postures I have mentioned, but more directly the consequence of the incorporation of professionalism within a large, complex organisation. When the relationship between broadcaster and public is inshrouded in a large array of other relationships, each bearing responsibility, and themselves arranged in a hierarchy – so that relationships with one's equals are usually of less consequence than that with one's superior, and less still than with his superior – it tends inevitably to become not so much obscured or extinguished as 'taken care of'. It is taken care of not simply by unloading the burden of the relationship on to superiors, but by the growth of certain institutional forms which empty it of personal involvement. It was possible to discern three such institutional forms: The 'responsible attitude' traditional in the Corporation and the ethical constraints which are implicit in the tradition; the cultivation of 'professionalism' in the special sense in which it is used inside the Corporation, and thirdly, by a limited, controlled use of Audience Research to provide crude audience figures (measured in millions) and an Audience Response measure; procedures which reduce awareness of the public to the safe dimensions of a percentage.

The 'responsible attitude' is familiar enough:

> The fact that if you're doing an hour's drama you're playing around with eight or nine thousand pounds of somebody's money – a lot of money. Again, the viewing figures – one producer was saying that on the night his show was being transmitted he was driving through a Cotswold village which seemed pretty unchanged from what it had been perhaps two hundred years ago, but through all the front windows he could see a little blue screen, and it suddenly came home to him that these people – most of them – were watching something that he had conceived – in an office – in his own mind. The implications of this are considerable, I think.
>
> *Yes. They're always with you, presumably in some form or other, though perhaps not quite in that concrete form?*
>
> They always should be with you.

> *This is, I suppose, the basis of the weight of responsibility which builds up as one approaches the time of recording or transmission?*

> Yes, especially with live transmissions, when you know that it only needs just one person to go berserk for say some fifteen million people to be influenced in some way . . . As Owen Reed said, if you show a hanging on a children's programme, the chances are that some of the children watching will have attempted to do the same, in imitation – which brings the responsibility home.

There seems, in fact, no way of attaining any direct relationship with an audience which will be more significant, or even realistic, than the 'viewing figures' or driving past the front windows of Cotswold cottages. 'Responsibility', for the broadcaster, is institutional. It has had to be generalised, turned into a routine of thought and behaviour, and, outside the context of occasions such as this interview, enclosed within the structure of the Corporation itself. Indeed, 'responsibility' was more easily and clearly registered among the engineers and others not directly concerned with programmes:

> In our organisation the pressures are not commercial but if I can . . . yes, I think this is a fairly sensible term – 'public service conscience'. It's not a nice thing to say, it sounds a but uppity, but if you do have a conscience the pressures in an organisation like this are tremendous.

Yet, like the other institutional forms of the relationship with the audience public, 'responsibility' has become subject to some ambiguity and manipulation. It can be dodged:

> The system in the organisation is such that you could either work very hard, or you could live happily – and it doesn't make an awful lot of difference either way to the immediate situation.

Among producers, on the other hand, there is a feeling that 'responsibility' is somehow at odds with 'artistic integrity'; and that the moral restraints or censorship traditionally exercised implicitly by heads of programme departments are now a set of conventions which it is smart, or wise, to out manoeuvre: one reaction to *That Was The Week That Was* is said to have been the relaxation of self-censorship over the themes and language of 'situation comedy' series mounted by Light Entertainment.

> We've got a thing coming off now, a confidence trickster
> dressing up as a parson, and slipping into some Euston Road
> flophouse. Well this thing was billed for April 17th. We found
> that it's Good Friday, and we've altered the date! But that's as
> far as we're prepared to go.

Standards of responsibility were now perceived as varying
between departments and even programmes:

> Partly because of the speed at which they have to work, there
> comes in a certain meretriciousness, a certain slickness, a ten-
> dency to do things in their programme, which, if the Press did
> them, they'd despise, and almost a certain degree of hypocrisy.
> I can give you one very good example of that. When Bennie
> Paret, the boxer, was killed, there was a telerecording of the
> fight, and the final blows were considered so – vile – that it
> wasn't shown. But 'Panorama', in the course of a discussion
> about boxing, says 'And now we will show you these ghastly
> thirty or forty seconds.' And you are shown this. And you
> come back, and then he says, 'Vile, disgusting, disgraceful,
> and now here is X, Y and Z to talk about this'.

These, and other passages in interviews, refer to isolated
instances and episodes. They are not as wholesale trends, even
in individual output departments, certainly not as a deliberate
policy change. Yet they reveal some unease, and point to the
present as a period of testing out an ethical tradition which is
proving hollow. This is not to suggest that a kind of Gresham's
law operates in broadcasting, but that, within the Corporation,
there is a widespread feeling not so much that the young lions
are taking over but that the Corporation in this one respect has
gone for a ride with a tiger.

The comment by one newcomer to the Corporation, if not
wholly serious, was at least half-serious:

> One of the interesting things to me about the BBC and what it
> does do and what it doesn't do, is that it has done everything
> except nudity. And since it has no real censorship from above,
> this is very strange. I remember that when they visited the
> Windmill, the girls put special clothes *on*. Well, if you're
> going to be politically uncensorable, and if you're going to
> have as much violence as you see on television it's strange
> that this hasn't been exploited. Because it's an audience
> puller, and if people care about viewing figures, I'd have half
> expected this. I think maybe there's a great opening there for
> somebody.

The word 'professional' has an extraordinarily wide currency in the Corporation. In the context of programme production, and of the BBC's relationship with its audience, it seems to have three separable, though not distinct, meanings. First, and most frequently, it means merely the opposite of 'amateur' – i.e. good of its kind, expert, finished; there seems to some people a danger of professionalism, in this sense, degenerating into 'slickness' or even 'journalistic slickness'. Secondly, there is the more conventional use of the word to mean 'qualified by prolonged and specialised training'. A professional engineer is obviously a professional in this sense, but so is a man who has become a producer after many years apprenticeship in the theatre or films, or a floor manager. Thirdly, there is the sense in which it indicates 'a code of behaviour where the first consideration is the need of the client and the quality of the work'.

This third sense involves the appraisal by the professional of what the needs of the client are, independently of the demands and wishes expressed by him, and the appraisal of the service he gives by standards other than appreciation or reward. The first direction of reference – to the client (i.e. the public) – was hardly ever invoked in discussion. The second bulked very large, and relates to one's own sense of successful accomplishment, possibly unreliable, and to the regard of the head of one's department, one's fellows and, most constantly and evidently, the studio staff with whom one works.

The insistence on professionalism arises at least in part from the need to protect oneself from or shelve consideration of the unseen, unknown audience. Even in those output departments in which constant and patent reference was made to audience figures and Audience Response percentages, it was said with great firmness that what counted was judgement by fellow professionals of a programme's quality.

Yet, it was also apparent – and frequently enough said – that producers hardly saw anything of each other. Two producers claimed they hadn't done more than exchange hellos with other producers for months – seven months, one said. Producers tend to isolate themselves, or to get isolated, in the show.

> One of the impressive things about watching a production going on is the special relationship which obtains between producer and cast, floor managers, and crew, and so on – a very difficult relationship, but all balanced on the isolation of the producer and the insecurity which necessarily comes from that. When the thing's in rehearsal, it seemed to me, he's going down a long slide.

Yes.

> *And he's got to end up at the bottom – safely, he hopes. He can't stop. The relaxation at the end, after the show, is very much a happy landing feeling. He's isolated because he's the steersman.*

> The isolation is the thing most producers are afraid of. They don't like it, they don't welcome it. That's why they stick so closely to the notion of the team. They're constantly referring to 'the team'.
> Particularly in this department, we're very much on our own . . . On my own programme, very often I have to do things which I know if I asked my boss he'd say no. It would be right for my boss to say 'No, you mustn't do that.'

Even in the studios, or rather, in the gallery above the studios and sealed off from it, the producer is physically isolated. To retain control and the feeling of control, requires intense concentration:

> When you're producing and you sit in the gallery, you see twenty people, all of whom are not merely expert – but incredibly slow. They seem to you to have a lot of inside knowledge, which you haven't got. But they seem at the same time not to be carrying out your instructions, because from the point of view of a producer speaking into a microphone, to get twenty people to do the right thing at any one moment is inevitably a long process, and it seems utterly endless. The producer must have a tremendous amount of patience to get anything done at all. Occasionally the patience cracks.

The utter absorption of the producer in his show – a commitment far more complete than I have encountered anywhere else – is the product of cumulative pressures. He may be, and often is, responsible for the original idea. The number of people involved, at least in television, is larger than any other form of presentation required. At the time of transmission he is responsible not for a film, which other people will market, or a performance which is now in the hands of the cast and the backstage workers, but for the output, at that time, of the BBC. More of the final product rests on his decisions than with other kinds of staged or filmed performance. And most important of all his responsibility remains throughout the performance, whether it is recorded or transmitted live.

This absorption demands emotional reinforcement and expressive demonstration. No kind of detachment is really permissible; commitment has to be – and be seen to be – deep,

sincere and binding, although surface cynicism, in the right circumstances and in the right company, enters in, as it does with
other professionals whose occupational values have nevertheless to be central to their lives – scientists, priests, doctors. For
producers, this aspect of professionalism develops naturally
from the conventions of the theatre. In rehearsal, the twentieth
repitition of a joke line or a comic sequence will be greeted
with the same appreciative laughter by the other members of
the cast and the other 'professionals' (producer, stage manager
and aspirant juniors) as they gave at the first rehearsal. The
producer, especially, must respond. He must, above all, it
seems, 'believe in' his show.

> *What has struck me is that a producer has got to feel that the show
> he is doing is really good, and that, moreover, he likes this kind of
> thing?*

> Yes. I think he must, even when he's offered an idea, and he
> takes it from this stage. It is rather like approaching a painting,
> for instance. One has to put as much of one's own personality
> into it as possible – but one has to rely on so many people
> around you. You have to work as a 'team'.

Subsequent discussion, too long to reproduce here, made it
clear that there did not exist an alternative professional attitude
of dealing competently and expertly, even imaginatively, with
a show – *Compact* for example, or *Juke Box Jury* – that one did
not regard as anything but unintelligent pop. Taking production responsibility, in these cases, would mean – if it were to be
done *professionally* – remodelling the content and presentation
so that it did represent one's own best, by any criterion.

The weight of commitments – of cast, studio crew, specialists,
engineers and of the Corporation itself – which bear on the
producer is met by a total commitment on his side. Given not
only the special unreality of theatrical or even film productions,
but the fact that the *Dunford Dialogues, The Billy Cotton Band
Show, Today, Z Cars, Panorama, Saturday Night Theatre* and *Don
Giovanni*, all represent quite different orders or species of
unreality, the producer must immerse himself in the particular
unreality in which his show exists, an immersion which
demands involvement of a far more extreme kind than we
accept under the ordinary dispensation of a 'willing suspension
of disbelief'.

The professional role of television or radio producer requires him, therefore, to insulate himself, for the duration of the rehearsal and production period, from the worlds of other productions, both his own past efforts, and those proceeding concurrently. He must match his production: 'A square show needs a square producer,' as one said, and, since this is not easy for people who live by being sophisticated, one must adjust one's perception of the outside world – including the public – so as to make it possible. So, if one is producing a show which I, as an outsider, suggest is very square indeed, the producer must reply, as one did, 'But this is the squarest country in the world.'

Insulation applies to audiences too. The relationship with the audience has to be reduced to the simplest possible terms. I found it difficult to discover whether any kind of reaction from the outside world had been regarded as relevant or worth attention in the days of monopoly broadcasting. Since competition – between sound and television, between the BBC and commercial television, between Third, Home and Light programmes – had been instituted, a little more information about the response of audience had become admissible. But the response elicited – viewing or listening figures, and an Audience Response quotient – applies only to the competitive situation itself.

Beyond the restricted use of Audience Research figures to measure the size of audience and the volume of applause, a use related exclusively to competition between rival broadcaster inside and outside the Corporation, there was, as one comment put it, I think rightly, 'no evidence, to the people inside Television Centre, of people at the top of the Corporation knowing, or indeed caring, what the audience makes of the service it receives'.

The Audience Research Department was not one of the subjects of this study, and its activities are referred to here only in so far as they serve as a constant connection between the BBC and its public.

Audience Research did not attract much attention from the Pilkington Committee. From the Beveridge Committee, however, the service received a good deal of criticism. This criticism still holds good. It does so, I believe, not because of any deficiancy in the department itself, but because of the constraints put on its role within the Corporation, constraints noted by the

Beveridge Committee (paras. 234–5) and which called forth the comment 'To whom is the broadcaster responsible? If it is only to his own conscience, the decision might better be described as irresponsible.'

What I have tried to suggest is that there are reasons for the constraints put on Audience Research and that these are not the irresponsibility, or arrogance, of broadcasters.[6] The pressure on those responsible for programmes is such that fuller or deeper analysis of audience reactions would amount to an intolerable strain.

Even the information contained in an Audience Response (AR) index may have to be rejected. The shock of a reported AR figure of 63 for a programme in a series which had touched 75 was enough to disrupt the first hour or two of rehearsal of a subsequent production. Very little work was done. The atmosphere of dejection deepened with every new arrival. Clusters formed around the leading actors, the floor manager and the assistant floor manager, with the producer circulating between them and the telephone. The whole assembly was, in fact, engaged in a more preoccupying task than rehearsal for the next show: the search for a reassuring explanation. It was found eventually in the concurrence of a sports film on the commercial network.

'This,' it was explained to me, 'is what it's like on the morning when you've got a low audience figure.' For cast and production team, it was 'the figure'. Even after rehearsal began, the figure returned to the centre of the stage during waits: '63 – and I thought it was such a bloody good show.'

For a sociologist, it was rather like watching the whole practice of medicine being reduced to the use of the thermometer. But its significance lay not so much in the importance attached to a statistical index as in the lack of curiosity about its meaning, the damage this particular return inflicted and the way in which the damage was repaired. The clear objective throughout was to restore the safe enclosure of the autistic world within which they could sustain the complex system of commitment and belief their work called for.

The world of autistic activity and belief which producers, programme departments and broadcasting as a whole can create around itself is liable to be construed as complacency, as it was by the Beveridge Committee.

238 *Description, Explanation and Understanding*

Entry into this closed world, with its private enthusiasms and its new absolutes based on the shortest of critical perspectives proved a disconcerting experience for newcomers used to the larger and slacker involvement of students or of writers and journalists, and led to some odd interpretations:

> There was one other thing which I did feel very uncomfortable about when I joined, and still do. I've been on two courses and each time there seemed to be an attempt being made by somebody to do a job of brainwashing. I don't think it was a conscious attempt. It was just that everything to a lot of the senior lecturers seemed to be for the best of all possible worlds. You were left with two uncomfortable thoughts. (a) Why it was necessary to try and brainwash like this, and (b) well if everything is so grand, why aren't the programmes better? And XX was a case in point – the first lecture on this course, about a man who'd travelled all over the world, and had come to the conclusion that home was the best and that we had nothing to learn from anyone. This, constantly repeated during both courses, generally from administrators or from people fairly high up in the Corporation, left a sort of uncomfortable taste in the mouth – that they considered there was some need for this.

These observations referred (by name, later) to heads of output departments ('administrators') who were regarded by producers as ruthlessly critical. 'Brainwashing' is an almost ludicrously inappopriate word in this context. But the fierceness of the reaction of this particular newcomer to the BBC jogs one into awareness of the almost deliberate and certainly perpetual effort made to domesticate the world the Corporation inhabits. Perspectives are drawn so that they terminate within range of its control or influence, considerations are reduced to a common Gestalt, public issues translated into internal politics.

To repeat – there is nothing peculiar to the BBC, in the creation of a private world out of an occupational milieu. It is, in fact, a necessary corollary of becoming committed to a job and an organisation. This withdrawal into a closed, isolated world of ideas, activity, involvement and resources is at its clearest and most intense in the producer's gallery of a studio. The elaborate provisions made to ensure that everything and everybody conceivably relevant to what is going on is available within the studio, and physically to exclude everybody and everything else – and the sheer necessity of these provisions for production to be achieved – afford a paradigm of the closed system the Corporation creates for its members.

NOTES AND REFERENCES

1. Howard Becker, *Outsiders*, Collier Macmillan, London, 1963, p. 7. See also Tom Burns, 'Micropolitics', *Administrative Science Quarterly*, vol. 6, 1961, pp. 257–81.
2. Stuart Hood, *A Survey of Television*, Heinemann, 1967, pp. 49–50.
3. I am here omitting a fairly lengthy discussion of the social function of the mass communication industries in contemporary advanced industrial societies.
4. M. Maruyama, *Thought and Behaviour in Japanese Politics*, Oxford University Press, 1963, p. 3.
5. R. Bendix and S. M. Lipset, 'Political Sociology', *Current Sociology*, vol. 6, no. 2, 1957. *Unesco*, Paris, p. 84.
6. The situation is not, therefore, one which can be met by a Public Representation Service, as the Beveridge Committee recommended.

12

Leisure in Industrial Society

This was yet another effort to expand what remained my
central interests, which were in organisation and industrialism, beyond the confines of empirical research. It had
begun life some years earlier as a paper presented to the
annual conference of the British Sociological Association in
1967.

I want to make this essay serve two purposes. First, I shall discuss and, to some extent, develop explanations of the nature of
leisure, and do so by relating what can be said about it to our
understanding of industrialism, and to the implications of both
leisure and work in the organisation of society. Secondly, I
shall arrange this account so as to exemplify a particular strategy for sociological explanation (or 'theory') in general.

1

Much of the earlier research into leisure was directly concerned
with the significances – the meanings – which were variously
attached to leisure. The most obvious of these seemed to be
afforded by the contrast with work, and empirical studies and
discussion of fifteen years ago were preoccupied with the connection and the contrast between leisure and work. Was it to be
regarded as in effect a pursuit of compensatory activities for

From M. A. Smith, S. Parker and C. S. Smith (eds), *Leisure and Society in Britain*,
Allen Lane, 1973, pp. 40–55.

the fatigue, the boredom, the alienation endured at work? Or did it provide for the free exercise of the skills and energy that workers sold to gain a livelihood? Or was it rather a re-affirmation in games and gambling of the sense of autonomous decision-making of which submission to the constraints of work organisations had deprived the industrial masses?

We can read the record of research in the sociology of leisure over the past ten or fifteen years as an exploration, to begin with, of the implications of this kind of interpretation and then an escape from them. Dumazedier, whose name more than anyone else's is associated with the sociology of leisure, mirrors this theoretical development in a sentence: 'Just as labour is more than the negation of idleness, leisure is more than the negation of labour. Leisure is also the negation of yet other obligations: familial, social, civic, religious.'[1] Leisure is seen as a reaction from the combined pressures of traditional institutions and the social forces of contemporary organisation, or more fundamentally, as a kind of delinquent escape from the impossible dilemmas of a situation midway between the Marxian view of man's destiny as a worker and a 'post-industrialism' image of him as a learning animal.

Some of the simplicities in the earlier interpretation we can now dismiss. A good deal of survey research in France, particularly, has been concerned to test and disprove the hypothesis that the form taken by leisure activities is determined by the need to compensate for the deprivation of constraints or demands of work, and the alternative hypothesis that leisure activities tend to reflect the direction and level of work performance. Both Dumazedier's Annecy studies and Crozier's survey of office workers[2] reach the same conclusion – that there is no evidence of either a direct or an inverse relationship between work and leisure.

These studies, and a large number of others, follow the main methodological convention of survey research and seek to enumerate leisure pursuits or to compare 'profiles' of leisure as whole or part of the description of communities, groups or categories of people. Inevitably, the development of 'social characteristics' research is governed by the need to account for more and more of the variance left unexplained, or to rope in more recalcitrant individuals left in minority or mixed categories by previous research; quite properly, this leads to an increasing refinement of characteristics, cannier (if not exactly more rigorous) sampling frames and smaller parcelling of categories. Also – and much more important – interpretations of data, explanation and theory are all couched more and more in terms of the extent to which each social characteristic combines with others (the 'predictive value' of characteristics). Lastly, the most important of all, the sociologist finds himself peopling the world with what Hans Paul Bahrdt has called 'sociological men' – crude identikit characters labelled 'the conservative working-class voter', 'the spiralist', 'the empty nester', 'the affluent worker' and so on. If the most significant task of contemporary sociology is, as Edward Shils claimed, 'the theorisation of empirical research', then it is one which will have to be accomplished not by buttering survey research with theory but by the reconsideration of the elementary relationship between the goals of sociological explanation and the methods to be used for attaining them.

Survey research, the almost exclusive research method for the empirical study of leisure, does not in fact make it easy either to develop hypotheses of a sociological kind or to develop theoretical explanations, since it is applied to individuals and their responses and presumes the possibility of inducing social characteristics from the study of populations. The task of obtaining causal connections and of developing explanatory categories is, as Durkheim has shown us, something which has to be done, not so much 'at another level', perhaps, as from a different, broader set of premises contextual to the always tiny assortment of first-hand facts empirical researchers can collect for themselves. If this is not done as itself an exercise in sociological explanation, as Durkheim did, then sociological explanation lapses into description by numbers (which gets us nowhere, except perhaps into market research, or into providing ammunition for those academic friends and neighbours who insist that 'those who count, don't') or into interpretation according to ideological slant.

Those who have followed the same research convention but used the strategic point of departure of the audience or public for a particular kind of entertainment or recreation (e.g., all audience research and the outdoor recreation studies commissioned by the US Department of Agriculture) have not fared better in the search for connections between leisure pursuits and social characteristics. Wilensky, in the paper that did so much to refine the treatment of the subject and relate it in a reasonably satisfactory way to some of the main preoccupations of sociology, concludes that:

> Television, the most 'massified' of the mass media, the one with the largest and most heterogeneous audience, has become central to the leisure routines of majorities at every level. The usual differences in media exposure and response among age, sex and class categories – easy to exaggerate in any case – have virtually disappeared in the case of television.[3]

Even for the very earliest students it was clear that leisure was not simply non-work; unemployment was also non-work, and to describe an unemployed worker as leisured is a very tired piece of journalistic irony. The key to the concept of leisure which seems to underlie these earlier studies is, I think, that leisure in industrial society is somehow the counterpart of industrial labour. This is put in its simplest form by Riesman, in his introduction to Chinoy's Automobile Workers and the American Dream. 'Chinoy's interviews,' he says, 'show work to be part-time imprisonment, through which one pays off the fines incurred by one's pursuit of the good – or rather the good time – life at home and on vacation.'[4] The converse of this, or its fuller meaning, is that adequate work performances and successful endeavour cannot be maintained in terms of aspirations and goals relevant to the work situation or the occupational career; these essential aspirations and goals have had to be transformed into values which can be realised in leisure activities. In this reading of the meaning of leisure there is a parallel (the implications of which we shall explore later) between the relationship of leisure and work and that between consumption and production.

2

I want now to give some consideration to the origin and implications of the simple contrast notions of leisure as time free from work and as a counterpart of work (and, by intention, a complement to it) – notions that sociologists may simply have seen as demonstrably appropriate within their academic niche in industrial society and treated as 'litmus-test' hypotheses for other milieux much as they did with notions like job-satisfaction and alienation.

First and most obvious is the significance which attaches to its being free time which has been won from the working day. Guy Chapman, in a book which anticipated an uncomfortable proportion of later sociological work, called 'the Ten Hours Act by far the most important landmark in nineteenth-century social history'.[5] There are two significant aspects of the agitation for this particular reform. First, it came from factory workers, mainly, of course, textile workers; second, it was the first legislative reform carried through by popular agitation among industrial workers, and formulated in direct response to their demands.

In pre-industrial society work was part and parcel of everyday life; and there was no sense in which leisure was a separate section of the day. Work was something which caught up and included a good deal more than work. It was carried on in the fields within sight of the home or within the home itself along with the cooking, child minding, the friendly conversations and quarrels, and the business of village life. It is only when work came to be done in a special place, at a special separate time and under special conditions that leisure came to be demanded as a right. This demand, moreover, seems to have taken precedence over any demand for increased earnings. Increases in prices were the usual occasion for demands for higher earnings, which were related to a fairly specific norm of working-class living standards. In any case, apart from negotiations about piece rates, it so happens that workers were, in the earlier decades of the nineteenth century, more concerned with prices than with wages. Chapman argues this point at some length and, I think, convincingly. In the earlier part of the nineteenth century, so far as earnings were concerned, demand seems to have been limited to 'the wages which will pay for the cost of living and a little more', among factory workers and non-factory workers alike. For instance:

> Leonard Horner, the factory inspector, examined a large number of workers in 1848 and found that 70 per cent of them were in favour of the ten hour day . . . The opinions of several men working 12 hours were taken . . . many of them said they would prefer working ten hours for less wages, but they had no choice.[6]

The unprecedented demand for leisure time was a response to unprecedented conditions. The working week for factory workers in the mid-nineteenth century was over seventy hours; this applied not only to this country but to France and America. Yet what evidence there is suggests that the pre-industrial urban proletariat had at least as much leisure as exists at the present day, when industrial workers throughout Western Europe and America work between forty and forty-six hours a week, and even less in Eastern Europe. Rudé remarks that saints' days and holidays were so frequent (111 in the year) as to have reduced the ordinary Parisian workers' average working week to something less than four days.[7] The change to a full working week must have occurred much earlier in England, well before the Industrial Revolution, along with the general change to wage-labour in the seventeenth century.[8] Under pressure from that peculiar combination of business acumen and high moral tone which we have learned to call the Protestant ethic, the ordinary working week was considerably expanded by the suppression of saints' days and church festivals. It was this longer – or fuller – English working week which was taken over as a prescriptive right by factory owners.

The achievement registered by the working-class movement which can be said to have 'created' leisure – in the manifest, historical, political sense – was threefold. It was the first successful challenge to the immersion of everyday life in industrial work. Secondly, it was a major episode in the development of a strategy of collective bargaining for improved conditions of work and, as it proved, earnings. The connection was soon learned. Very clearly, pressure for a shorter working week maintains the character of a tactical device that can, if successfully employed, result in increased earnings as well, although the preference for increases in leisure over increases in earnings still prevails among industrial communities (e.g. miners) whose institutional life was formed in the early years of industrialism. Thirdly, however much the Parliamentary success of the movement was due to chance political combinations of the time, the working class did score a specifically political gain in the face of the power of industrial capital. And since then the most striking *political* successes of organised labour versus organised capital in this country have been in terms of restriction of hours of work much more than of increased earnings.

We thus have the spectacle of everyday life being swamped by the tide of capitalist industry, and subsequently of this tide receding under pressure from workers, to leave an increasing number of hours of freely disposable time.

The second aspect of leisure regarded in terms of its historical development is logically connected with the first. There is a qualitative difference between the popular social pursuits which formed everyday life along with work before the Industrial Revolution, and what later emerged as leisure. Release from work was demanded or excused only on church and civic festivals, and took on always the guise of a sacred occasion, however secular or mundane the actual pursuits were. (It was one of the more often repeated, as well as more serious, charges against the theatres in London that they drew apprentices and journeymen from their work, and one of the substantial reasons for their eventual closure.) Time out from work not only had to have its own particular justification and sanction in public ritual or celebration, but the kind of pursuits appropriate to each occasion were defined and organised in terms of meaning and significance attached to the occasion.

Leisure, under industrialism, was sanctioned, defined and organised in entirely different terms. The new leisure of the working classes represented a vacuum which was largely filled, even to begin with, by amusement industries. The new middle classes of bureaucratised industry and commerce and of government service obtained their release later than the textile workers. Lloyds closed on Saturday afternoons from 1854 on, but the Stock Exchange remained open for another twenty years. The Civil Service gained its Saturday half-day in the 1860s. Shop assistants, of course, had to wait until the end of the century before they were allowed some remission of their eighty-four hour week. Nevertheless, 'by the end of the sixties, amusement for leisure has become an undertaking worthy of commercial exploitation'.[9]

Drinking was the first and most general pursuit to be commercialised. During the last quarter of the nineteenth century an increasing amount of the profits of the brewing trade were invested in building licensed premises where evenings could be spent; the drink shop was replaced by the gin palace and the public house. Racing, a disreputable racket in the 1850s, was reconstituted, heavily capitalised, and a popular mass entertainment by the 1880s. Professional football and boxing followed the same path even more rapidly. Absorbing more time than either, the popular press cashed in on a public formed earlier by cheap prints and broadsheet reports of criminal case and expanded rapidly by the 1870 Education Act.

Just as organised working-class demand for improved working conditions was first successfully articulated in terms of leisure, so the commercial response to improved living standards made itself apparent first in the provision of new services. Increase in the supply and variety of consumer goods, which meant so much to the new middle classes and to the ways in which the system of social stratification worked itself out in the twentieth century, was a subsequent development. But in both cases there is a complementary relationship between the growing subdivision, specialisation and organisation of labour on the one hand, and the increased hourly earnings and pressure for a shorter working week on the other which the self-same industrial development generated and facilitated. There is also a parallel relationship between the increasing constraints which larger and more elaborate structures of industrial organisation imposed on the work situation, and the increasing definition of leisure pursuits in terms of the organised provision of services and goods by new forms of commercial and industrial enterprise.

The force of Chapman' remark, 'The Ten Hours Act effected the greatest change in the work situation of ordinary people since Moses brought the six-day week down from Mount Sinai' lies not merely in the separation of leisure and labour which it began. Besides initiating this crucial stage in the differentiation of everyday life, the Act also made way for the development of commercial, industrial and other organisations that would provide a structure of activities ordered for individual choice and preference, individual satisfactions and rewards. The point is that these pursuits are wholly secular, organised for a commercial market, or at least for a user public, and, by and large, limited to what can be so organised.

This puts a new light on the thesis, which has gained some currency, of the increasing dissociation of social stratification from social class. Individual consumption has had to be expanded to become the necessary prime mover of economic expansion; secondly, this replaces the directly exploitative relationship between capital and labour by a relationship which involves the fostering of the propensity to consume among the masses of the population in the self-interests of the industrialist entre- preneur; thirdly, both the development of modern industrial organisation and of new ways of organising the spending of disposable means and time led to the evolution of new stratifi- cation systems and the blunting of the structural definition of classes through conflict.

I have dwelt on the implication of the elementary idea of leisure as contrasted with labour because it seems to me that sociologists have been in rather too great a hurry to dismiss this interpretation as *simpliste* and to hurry on to more rewarding data and interpretations; they have thus ignored some of the more profound and durable contributions to our knowledge of the social structure, and especially of recent changes in it, which this notion has made. The thesis argued in this section is that the swamping of everyday life by industrialism has not been succeeded by a mere ebbing, or forcing back, of the flood. Social life outside the work situation has not re-emerged; it has been created afresh, in forms which are themselves the crea- tures of industrialism, which derive from it *and which contribute to its development, growth and further articulation.*

3

When the elementary idea of leisure as contrasted with work is set in the context of a straightforward, even superficial, account of the historical developments of the relationship, there is an immediate expansion of the explanatory force of the contrast. Together they make more sense than does either singly; but this is not to say that one *illuminates* the other. If the first orien- tation of study springs from a particular consensual view of some symmetry obtaining between the two halves of everyday life which has a peculiar force for contemporaries, then the second derives from an equally consensual apprehension of history as development. A third perspective is afforded by the appreciation that there are limits to the shared meanings action can have. Groups and categories of people standing in some asymmetrical relationship to one another may ascribe *different* significances to *similar* patterns of behaviour.

The connection between the second and this third orientation to the theme lies in the political significance which attaches to the movement for the reduction of the working week during the nineteenth century. The historical circumstances of the movement itself, and its later incorporation in the strategies of organised labour, give some support to the speculative remarks of Pizzorno (also applied to nineteenth-century development) about the ideological function of leisure.[10] In a society devoted increasingly to the values of leisure and consumption rather than to those of production, leisure presents itself as an alternative source of ethical values to those founded in production and work, and which are identified with the middle class. But the choice between the alternatives is not open and individual. Pizzorno suggests that, during the earlier period of industrialisation, the bourgeois values of thrift, austerity and production were adopted by (or it could be more plausibly said 'wished on to') the working class, but became obviously incompatible with their situation in industrial society. Further, leisure values developed as a counter-system in much the same way, he suggests, as the virtues of bourgeois capitalist society developed as an alternative counter-system to those of the aristocracy and gentry.

There is some parallel between this suggestion, with its Orwellian overtones, and the findings of Alberoni, another Italian student of leisure and consumer behaviour (see pp. 189–91 above).[11] His point of departure is the assumption, which American economists and sociologists have taken over from Veblen, of social differentiation as one-dimensional – that there is unanimity about the value of having more goods or more leisure for use and display.

The Veblenesque view, current in America and reflected in the 'embourgeoisement' thesis of European social scientists, of the effect of a general rise in working-class living standards is simply that of emulation of the better-off. In Alberoni's view, the effect of greater affluence on lower-class families is that they reject the models presented by their social superiors in the local community – who also possess political and economic power in it – in favour of those they see as socially superior to everyone else and who, moreover, are essentially powerless in political and economic terms. These are the 'powerless élite' – the select few who are exceptionally privileged but who nevertheless have nothing to do with the structures of economic and political power which controls the world that people actually live in. Hence, Alberoni concludes, the preference for a television set as against all those other useful possessions of the well-to-do among those who can at last choose between them. The television set provides an escape from the power and oppressive presence of their immediate social, economic and political superiors and entry into a larger world in which they participate along with the '*divi*'.

When we move, with Pizzorno and Alberoni, to this new plane of analysis, a good deal more is changed than merely the scope of considerations relevant to the study of leisure and consumer behaviour. What they have done is to demonstrate, once again, that sociological explanation has to be sought in bringing structural connections to bear on individual connections; to exploit the basic assumption of sociology – which is that social structure influences the behaviour of individuals – one has to do more than merely invoke it.

At all events, at the level of the considerations drawn in from Pizzorno and Alberoni, there is a direct regard for the implications for each other of changes in the social structure and in the development of leisure. There are two ways in which, for example, their findings and comments challenge orthodox concepts of social stratification.

It is now common ground that in leisure and consumption, no less than in other respects, it is difficult to regard the stratification system in unilinear terms: i.e. as a continuous gradient of status differences produced by the deflection of a principle of distributive justice by another principle, effecting an asymmetrical ordering of power and rewards. Pizzorno's and Alberoni's work raises again and suggests possible solutions to the old unanswered questions about why there is still no direct challenge to the power and authority of capitalists and managers, why Chinoy's and Andrieux and Lignon's and Popitz' workers direct their aspirations to acquisitions, 'fun' and independence instead of towards promotion or a redistribution of power and rewards within the enterprise, why production committees and *Mitbestimmung* failed and were not succeeded by other devices and other claims for a share in management.

Second, their work rescues the concept of 'style of life' from the status to which it seems to have been relegated, of a dependent variable, an extra and perhaps superfluous appendage of class or occupational status. The way in which people spend their disposable money and time is a mode of organising their lives and, therefore, one of the concrete forms in which the social structure is manifest in action. The appropriate sociological category, one could perhaps say, becomes 'way of life' rather than 'style of life'.

One is not, therefore, arguing for a simple class-determined view of leisure to replace an occupationally-determined one, still less following Henri Raymond's tentative suggestion that 'affiliation to one social stratum is determined by choice of leisure'.[13] Rather, one is confronted on this third plane of analysis with the appearance of different, autonomous, even rival structures which pertain to the ordering of social behaviour and of society in terms of stratification, occupational system and styles of life, and which are certainly interrelated, or even 'multi-bonded' or 'crystallised', if you like, but between which the causal flow of dependence is not easy to determine. For example, from some of Dumazedier's work it seems that the organising principles at work in the articulation of leisure activities extend beyond leisure itself. Occupational choices may be made not so much to provide the income which will support the highest standard of living as to consort with a preferred way of life. Preference for particular forms of leisure impose constraints on choices made in the rest of life and especially in terms of hours of work, opportunities for supplementary earnings and the social milieu offered by the workplace. In addition, of course, such preferences affect actual decisions (in the case, for example, of married women, about whether or not to seek employment) and they affect location and mobility.

4

One can leave the matter here, at the point at which a strong case has been made for the implication of leisure in the system, or systems, of social stratification in industrial society, and for increasing the weight to be attached to characteristic leisure activities when considering the structural location of individuals.

If one remains unsatisfied, one does not *solve* the residual problem by adopting a new perspective, moving to yet another plane of analysis. What one has to attempt is explanation in *contextual* terms, too, as a necessary conclusion to the various levels of considerations already invoked. This context concerns the relationship between the way in which social facts are defined for the individual by himself and by sociologists. In Bendix and Berger's terms, we have to 'consider not only the social conditioning of the individual but also his capacity for independent action for which that conditioning is only the necessary basis'.[14]

In his study, *Le Monde des employés de bureau*, Michel Crozier ends by insisting on the plurality of the office-worker's world, on the variety of ways in which he can select and arrange and organise his life in terms of work situation, of commitment to the organisation, of collective action, of social groupings and of differentiation of leisure pursuits. In fact, he points out the strategic advantage to the individual of the very lack of correspondence between sections of the structure to which Marshall has referred.[15] In a sense, perhaps, this choice of a hand from the cards one is dealt is no more than a choice among an array of alienated positions, but, he says, 'The multiplicity of the kinds of alienation possible, and the consequent incoherence (of the systems of social ordering and of values obtainable) tend to liberate the individual'.[16]

This is more than a restatement of the basic Simmelian position, in which 'The number of different social groups in which the individual participates is one of the landmarks of culture'.[17] It is nearer, perhaps, to Simmel's development of the same notion:

> As individuals, we form the personality out of particular elements of life, each of which has arisen from, or is interwoven with, society. This personality is subjective *par excellence* in the sense that it combines the elements of culture in an individual manner. There is here a reciprocal relationship between the subjective and the objective. As the person becomes affiliated with a social group, he surrenders himself to it. A synthesis of such objective affiliations creates a group in an objective sense. But the person also regains his individuality because his pattern of participation is unique.[18]

The implication of Crozier's conclusion is that, in a world of organisation and organised activities, while it renders self-realisation (or autonomy) through identification of the individual with his work and its product impossible, a kind of second-order self-realisation and autonomy is available in the ability to choose both *which* commitments of all those preferred him by work, associations and cultural pursuits he will engage in, and also *how much* 'psycho-social capital' he will invest in those he chooses.

A similar strategic inversion of the notion of alienation has been developed by Touraine in the concept of *projet*. For Touraine, the total apparatus of industrial society, in work, in leisure, in the political order and in the cultural world – the detritus of the total historical development of society – constitutes the inescapable datum of existence for the individual, who must live within the constraints imposed by the apparatus on the several status positions he occupies. But the same apparatus is also *data for* existence, in that he orders his life in terms of the commitments he enters into each status, and can, from that position, view the apparatus of society as means whereby he can realise his *projet*.

There are many other forms taken by this perception of an analytical component representing the individual as interacting positively with the social order. Raymond Firth, in his essays on social organisation, expands the limited play allowed for truly individual choice in Crozier's and Touraine's formulations and affirms the connection with analysis in terms of structure for which Bendix and Berger argued.

> One may describe social organisation, then, as the working arrangements of society. It is the processes of ordering of action and of relations in reference to given social ends, in terms of adjustments resulting from the exercise of choices by the members of society. This is not the same as describing social action as the working *rules* of the society, which implies a conformity and an imperative in the ordering of the activities of the society which may be only partly true.[19]

A clearer lead still is given by Goffman in his earlier treatment of the notion of the styling of activities, as of demeanour and choice of furnishings and accessories, as an element in the individual's purpose of conveying to others the impression of himself he wishes to convey, and by this means to control the social situation into which he enters. Styling is thus the overt expression of the positive aspects of the self-image – it displays the upper frequencies of an oscillating self-consciousness forever rebounding between self-doubt and aspiration. In its most articulate and successful form, it is encountered among individuals who have modelled their behaviour on a specific social identity which overrides both occupational position and the organised apparatus of leisure and consumption, and fixes an appropriate 'distance' (again in Goffman's terms) between this identity and the several roles they occupy. Youth culture provides the more familiar styles but, at a more sophisticated level, it is possible for identities to be developed which do not merely override but manipulate and exploit the apparatus of the organised world of work and leisure.

The behaviour process this represents is most clearly visible in the world of the powerless élite itself – at least, to take one representative milieu, in the social territory of television studies. The styles cultivated there derive from the implication of the whole occupational community (of television) in the world of the theatre and of social sophistication in the commonly accepted sense. So people are divided into professionals and amateurs, and, more significantly, into camp, butch (terms now used without any hint of their nineteenth-century origins as homosexual cant) and square. Individuals can be camp – i.e. act habitually with an edgy elegance or sophisticated charm, or 'play it camp' for a social occasion; groups, occasions or whole departments can be 'campish'. 'Butch', which carries an equal connotation of being sophisticated and on the inside, allows of an alternative mode – plain or coarse-spoken cynicism or directness. Both terms clearly denote not personality types but manners and styles of conduct which can be assumed, and which relate to traditional 'characters' or even 'humours' in the English theatre as old as the seventeenth-century stage, where both types are clearly discernible and, indeed, explicitly portrayed. To reject both, and to be square, is, in this milieu, an equally positive choice, equally a style which has to be cultivated from models and consciously maintained.

The sense of purposed fabrication which runs through the notions of *projet*, or strategy, or the organisation of commitments, or the presentation of self, or – at a more conscious level – styling, relates to the individual's attempt to organise his behaviour in everyday life so as to give it significance and meaning. Analytically, the concepts seem to allow for the construction of connections between work and leisure and social structure which can contain the otherwise confusing two-way flow of causal relationships that survey research has shown to exist between the world of work and that of leisure, and also to round out the more general explanatory theses of Pizzorno and Alberoni, which invoke larger considerations of a structural kind but which also suffer from both a bias towards socio-logical reductionism and a still sizeable weight of variance unaccounted for. It also seems to me both to be in line with Wilensky's findings and also to offer a more satisfactory solution than the elaborate structural interpretation he rather tentatively advances. At least it avoids the decline into deter-minism in the manner of Whyte's *Organization Man* with which Wilensky concludes:

> As rich countries grow richer, harmonising structures in poli-tics, education and mass communications combine with an already high level of cultural uniformity to reduce the hold of differentiating structure of age, religion, work and locality, and bring about a greater consistency of structure and culture – a new combination of 'mass society' and 'industrial society', mass culture and high culture.[20]

One is sometimes tempted to regard congruence theory as an occupational disease of sociologists.

5

Finally, one has to ask what human purposes are involved in the projects, strategies and stylisations of life which organise the worlds of work and leisure for individuals?

There is a fundamental contrast suggested by the historical origin of contemporary leisure in industrialism, and what stood in pre-industrial life in place of leisure now. Everyday life, in so far as it was explicitly freed from work, was organ-ised in terms of religious and civic festivals. It derived mean-ingfulness from permanent (sacred, as Weber says) and ritual-istic elements in human life. There is a sense in which leisure activity in contemporary society represents an attempt to recapture the same quality of meaningfulness for everyday life now. This is certainly the thesis which runs through the work of Henri Lefebvre; leisure, he suggests, is an attempt to break away from everyday life, which is characterized throughout by frustration, into a factitious world which will endow everyday life with meaning and worthwhileness.[21] In a somewhat similar sense, Edgar Morin's social criticism of the cultural role of the cinema confers on it the function of an experimental, innovative composition of the potentialities of life for industrial man, a composition which remains, however, imaginary and unrealised.[22]

Leisure, and the games and entertainments which fill so much of it, may therefore be a substitute for ritual. The significance of the connection between ritual and, if I am right, the displaced behaviour which serves as its modern counterpart is indicated in Lévi-Strauss' brief analysis:

> Games thus appear to have a *disjunctive* effect: they end in the establishment of a difference between players or teams where originally there was no indication of inequality. And at the end of the game they are distinguished into winners and losers. Ritual, on the other hand, is the exact inverse: it *conjoins*, for it brings about a union (one might even say communion in this context) between two initially separated groups . . . In the case of games the symmetry is therefore preordained and it is of a structural kind since it follows from the principle that the rules are the same for both sides. Asymmetry is engendered: it follows inevitably from the contingent nature of events, themselves due to intention, chance or talent. The reverse is true of ritual. There is an asymmetry which is postulated in advance between profane and sacred, faithful and officiating, dead and living, initiated and uninitiated, etc., and the 'game' consists in making all the participants pass to the winning side by means of events, the nature and ordering of which is genuinely structural. Like science (though here again on both the theoretical and practical plane) the game produces events by means of a structure; and we can therefore understand why competitive games should flourish in our industrial societies. Rites and myths, on the other hand, . . . take to pieces and reconstruct sets of events (on a psychical, socio-historical or technical plane) and use them as so many indestructible pieces for structural patterns in which they serve alternatively as ends or means.[23]

Mass entertainment now offers the same re-composition of events and action so as to provide initiation into secrets, inclusion among the survivors, and acceptance by the officiating élite, for all. And there is a sense, known to all of us, in which events and places remain 'unreal' (i.e. unattached to our ordered knowledge of things, and therefore unmeaningful) until they have been recorded, processed, and presented on television, in films or in the newspapers. Just as games re-enact both the constraints of the social structure ('the rules of the game') and the latitude still left the individual (who exercises autonomy in exploiting the rules of the game), so entertainment, on the other side of organised leisure, can be construed as contemporary society's response to the enduring need to ritualise the unfamiliar and disconnected, the unattainable and the threatening, to reduce the increasing range and strangeness of the individual's world to the synthesised and safely repeatable form of a composed story, or documentary, or performance. The structures of leisure exist to serve as repositories of meaning and value for everyday life.

NOTES AND REFERENCES

1. J. Dumazedier, *Toward a Society of Leisure*, Collier-Macmillan, 1967.
2. M. Crozier, *Le monde des employés de bureau*, Seuil, 1965.
3. H. L. Wilensky, 'Mass Society and Mass Culture', *American Journal of Sociology*, April 1964.
4. E. Chinoy, *Automobile Workers and the American Dream*, Doubleday, 1955.
5. G. Chapman, *Culture and Survival*, Cape, 1940.
6. Ibid.
7. G. Rudé, *The Crowds in the French Revolution*, Oxford University Press, 1959.
8. C. B. Macpherson, *The Political Theory of Possessive Individualism*, Oxford University Press, 1962.
9. Chapman, op. cit.
10. A. Pizzorno, 'Accumulation, loisirs et rapports du classe', *Esprit*, 1959.
11. F. Alberoni, *Consumi e società*, Mulino, 1964.
12. This rendering of Alberoni's conclusions is largely that of Dr Gianfranco Poggi, to whom I am indebted for introducing me to Alberoni's work.
13. H. Raymond, 'La Sociologie du loisir en France – résultats et perspectives', *Information*, 1964.
14. R. Bendix and B. Berger, 'Images of Society and Problems of Concept Formation in Sociology', in L. Gross (ed.), *Symposium on Sociological Theory*, Harper and Row, 1959.
15. T. H. Marshall, 'Changes in Social Stratification in the Twentieth Century', in *Sociology at the Crossroads*, Heinemann, 1963.
16. Crozier, op. cit.
17. G. Simmel, *Conflict, and the Web of Group Affiliations*, Free Press, 1955.
18. Ibid.
19. R. Firth, 'Social Organization and Social Change', in *Essays on Social Organization and Values*, Athlone Press, 1964.
20. Wilensky, op. cit.
21. H. Lefebvre, *Everyday Life in the Modern World*, The Penguin Press. 1971.
22. E. Morin, *Le Cinéma, ou l'homme imaginaire*, Editions de Minuit, 1956.
23. C. Lévi-Strauss, *The Savage Mind*, Weidenfeld and Nicolson, 1966.

13

The Organisation of
Public Opinion

A by-product of the study of the organisation of the BBC rather than an excerpt from it, this was written in response to a request from the editors of one of the many books on 'mass communications' which appeared during the 1960s and 1970s. The quite extraordinary fuss created by Marshall McLuhan's *Gutenberg Galaxy* is now almost forgotten, but it did lead on to – rather than provoke – a fairly intense discussion about the growing power widely attributed to newspapers and broadcasting organisations or sometimes, and more discreetly, claimed by them. Interestingly, the public debate died down during the 1980s, to be resumed in the next decade, this time in terms very like those of the 1920s, when the central issue was the intellectual, cultural and moral debasement of 'the masses' and the concentration of power in the hands of a few newspaper proprietors.

From the very beginning, controversy about broadcasting has been dominated by strong and almost universally held beliefs about its immense potentialities as a means of influencing, and possibly even controlling or directing, public opinion. This belief rests on a single and manifest truth: broadcasting makes it possible for one man to address an audience of millions, indeed, nowadays, of hundreds of millions. For the first two or three decades the power of broadcasting was seen as vested in

From J. Curran, M. Gurevitch and Janet Wollacott (eds), *Mass Communication and Society*, Edward Arnold for the Open University Press, 1977, pp. 44–69.

its possibilities as an instrument of propaganda. Indeed, the very first use of broadcasting made in Britain was the foreign broadcasts operated directly by the Foreign Office immediately after the end of the First World War. Twenty years later, the BBC's European services were begun to counter the foreign broadcasting services mounted by Germany, Italy and Russia. After the Second World War, claims about the propaganda power of broadcasting, both political and commercial, tended to become more modest. Even so, the fact of the sheer pervasiveness of broadcasting still carried with it the belief that it is powerful *because* it is pervasive, and a corresponding fear of the ways in which, and of the groups by whom, that power might be exercised.

More recently, fear of the persuasive power of broadcasting over 'the masses' has tended to slacken, much in the way that fear of broadcasting as propaganda faded earlier on. Neither fear, though, has entirely disappeared. It is revived from time to time by claims still being made by interested parties about the effects of propaganda and persuasion through broadcasting. Social scientists and specialist writers on mass communications find it equally difficult to surrender the belief altogether, despite the accumulation of almost entirely negative findings from research over thirty-five years into the extent to which broadcasting actually influences political opinion and voting behaviour. In retrospect, concludes Denis McQuail, 'the expectation of great persuasive power from the new media has been largely misplaced' (McQuail, 1969), and many others have reached much the same conclusion. Yet McQuail, two or three pages away from that statement, asserts that the media 'are largely responsible for the creation of public opinion'. The Langs, equally short of supporting evidence for the political persuasiveness of television, nevertheless conclude that 'The media also structure a very real political environment which people can know about only through the media. Information about this environment is hard to escape. It filters through and affects even persons who are not directly exposed to the news' (Lang and Lang, 1968, p. 305).

1

We are dealing, in fact, with a set of beliefs much older than broadcasting. During its own formative years (which extended from the beginning of the eighteenth century until well into the nineteenth), the press was regarded with even greater alarm and suspicion. Windham, says Aspinall, laid most of the blame for the mutinies at Spithead and the Nore at the doors of the press, and Burke saw in it 'the grand instrument of the subversion of order, morals, religion, and human society itself' (Aspinall, 1949, p. 1).

To draw on Aspinall's opening pages again, he quotes Sir James Macintosh remarking in 1803 on the great change which had taken place in the discussion of public affairs: 'The multiplication of newspapers has produced a gradual revolution in our government by increasing the number of those who exercise some sort of judgment on public affairs' (Aspinall, 1949, p. 1) and cites Brougham's considered assessment in 1831 of the importance of the press in the pre-Reform era: 'it alone rivalled the House of Commons, in that it was the only organ of public opinion capable of dictating to the Government, since nothing else could speak the sense of the people' (Aspinall, 1949, p. 3). This is the press in the full panoply of its classic Fourth Estate role, and it is no historical accident that this particular term was coined to designate the political role of the press towards the end of the eighteenth century.

It was probably Burke who first used the term to signify the political power (a usurped and malignant power) of the press, and certainly Burke would have relished and exploited the full historical irony only partially evoked by the words 'the fourth estate' when they first gained currency. For, during the fifty years (1780–1830) when the unreformed Parliament assumed the political stance, the attitudes, the strategy and the legislative and administrative tactics of the absolutist *anciens régimes*, it was the press which took up the original role from which the third estate proper, the Commons, had apparently abdicated.

Herein lies the key to the perpetual ambivalence which dogs the political role of the press and, later, of broadcasting. For the Commons itself had begun life as the spokesman – and merely spokesman – of public opinion. The primary purpose of including representatives of the *bourgeois* and of propertied countrymen (the burgesses and the knights of the shire) in the Model Parliament of 1295 and in subsequent Parliaments was 'to inform the crown about local conditions and help it to influence public opinion' (Lapsley, 1936). They discharged this function, moreover, by acting as the bearers, intermediaries, or discussants of the large number of petitions for relief or remedy presented to the king in Parliament – petitions of a kind that, 'whatever their origin, were held to be of interest to the community at large' (Lapsley, 1936, p. 5). This particular function, what is more, seems to have been anterior certainly to any legislative powers and probably to any contributory legislative function which the Commons later, along with barons, bishops and the king's counsellors, ministers and servants were called upon to discharge. In fact, the earliest discernible functions of Parliament are much more those of what might be called a national jury of public opinion than of the supreme body of legislative, executive and judicial power which Parliament became five centuries later. For Edward I, summoning representatives of the Commons to a parliament provided an effective instrument for consulting – and for influencing – public opinion. It was only when the voices of that public opinion became organised themselves, during the following century, that the Commons began to encroach on the legislative powers of the king and his council. But such power as the Commons acquired then and later rested on the validity of its claim to speak for the people – to be, in fact, public opinion made articulate. By the eighteenth century, the Commons was not only the voice of the people; constitutionally, it was the people:

> The British Parliament had always been, was then (1789) and remains now, a sovereign and constituent assembly. It can make and unmake any and every law, change the form of government or the succession to the crown, interfere with the course of justice, extinguish the most sacred private rights of the citizen. Between it and the people at large there is no legal distinction, because the whole plenitude of the people's rights and powers resides in it, just as if the whole nation were present within the chamber where it sits. In point of legal theory it is the nation.
>
>   (Bryce, 1914, pp. 35–6)

Applied to an age which extended from the Black Act of 1723 to the Combination Acts of 1799 and 1800 and beyond to Peterloo and the Six Acts, such a statement stands condemned as the most cynical of paradoxes. So it is. But it is a paradox which actions and events within the framework of the British political system worked, ultimately, towards accommodating rather than emphasising, in much the same way as they did in the parallel case of the law (Thompson, 1975, p. 269). The political role of the press evolved as it did during the eighteenth century largely *because* the practice of Parliament and the relationship of Parliament to the commons departed so grossly from the constitutional principles on which the authority and powers of Parliament were claimed to rest.

The first politically flavoured journals, towards the beginning of the century: Defoe's *Review*, Tutchin's *Observator*, Swift's *Examiner* and, later, Bolingbroke's *Craftsman*, were merely indicators of the emergence of parliamentary parties (rather than the critical organs of a politically minded public that Habermas saw in them (Habermas, 1965, p. 72)). Such journals did undoubtedly play a part in the articulation of distinctive principles and policies for the parties of Government and of Opposition, but it was not until the 1760s that the extra-parliamentary political role of the press becomes visible. Until that time, as Blackstone's *Commentaries*, written in that same decade of the 1760s, indicate, freedom of the press meant no more – and no less – than freedom of speech, one of the three basic constitutional rights secured by the 'Glorious Revolution' of 1689 (the other two being the right of public meeting and the right to petition Parliament). In formal, constitutional, terms, freedom of the press had been established in 1695 with the expiration – at the express instance of the House of Commons – of the Printing Act, by which press censorship had been maintained. Anyone was free, thereafter, to publish anything they liked, but it was in law as well as in practice a heavily qualified freedom, as Blackstone made clear:

> The liberty of the press is indeed essential to the nature of a free state; but this consists in laying no *previous* restraints on publication, and not in freedom from censure of a criminal matter when published. Every freeman has an undoubted right to lay what sentiments he pleases before the public: to forbid this, is to destroy the freedom of the press: but if he published what is improper, mischievous, or illegal, he must take the consequence of his own temerity . . . Thus the will of individuals is left free; the abuse only of that free will is the object of legal punishment. Neither is any restraint hereby laid upon freedom of thought or inquiry: liberty of private sentiment is still left; the disseminating, the making public, of bad sentiment, destructive to the ends of society, is the crime which society corrects.
>
> (Blackstone, 1857, pp. 161–2)

Of course, the decision as to what was 'improper, mischievous, or illegal', or which sentiments were 'bad' or 'destructive to the ends of society' rested with Parliament and the courts – as John Wilkes was discovering at the very time that Blackstone was writing. The significance of Wilkes's eventual victory in 1771, when the House of Commons tacitly abandoned its right to forbid reporting and even prevent publication of its proceedings, does not lie in any shift of the boundary between legitimate freedom and illegitimate abuse of freedom to which Blackstone's words refer; it lies in the acknowledgement of the existence of extra-parliamentary political interests and processes. In a way, 1771 is as crucial a date as 1295. Then, the king in Council – the supreme executive, judicial and legislative authority – sought to inform himself about the condition, needs, opinions and desires of his subjects by summoning representatives of the Commons to his Parliament. In 1771, Parliament, now itself the supreme executive, judicial and legislative authority, acknowledged the right of the electorate – and, consequently, the common people at large – to be informed about the way in which their needs, opinions and desires were expressed or interpreted in Parliament.

But the confinement of the role of the press to serving as a 'medium' for purveying information about Parliament to the people was even more short-lived than had been the role of the Commons in merely purveying information about the people to the king in Council. Moreover, significant as the date, 1771, became for later developments, the impact of the change it represented was hardly noticeable at the time. After all, there were only nine daily newspapers published in Great Britain in the early 1780s; no less than five of these were advertising journals; in the other four, news filled less than half their rather scanty column space. Yet there was a change, and a change of decisive importance in the development of the political role of the press. Parliamentary reports and political information formed an integral part of the staple of such news as was purveyed. Second, and more important still, in acting as 'media' for the dissemination of this kind of news, newspapers tended to assume the stance of independence of political parties.

Thus, albeit tacitly, two fundamental principles were established before, to quote Aspinall, 'the progress of revolutionary doctrines in France, the outbreak of hostilities on the Continent, the threat of war between Great Britain and France, and the existence of much popular discontent at home, made the *regulation* [my emphasis] of public opinion a matter of prime importance to Pitt's Government in 1792'. (Aspinall, 1949). First, the very existence of newspapers, and the nature of their contents, presumed the existence of a public, political, opinion external to the small and enclosed world of parliamentary politics. Second, their role was assumed to be that not merely of purveying information but of articulating and expressing public opinion; in so far as they were successful – i.e. in so far as their sales grew, and their views were taken seriously by government ministers – they were not only the 'independent and responsible organs of public opinion' they claimed to be, but *organisers* of public opinion. That they were taken to be no less than this is plain from the quantity of money spent by the Government in buying editors and journalists,[1] founding new newspapers and subsidising others, and harrassing its critics. Money was not the only weapon. The Attorney-General could take proceedings against anyone on the grounds of information laid before the Crown (*'ex officiis'*); the 1799 Act required every printing press to be registered and the names and addresses of the printer and publisher of every book, pamphlet, poster and newspaper to be recorded. Superimposed on the libel laws alone, the 1799 Act put a powerful instrument into the hands of government for suppressing news or views which it chose to regard as contrary to the 'national interest'; but, beyond this, an act passed the year before, in 1798, had provided more ample grounds for proceedings: persons printing or publishing any 'matters tending to excite hatred and contempt for the person of His Majesty and of the Constitution and Government established in these Kingdoms were liable to a year's imprisonment.

As in other cases, the rapid accumulation of suppressive measures is an index of the strength, frequency and variety of the activities they are designed to suppress as much as of the anxiety and determination of the government. There was plenty to be anxious about. In 1793:

> A convention met in Edinburgh where delegates from popular societies made preparations for secret meetings of delegates to deal with a foreign landing or resist government interference. For this three of the leaders . . . were transported. The response of the radicals was to issue appeals in 1794 for a

further national convention. In doing so they obviously challenged the authority of parliament. However moderate their
proposals for reform, they were, in proposing to meet on a
national scale, claiming to be a rival body expressing the will
of the people better than the House of Commons.

(Watson, 1960, p. 359)

Such conventions were difficult and expensive to organise, and
rare even before they became illegal. Hence the importance of
the radical press – pamphlets as well as newspapers – which
were not only easier and less dangerous instruments for articulating and promoting opposition and protest than were meetings, but could themselves provide the occasion for regular,
semi-clandestine, meetings, it being common practice for them
to be read aloud in public houses and coffee houses throughout
the country. 'The "Jacobinical" Societies of United Irishmen,
United Scotsmen, United Englishmen, United Britons and the
London Corresponding Society had been publishing and circulating large quantities of "irreligious, treasonable and seditious" literature among the "lower classes of the community,
either gratis or at very low prices, and with an activity and pro-
fusion beyond all former example"' (Aspinall, 1949). As early
as 1793, a minister claimed that almost all newspapers 'were in
the pay of the Jacobins'. Even when the threat, real or imag-
ined, of Jacobin revolution had passed, *Black Dwarf*, Cobbett's
Political Register and other journals kept alive the movement for
radical reform which the Opposition tacitly disowned for a
whole generation after 1797, when the Whigs, having 'nailed
their colours to the mast', in Trevelyan's phrase, with the for-
lorn gesture of a parliamentary motion for reform, 'proceeded
to desert the ship'.

2

The ambivalence which besets the political role of the press is
integral to it and therefore inescapable. But at least around 1800
the line which could be drawn between the press which the
opposition, both Parliamentary and radical, regarded as a
medium for the 'expression' of public opinion, and the press
which the government saw as a means of 'regulating' it was
clear, and individual newspapers could be identified as lying
on one side of the line or the other. Later in the century, while
Lord Grey could write that, 'newspapers could be divided into

two classes: those which sought to mould public opinion, and those which took their tone from it', in either case, as he had good cause to know, newspapers chose which political side they pleased to support; in 1830 there was scarcely one newspaper which found a good word to say for the Tories, and ten years later most of them were against the Whigs (Aspinall, 1949).

There are other ambivalences. Those newspapers which became profitable became, eventually, financially independent of Treasury subsidies and party payments and shed their party ties; the people's press, which had flourished when it had been bullied in the courts and persecuted by high taxation, dwindled into extinction in the very years, from 1825 to 1861, when restrictions in size were removed, tax on pamphlets repealed, advertisement duty reduced and stamp duty and paper duty finally abolished.

So the axis, along which the antithetical positions visible in the role of the press are drawn, itself changes. In the twentieth century this applies with equal force, though in different ways, to broadcasting as well as to the press. In the 1920s, mass circulation 'popular' newspapers had long filled the vacuum left by the demise of the people's press. Along with popular weeklies, pulp fiction and children's comics, they had subverted the role of the printed word as an instrument of religious, cultural, social and political enlightenment; in a later view, indeed, they had become elements in, and supporters of, the institutional structure of established authority and of economic and political power which it had once been the primary task of the press, and its chief boast, to expose, discuss and criticise. Geoffrey Crowther, in his history of *The Economist*, was able to say with some justice that, 'The printed word has always been the chief lieutenant of discontent. If the hope of better things cannot find a lodging in the press, much of the leaven will have gone out of society' (Crowther, 1943). He was, in using those words, reformulating a journalists' credo which had been inserted into the credo of political democracy some two hundred years before *The Economist* began its life, at the cost of some blood and much misery, but which, in the form of words he uses, would in the twentieth century be better described as a shibboleth. Suspicion of the malign influence of the popular press had been expressed at the turn of the century by no less a person than

Lord Bryce (1914). His observations concerned American news-papers, but they were made at the very time when Harms-worth's *Daily Mail*, taking the American popular press as its model, had begun to sweep the board in Britain.

The astonishing thing about the political role assumed by the press in the 1920s was the unabashed arrogance with which it was exercised, and was claimed to be exercised, by its propri-etors. A. J. P. Taylor in his *Beaverbrook* quotes a remark made by Rothermere to Beaverbrook about what he could do for Bonar Law: 'If Bonar places himself in my hands I will hand him down to posterity at the end of three years as one of the most successful prime ministers in history, and if there is a general election, I will get him returned again. This may sound boastful but I know exactly how it can be done.' How much power over elections the press barons actually had is doubtful; in the elec-tion in which it was exercised most blatantly – 1923 (when the *Daily Mail* published the 'Zinoviev letter') – the Labour Party, against which the forgery had been directed, increased its vote by a million. Empire Free Trade, the policy Beaverbrook invented in order to champion, quickly became a dead letter – indeed, as A. J. P. Taylor remarks, 'Perhaps it was ruined by the support of the press lords' (Taylor, 1965, p. 283), a remark-able historical verdict on what was, in the same writer's view, a great attempt made 'for the first and last time . . . to change party leadership and party policy by a battery in the columns of the popular press' (Taylor, 1965, p. 283).

Not surprisingly, it was during the 1920s that the 'freedom of the press', like other freedoms since, was beginning to shed its quality of absoluteness, and 'freedom for what?' became an increasingly pertinent question. It was a notion that was slow to gain acceptance. Throughout the inter-war years, in fact, it became evident that mass circulation newspapers were putting their own arbitrary constraints on what constituted news, and even firmer constraints on free and open discussion. For older people then – and politicians among them – they provided a deplorable contrast with the press they had known in their youth, of which descriptions like R. C. K. Ensor's, published in 1936, so poignantly reminded them.

It is worth quoting at length, because the press of the last quarter of the nineteenth century (or at least this kind of vision of it) so obviously provided the 'folk-memory' benchmark (for

Ensor no less than his readers) against which what happened
later was measured:

> These penny dailies conformed very much to one character.
> Originally modelled on *The Times*, they catered distinctively
> for the upper and middle classes, and almost exclusively for
> the male reader. Though, as a rule, they earned comfortable
> profits, their ownership was not primarily commercial, and
> the newspaper world was about the last quarter in which any
> one then would have looked for a millionaire. Nearly all of
> them were family properties. Their controllers were usually
> well-educated middle-class people, cautious rather than
> ambitious, seeking no new worlds to conquer, valuing their
> papers chiefly for the political and social influence which
> accrued through them, and disposed in most instances to
> view the proper exercise of this influence very seriously as a
> sort of personal trust. On the contents side they were over-
> whelmingly political. They gave some space to business and
> religion, and some to racing and cricket; while for 'human
> interest' they relied on sensational law cases, and brought
> leaders of the bar and bench into a brighter limelight than
> ever before or since. But the staple was politics, especially
> speeches; and proceedings in parliament were reported and
> read all over the country at full length. The way in which the
> news-matter was handled would today be thought incredibly
> dull and matter-of-fact. Headlines were few and paragraphs
> long. But the reader was at least fairly given the facts, on
> which he could form his own judgment. Editorial opinion
> was more or less confined to the leading articles; which were
> written by the highest-paid men in the office, or occasionally
> (though always anonymous) by good writers outside.
> Propaganda was made by open argument; not, as in the twen-
> tieth century, by the doctoring of news.
>
> (Ensor, 1936, p. 144)

The slighting reference to the contemporary press is significant.
For there is little doubt that the conception of 'public service
broadcasting' which was formed during the 1920s owes as
much to the low esteem in which the popular press of the day
was held as to J. W. C. Reith's missionary zeal and masterful
ways. In the view of people like Reith and the conservative
party politicians and civil servants who made the crucial decisions, the products of the newspaper industry, no less than
those of the film industry, represented the consequences of
giving the public what it wants' and were consequently silly,
vulgar, false and contemptible. Broadcasting, if they were to

have anything to do with it, had somehow to be developed in the completely opposite direction. Yet, despite this determination – perhaps, indeed, because of it – the decisions they made which were written in to the original constitution of the BBC, which have been hailed as a masterpiece of foresight and characteristically British political wisdom, at this distance seem like a masterpiece of calculated imprecision.

It was the work of Mitchell-Thomson, then Postmaster-General in Baldwin's government. He followed, in the main, the recommendations of the Crawford Committee, which reported in April 1926, with one or two notable exceptions. The Crawford Report envisaged the new broadcasting organisation operating, as before, very much as an ordinary private firm under the provision of the Companies' Act, but consisting of a number of Commissioners, 'persons of judgement and independence, free of commitments, with business acumen and experience in affairs', who would act corporately as Trustees for the national interest. An alternative arrangement, also canvassed by the Crawford Committee, was that the 'British Broadcasting Commission' should be set up by Act of Parliament. Mitchell-Thomson rejected both those proposals, the first because 'it would lack a certain amount of status and dignity' and the second because the Corporation might be invested 'in the mind of the public with the idea that in some way it is a creature of Parliament and connected with political activity' (Mitchell-Thomson, 1926), pp. 4,466–8).

Having argued the case for giving the new Corporation a privileged position, and at least the appearance, in the mind of the public, of *not* being a creature of Parliament, the Postmaster-General provided himself with overriding rights over transmission (including the wavelengths to be used, the location and the power of transmitters) and powers over the content of broadcasting; indeed, even before the corporation came into being on the last day of 1926, the Postmaster-General had instructed it not to broadcast on matters of political, industrial or religious controversy; nor was it to broadcast any opinion of its own on matters of public policy.

These instructions, which rejected the Crawford Committee's recommendations, were a belated affirmation, in explicit terms, of the control exercised over the British Broadcasting Company by the government a few months previously at the time of the General Strike. In fact, they were no more than an insurance – a stick held well behind the back of the government – and used very rarely. A broadcast by Ramsay MacDonald during the General Strike had been forbidden, even though his general line fully supported the government's stand; five years later, with a Labour government in power, Winston Churchill was denied the right to broadcast his own views of the Conservative Party line on India, his violent opposition to which had led to his resigning from the Shadow Cabinet. (It was the Secretary of State for India, and not the PMG who applied the veto – which it was, although Reith's own words for it was 'a request emphatically made by the Minister responsible'.)

'Control', then, becomes an inapposite word. The powers assumed by the Postmaster-General have never been exercised publicly and officially. It was, in fact, hardly necessary to do so. The kind of arrangement arrived at between the Government and the BBC at the time of the General Strike provided the mould for the kind of compromise solution and understanding which has prevailed since then.

In 1926, Reith made it quite clear, in a memorandum to Baldwin, that the BBC could be relied on to support the Government:

> Assuming the BBC is for the people and that the Government is for the people, it follows that the BBC must be for the Government in this crisis too.
>
> (Reith, 1949, p. 108)

An *obiter dictum* inserted by a High Court judge on a case which came before him towards the very end of the General Strike, to the effect that the 'so-called General Strike was illegal', gave Reith an opportunity to assert to his senior staff that 'we were unable to permit anything which was contrary to the spirit of that judgement, which might have prolonged or sought to justify the Strike'. But on their side, the Trade Unions saw the picture differently, and, according to their lights, much more clearly; at the start of the General Strike, the TUC warned its members against believing the BBC, 'because radio would be just another tool in the hands of the Government', and Beatrice Webb noted that 'directly the news began, it was clear that the BBC had been commandeered by the Government and the main purpose was to recruit blacklegs for the closed services' (Cole, 1956, pp. 91–2)

It took seven years, which included two years of a Labour Government, for the situation to ease sufficiently for the Parliamentary Opposition to be given the chance to respond to 'political' (as against 'ministerial') broadcasts by the Government. Almost certainly, it was the exaggerated fears of the 'power of broadcasting' which prevailed at the time which led to this development, since every time the Government used it for blatantly political purposes (as for example Churchill did in his broadcast on his 1928 Budget) there were counterblasts from the Opposition in Parliament and in the Press; the BBC felt able 'not to invite' Churchill to repeat the performance in 1929. At times of crisis, of course, the BBC could prove as reliable as it had in 1926; during the critical months of 1931, after the National Coalition Government had been formed in August, but before the election campaign opened in October, no Labour speaker broadcast (although in the three weeks of the election campaign itself, time was doled out between the contending parties, fractured as they were). After the election, Attlee raised the first demand for 'equal time', a demand which was laughed out then, but eventually became the principle governing 'access' by major political parties to broadcast time.

On the other hand, political altercation about 'fair play' between Government and Opposition seems, if anything, to have strengthened Government control, both direct and, more effectively, indirect, over the broadcasting of anything controversial. Throughout the 1930s, the BBC was ridden with a tight rein. Mild as the incursions by commentators into foreign politics and genteel as discussions between political figures were, there were frequent occasions on which objections were raised in the House and in the Press to what were labelled errors in editorial judgement or lapses in taste. Such occasions reinforced the propensity of the chief officials of the BBC to prove themselves even more 'reliable'; and, as ever, self-censorship proved to be the most effective form of censorship. As Andrew Boyle remarks, 'BBC controllers and producers were not encouraged to flaunt their consciences or to demonstrate their powers of initiative. The most sensible course, especially for newcomers in the early 1930s, was to dispense outright with such luxuries.'

The formal terms of the relationship between the BBC and Government were laid down explicitly by the Ullswater Committee, and have never been challenged or amended. Paragraphs 51 and 52 of the Report read:

> 51. The position of the Corporation is thus one of independence in the day-to-day management of its business, and of ultimate control by His Majesty's Government. We find that this line of demarcation has been observed in practice, and we are convinced that no better can be found. We agree with those who in recent years have examined the question that the constitutional independence of the BBC brings advantages to the general public and to listeners which could not otherwise be secured. Our proposals under this heading are designed to make both sides of this two-fold position simpler and more evident.
> 52. It is inevitable that the State, in establishing a sole broadcasting authority, should reserve to itself those powers of ultimate control; but we have no reason to suppose that, in practice, divergent views of the lines of public interest have been held by the Corporation and by Government departments, or that the Corporation has suffered under any sense of constraint or undue interference. Where the interests of the State appear to be at all closely involved, it is open to the Corporation to consult a Minister or Department informally and of its own accord. This method leaves decision and discretion in the hands of the Corporation and is consistent with the independent status which was formulated ten years ago as the desirable objective.
>
> (Ullswater Committee Report, 1936)

Nevertheless, the BBC's relationship with Government, Parliament and political parties, and its handling of current political affairs have confronted it with a perpetual and unresolvable dilemma. From time to time, the terms in which the dilemma manifests itself have changed. In its contemporary form the BBC has come to be regarded as occupying a position of political power, while it sees itself as the custodian of the nation's interests in the uses to which an instrument for the exercise of political power may be put. In reality, the BBC's position may be construed as having responsibility without power – the privilege of the servant throughout the ages.

The contemporary dilemma is revealed fairly clearly in two quotations, one from the report of the Select Committee on

Nationalised Industries (Sub-Committee B) published in 1972:

> There has been a shift of emphasis from considering the broadcasting media solely in terms of the programmes they produce to one in which the BBC and the Authority are seen as powerful institutions in their own right, whose whole style of decision making and action profoundly affects the community.

The other is taken from an article in *The Listener* (6 June 1974) by Oliver Whitley, formerly Assistant to the Director-General of the BBC:

> Neither the broadcasting organisations nor the public in this country really know what the objectives of the broadcasting organisations are supposed to be, because these objectives have never been properly and officially defined . . . If you reflect that broadcasting is the medium which everyone nowadays seems to regard as chief public-impression former, is it not very strange, indeed rather alarming, that Parliament, which decides who should provide these uniquely influential services, apparently has nothing of practical significance to say about their main purposes?

Parliament, he went on to say, was 'particularly inept in its handling of broadcasting'. A reading of parliamentary debates over the years since the early 1920s suggest that, while this is not an altogether fair judgement, it is true that, for the most part, leading politicians have treated broadcasting very much as the Post Office did at the outset – as a nuisance. On the other hand, the kind of interest which leading politicians like Churchill in the 1920s, Kingsley Wood in the 1930s, and Wedgwood Benn in the 1960s have occasionally taken in broadcasting, has not been altogether welcome to the BBC.

Not surprisingly, therefore, the BBC's relationships with national politics, political parties and politicians, uneasy at the beginning, have been more and more difficult and troubled. Throughout, BBC programmes have become at times increasingly circumspect, at other times increasingly adventurous, its pronouncements increasingly simple-minded and increasingly devious, and its handling of individual politicians and groups increasingly clumsy and increasingly finicky.

There is a world of difference between the picture of Reith editing and polishing the script of *Message to the Nation* during the General Strike, broadcast from Reith's home, or 'titivating' Baldwin's election broadcast in 1929 (Adam, 1927, p. 208) and that of the anxious trimming of the course of balance and impartiality by constant consultation with Party Whips. On the other hand, the decision to risk presenting programmes like *The Question of Ulster* and *Yesterday's Men* is even farther removed from the time, in 1930, when Wedgwood Benn *père,* as Secretary of State for India in a Labour Government, could deny Churchill the opportunity of airing his views on the Conservative Party's India policy, over which he had just resigned from the Shadow Cabinet, or when Chamberlain, as Chancellor of the Exchequer, could forbid any Opposition reply to his broadcast talk on the 1933 Budget.

In the 1950s, the 'fourteen-day rule' forbade any broadcast discussion of matters which were to be the subject of Parliamentary debate at any time within the next two weeks, an embargo which seems improbably crude and arbitrary compared with the gentlemanly provision recommended by the Crawford Committee in 1926, which was that 'a moderate amount of controversial matter should be broadcast, provided that the material is of high quality and distributed with scrupulous fairness, and that the discretion of the Commissioners [i.e. Governors of the BBC] in this connection should be upheld.'

Yet again, the crude stopwatch conception of 'scrupulous fairness' that operates nowadays is accompanied by a quite extraordinary acceptance of the notion that 'when politicians or any public figures have access to the powerful platform of television, they should be open to questioning of a critical and challenging nature'[2] – by 'television journalists' or by 'invited audiences', themselves selected, and their interventions stage-managed, by broadcasting producers or by the television journalists themselves.

Every year seems to reveal more depths and more versions of the basic dilemma. Reporting on the television coverage of the February 1974 Election, Blumler wrote that much of the effort 'was channelled into the main evening TV news programmes. Fully merging its news and current affairs staffs, the BBC devoted a further half hour of each edition of the *Nine O'Clock News* to the Election, and often presented campaign items in the more topical first half as well . . . But the disturbing consequence of the campaign role of television news was a tendency for news events to dictate much of the flow of the subsequent argument.' He goes on to detect an even more indefinable and unmanageable source of bias: 'The British communication media are apparently so organised that the Conservatives may count on the entirety of their message, whatever it may be, receiving a thorough airing. In so far as Labour is a Party for egalitarian redistribution and radical social change, it cannot rely on the same treatment . . . The bulk of the mass media tended to present the Election issues in middle-class terms.'

It is variously argued that this fundamental dilemma is inescapable, given the nature of broadcasting itself, given the fact that broadcasting was a monopoly, or alternatively, that it is now dominated by competition between the BBC and Independent Television for numbers of viewers; that, being so powerful a means of influencing opinion, it must be subject to governmental control, or, that being so important to the functioning of a democracy, it should be free from government control; that being so expensive, its programmes must be such as to appeal to the majority most of the time, or, at the very least, not offend the majority, or, being so important a medium of communication, it must make room for the expression of minority views and dissenting opinion (Blumler, 1974, p. 572).

In considering the political role of broadcasting in particular, in the contemporary situation, it is as well to remember two things. First, despite the intentions of the people who founded public service broadcasting, and the constitutional machinery which was applied to see their intentions were carried out – machinery which applied as much to Independent Television as to the BBC – they could not alter the fact that in the beginning, broadcasting existed to provide entertainment, free entertainment. Later on, broadcasting entertainment served as a carrier for advertising in the United States and elsewhere, and for cultural improvement in Britain. But even now the primary function of broadcasting, so far as its audiences are concerned, is to provide entertainment, and whatever else it provides depends very largely on its capacity to deliver enough, good enough, and varied enough entertainment.

The second point is that the political role of broadcasting was thrust on it by politicians – by Baldwin in this country, and by Roosevelt, with his fireside chats, in America. The use of the press in this way (conceivable as it may have been in the eighteenth century) is inconceivable in the twentieth century. Chief executives in every country have the right to claim the use of broadcasting services for the purposes of government. R. S. Lambert, in writing of his experiences of the Reith era, said as much: 'Today, the BBC holds – in the field of art, intellect and politics – the power once exercised by the Court. It has become the main indirect organ of government, all the more potent because its influence *is* indirect' (Lambert, 1940, p. 317).

Such freedoms as broadcasting authorities in this country and elsewhere have in the publication of news and the discussion of public issues are probably due more to the gradual takeover of the constitutional doctrine of 'the freedom of the press' as they are to any strenuous assertion on their own part of political independence. The assimilation of broadcasting into the fourth estate role has been furthered, especially in the last two decades, by the increasing tendency of journalists, political and other, to pursue their personal careers in both newspapers and broadcasting. Nevertheless, broadcasting in all countries is controlled by government licence in a way that the press is not, and in most European countries is further subject to direct financial control by the government, in the way that the press, at least in Western democracies, is not.

From one point of view, therefore, the degree of political independence achieved by broadcasting systems is remarkable. American broadcasting can exercise far more licence in its treatment of politics and political issues than it can in the treatment of sex or the use of obscene language – a licence, moreover, which it owes as much to the decision of Congress to allow live television broadcasts of committee and other proceedings, and the desire of politicians to make their own use of broadcasting facilities, as it does to the public-spirited endeavours of broadcasting organisations and journalists.

This, I believe, explains to some extent the extraordinary sense of shock with which Vice-President Agnew's Iowa speech was received:

> The purpose of my remarks tonight, is to focus your attention on this little group of men who not only enjoy right of instant rebuttal to every Presidential address, but, more importantly, wield a free hand in selecting, presenting and interpreting the great issues of our nation . . . They decide what forty-fifty million Americans will learn of the day's events in the nation and the world. We can't measure this power and influence by the traditional democratic standards, for these men can create

national issues overnight. They can make or break by their coverage or their commentary, a Moratorium on the war. They can elevate men from obscurity to national prominence within a week. They can reward some politicians with national exposure and ignore others. The American people would rightly not tolerate this concentration of power in government. Is it not fair and relevant to question its concentration in the hands of a tiny, enclosed fraternity of privileged men elected by no one and enjoying a monopoly sanctioned and licensed by the Government.

(Barrett, 1969–70)

Three years later, Clay Whitehead, the Director of the Office of Telecommunications Policy appointed by the President, urged on the management of local stations their duty in buying network news and other programmes:

The station owners and managers cannot abdicate responsibility for news judgement. When a reporter or disc jockey slips in or passes over information in order to line his pockets, that's plugola, and management will take quick corrective action. But men also stress or suppress information in accordance with their beliefs. Will station licensees or network executives also take action against this ideological plugola?

(Barrett, 1971–2)

One can match these statements by one made by Norman Angell forty years earlier, about the popular press:

A few newspaper proprietors – Northcliffe's, Hulton's, Beaverbrook's, Bottomley's – come nearer, at just those junctures which are crucial, really to governing England and 'making it what it is' than Commons, or Cabinet, Church or Trade Union . . . One used to hear many an English householder talk most contemptuously of 'those Harmsworth fellows and their ha'penny sensations' and become indignant at the notion that he could be influenced in his opinions thereby . . . 'But I don't take my opinion from the papers; I never read their leading articles'. If one led him on to expressions of opinion concerning the government of the day, its merits and demerits; his estimate of the persons that composed it; his ideas of the character of other nations; his notions of fiscal policy, and national education, of the country's past and future foreign policy, and so on, one would discover that every single opinion he expressed responded accurately to just that distribution of emphasis in the news of our time which marks the Northcliffe press. Given the facts as this householder conceived them, he could conjure no other opinion; and those facts – one group of them stressed day after

day, and another group, intrinsically as important, hidden
away in corners, were presented as Lord Northcliffe had
decreed they should be presented.

(Angell, 1933, pp. 10–11)

Power has many forms. The critics of newspapers and broadcasting see their power as lying in controlling the agenda, in
their ability to select certain issues for discussion and decision
and to ignore others, or to treat them as non-existent; and in the
ability to treat certain conflicts of interest as manifestly proper
material and others as too complex, or marginal, or unmanageable. Perhaps the greatest constraint of all lies in the conventions of what is called 'news tasting' – the job of the aide to the
chief sub-editor who has to decide, almost instantly, which
messages coming through to the office are to count as news,
and which aren't. This constraint is even stricter on broadcasting
than on newspapers. Writing of the 1968 Democratic Convention
at Chicago, Whale saw this innate handicap as more serious
than any other of the many constraints, technical and visual, on
the presentation of television news and current affairs. 'Television viewers were never given more than a cursory explanation of why the mayor [Mayor Daly of Chicago] of a provincial
city was able to rule not only his own region but a national
political convention with an iron fist. They could not have
been: the juncture of patronage was too complex, too abstract,
too private to be set out on television. There was nothing to
photograph.'

Nevertheless, five years later, there was Watergate – far
more complex, more abstract, and much more private, but
which was nevertheless set out in extraordinary detail in all its
complexity – and on television.

The response of the controllers of the press and broadcasting
has always been that the media serves as a mirror to society.
R. D. Kasmire, giving evidence to the US National Commission
on the Causes and Prevention of Violence, said, 'There is no
doubt that television is, to a large degree, a mirror of society. It
is also a mirror of public attitudes and preferences.' The
President of NBC, Julian Goodman, claimed that the medium
was being blamed for the message, while the President of CBS,
Frank Stanton, claimed that, 'what the media do is to hold up a
mirror to society and to try and report it as faithfully as possible'. Closely allied is the view of the news as essentially a

random process. 'Newspapers and news programmes could almost be said to be random reactions to random events. Again and again the main reason they turn out as they do is accident: accidents of a kind which recurs so haphazardly as to defeat statistical examination.'[3]

David Brinkley, in an NBC news special, remarked, 'What television did in the sixties was to show the American people to the American people . . . it did show the people places and things they had not seen before. Some they liked, and some they didn't. It was not that television produced or created any of it' (Epstein, 1973, p. 10).

Perhaps the biggest change over the past ten years has been the enormous increase in the criticism of the claim by newspapers and, especially, broadcasting, that it served as a mirror, whose due task was 'to reflect society as it is'. This was certainly the dominant view of television's role in the early 1960s, when Hugh Greene's 'Young Lions' were winning back audiences from ITV with their new-style magazine programmes. The claim that the media serve as a kind of inertial guidance system for the nation, casting a neutral, impartial, balanced, but observant eye on the life of the nation and the world at large, and giving an inevitably selected, but honest, account of what is there, has been challenged by the conception of newspapers and broadcasting as instruments of power.

While this radical view is articulated and backed by minority groups of the political left and right, it has some support from large sections of the population, some of them organised (e.g. trade unionists). It is also an occasional presence in the minds of an increasing proportion of people as one moves farther from London and Washington.

In published writings, this interpretation manifests itself under a number of different titles. To a large extent, however (much larger, I should make it clear, than the proponents of any one of them would admit), all of them are variants on one theme. Shifts from one form of expression to another, therefore, represent not so much increased insight and knowledge, as varieties of the same basic belief which becomes dominant at different levels of political or social or economic stress.

This is most obviously the case with the first two: conspiracy theory and the 'power élite' notion. In the earlier part of the century, conspiracy theory was much favoured by left-wing critics, but was successfully taken over by the right wing (notably, of course, by the Nazis). After this happened, the Left seems to have developed the notion of 'power élite', fully articulated by C. Wright Mills in his book of that title (Mills, 1986).

Since the Second World War, the most striking exploitation of conspiracy theory was undoubtedly Senator McCarthy's, who very successfully married it to traditional populist hostility towards the traditional élite – the east-coast establishment of bankers, government officials and intellectuals.

Conspiracy theory has almost as long a history as journalism itself. It is the inevitable consequence of assumptions about the power and pervasiveness of the 'media'. Spiro Agnew spoke for more than himself when he claimed that a few journalists held 'a concentration of power over American public opinion unknown in history'.

The attack on the power élite, the core of which is what C. Wright Mills (and President Eisenhower) called the 'military-industrial complex' has remained much the same since 1950; broadcasting, in this case, features as an instrument – if not *the* instrument – by which the power élite maintains itself. The general position, which may be regarded as common to the militant left in Britain, as in the United States, has been most clearly stated by Ralph Miliband in *The State in Capitalist Society* (1969), in which he writes of the 'ownership and control of the means of mental production'.

Among the New Left, however, in broadcasting and outside it, the tendency is to plump for the third variant form: ideological hegemony. Miliband himself occasionally makes the slight shift necessary to assume this more general, and much more powerful, critique:

> The agencies of communication and noticeably the mass media are in reality, and the expression of dissident views notwithstanding, a crucial element in the legitimation of capitalist society.

> The mass media in advanced capitalist societies are mainly *intended* [my emphasis] to perform highly 'functional' roles; they too are both the expression of a system of domination, and the means of reinforcing it.
>
> (Miliband, 1969, pp. 197, 198)

Hegemony, a term adopted at two or three or even more removes from Gramsci's writings, represents a social order held in equilibrium by a consensus, which is both moral and intellectual and is diffused throughout the whole of the population and informs their daily lives. As applied to broadcasting, it has some long standing in Britain. During the 'Golden Days of Wireless', right through to the 1950s, it was seen in very explicit terms as identified with 'BBC culture', 'BBC types' and indeed 'BBC English'. The Ullswater Committee, in 1935, was at one point driven to defend the BBC against the 'suspicion that in appointments an undue preference was given to candidates with Oxford or Cambridge degrees'. They regarded this contention as disproved by quoting figures that, out of all monthly-paid non-engineering staff who were graduates, only 60 per cent were from Oxford and Cambridge!

It is not that broadcasting organisations, among others, are instruments of a power élite, of the establishment, or of an existing social order whose rulers are determined to maintain the status quo – if necessary, by making marginal concessions. The picture is much more of a recruitment and promotion *process*. The hierarchy of a broadcasting organisation appears not so much a hierarchy of power as a hierarchy of models, power consisting not so much in the issue of directives, instructions, or even policy documents, but in the laying down of a set of tacit principles by which individuals can gain membership, in the first place, of the organisation, and thereafter, by a sedulously monitored appointment system, the rewards of 'interesting' jobs and promotion.

Of course, the small population from which recruits are selected itself changes; so does the cultural and social and political ambience within which broadcasting organisations exist. Thus, in 1972, in his *Sunday Times* article ('What's to become of the BBC?') Peter Jay could write:

> There is [in the BBC] a kind of consensus, a pool of shared social and political assumptions, which on many subjects – abortion, divorce, censorship, drugs, emigration, promiscuity, capital punishment, penal policy, education and so on – are at the best partisan opinions and at the worst the opinion of a small educated middle-class and left-wing minority.

It is into this area that the main debate over the political role of broadcasting and the press has shifted in recent years. In this regard, as in others, both the area of debate and the national circumstances in which debate occurs have changed.

Before the war, Reith saw his public service broadcasting system acting as 'a dependable keeper of the nation's conscience', standing as 'an arbiter above the clamour of all political and social factions' and regarded as 'the paragon of impartiality, honesty and respectability'. He pursued his objectives with missionary zeal, and quite openly. He did this by bringing to bear what he called 'the brute force of monopoly' as his instrument. In fact, although his motives and his aims were utterly different, his view of broadcasting as an instrument was much the same as Rothermere's or Beaverbrook's. Government and influential public opinion supported his objectives, seeing them, as he did, as a means of promoting at least an appearance of national social and cultural integration in a country deeply divided but fearful of the destructive forces present and gaining strength in Britain and abroad. The 1940s and 1950s did bring integration, but of a totally unprecedented kind. They seem now to have been a curious historical interlude, a social interregnum in which fundamental political differences and the whole structure of social and economic inequality seemed to be made either irrelevant because of the war, or obsolescent through the magic of technological progress.

The imposed consensus of the 1930s, the consciousness of national unity of the wartime years and the surface appearance of inevitable progress towards improved economic welfare and social equality had all dissipated by the mid-1960s. Conceivably, the country by then had recovered sufficient assurance and essential unity for people to acknowledge once again the existence of the divisions which had always been a familiar part of everyone's common experience and awareness as a citizen, and which had, moreover, though latent, persisted since the 1920s. But, so far as broadcasting, broadcasting authorities and broadcasters were concerned, dissensus of the kind which then revealed itself and has remained with us since was a shatteringly novel experience.

It seems to be common ground that 'a dangerous gulf' has opened between leaders (i.e. politicians) and led (i.e. voters); that the consensus which has prevailed in Britain (seemingly from time immemorial) has broken up, and divisions which previously did not exist, or at least were unrevealed, had become obtrusively apparent; that trades unions, and trade unionism, have become much more militant, both industrially and politically; that Scottish and Welsh nationalism, as well as Irish, within the United Kingdom, has gained enormously in strength; that re-politicisation, especially among the young, has led to extremism, both of the Left and the Right, with a consequent increase in the use of the vocabulary of Marxism and Fascism; that a new wave of feminism has emerged with much broader claims to equal rights; and, finally, all these manifestations of 're-politicisation' are, for the most part, particularistic and have been quick to adopt the organisational structure, the tactics and the armoury of pressure groups within the Parliamentary system, and of dissident factions outside it.

There are striking resemblances between what has been happening in Britain since the mid-1960s and the period between 1830 and 1870, so comprehensively and admirably documented in the collections of writings edited by Patricia Hollis: *Pressure from Without* (1974).

Changes in the power structure (or, more precisely, the distribution of rights and privileges within society) are brought about in ways that can be broadly classified into two: Parliamentary and extra-Parliamentary political processes.

By itself, Parliamentary process is lengthy, arduous and tedious. Institutionalised as it now is, and mediated, as it now is, by the institutionalised process of party politics, Parliament, if left to itself (i.e. shielded or safe from outside pressure, as it was for the most part during the inter-war years), follows a single principle: inertia. But, though Parliament is not in any statistical (i.e. J. S. Mill) sense representative of the people, it 'represents' the people.

However, changes in the structure of society are implemented through the Parliamentary process. It does so by responding to 'pressures from without', although the response is not necessarily adequate, direct, correct or even positive. It does so most obviously and formally at election times, but this response is, again, mediated by the machinery of party politics. At election times, and at all times, it can be made aware of 'pressure from without' by four main means:

1. Public opinion as manifested in public meetings and demonstrations.
2. Public opinion as manifested in public utterances, spoken or written.
3. Action that focuses attention on grievances or demands

through attacks on property, through riots, through assassi-
nation.
4. Action designed to enforce change either through the
   organised disruption of civil life or by revolution.

Extra-Parliamentary political action has taken all four forms in
this country, as in others. Historically, the English and Irish,
and to a lesser extent, the Scots and Welsh, have been no more
docile politically than the people of any other country. The
major difference, in the past, has been the greater responsive-
ness of the Parliamentary process to pressure from without.
Even during the nineteenth century, it was the first two forms
of pressure which gained the real successes, but how far this
was so because these two forms had gained a legitimacy which
they did not have elsewhere, or because they were recognized
for what they were: the milder manifestations of pressure
which could easily range into the more violent forms; how far
the breadth and intensity of the first two kinds of manifestations allowed Parliamentary politicians to assess the strength of
the pressure; or how far these modes of manifestation of
pressure ('public opinion') have become recognised and institutionalised as modes of political action, it is impossible to say.

But during the past decade or so, things have changed, and
the reason for this rather lengthy excursus is that what seems
to have changed is that the first two modes of expression of
'pressure from without' have become ineffective.

There are three reasons for this:

1. Increasingly, from the 1930s on, the 'pressures from without', political, economic and social, have come from outside
   the country, so that the Parliamentary system has had to
   respond to them, as well as to pressures from within society. (Before a generation or so ago, these pressures were
   largely political – i.e. concerned diplomacy or war; over the
   last generation they have become increasingly manifold,
   complex and unmanageable, so far as Parliament itself is
   concerned.)
2. The diminution of British power and prestige, which has
   been concomitant with, and the consequence of, the increase
   in extra-national pressure, has diminished the supreme sovereignty of Parliament. Both factors have combined to reduce
   both the effective and the apparent force of the first two

modes of exerting pressure on Parliament from without.

3. There has been a very great reduction in the number of different means by which public opinion can be made manifest, together with – an almost inevitable consequence – firmer and more comprehensive control by professionals: professional politicians, professional journalists, professional broadcasters, professional publicists.

This situation, I believe, lies behind (and is largely concealed by) Mr Wedgwood Benn's by now familiar pronouncement on the matter:

> The whole political process in a democracy rests on the maintenance of a delicate fabric of communication within society which reveals the common interest that exists, identifies conflict where it arises and painfully builds the consent which leads people to accept the policies that emerge as these conflicts are resolved by upholding the ground rules of the system.
>
> The media are engaged in the same process and are so much more effective in disseminating information simultaneously to large groups of people that they not only supplement the political and educational systems but in some respects supplant them, because of their enormous power.[4]

But the power of the press barons, claimed with such assurance during the 1920s and acknowledged by Baldwin even as he challenged it, has gone, to be replaced by the power of the balance sheet, which drives newspapers to compete not for numbers of readers, but for the numbers of pounds their readers have for spending on consumer goods. It is this which has driven the national press into the narrowly confined consensus not of opinion but of the agenda for discussion which they now display, and which, as Hirsch and Gordon so clearly document, is based on a minority of the well-heeled professional and managerial middle classes.

> The consensus is a broad band, not a party line – not even a Fleet line. The picture that we suggest of the quality press is of a band of opinion and approaches occupying the broad centre of British politics from about half-way into the moderate Left through to the edges of the extreme right; with individual papers occupying different and sometimes shifting positions within the band, and the band itself moving over time in response to events and political changes. But the most important characteristic of the consensus band lies not in the nuances of the attitude taken on different items on the

political agenda, but rather in the common agreement on that
agenda itself – on the issues for discussion and the way in
which they should be approached.

The consequence of all this is that, so far as the representation of opinion among the public is concerned, 'minorities with
high spending power find themselves excellently catered for.
Minorities who have less pull on advertisers find themselves
neglected. There is no newspaper their money can buy.'

Of course, the remedies are there, and are found: the creation
of new publications which do cater for minorities. And it is significant that the 1960s and 1970s saw the appearance of a number: *New Society, Private Eye, Socialist Worker, Black Dwarf,* which
added themselves to *Tribune* and the *Morning Star* to preserve a
modicum of unestablished political opposition, informed criticism, and to serve, in Geoffrey Crowther's words, as 'the chief
lieutenant of discontent'. The response to the claim for 'access'
is always to hand.

But the press, nowadays, is only half the matter – perhaps
less than half. The increasing concern about the press which
has expressed itself in the institution of three Royal Commis-
sions since the war is centrally concerned with the shrinking of
the number of national newspapers and the consequent shrinkage of the 'band of consensus' within which they operate. The
quality newspapers may have survived, at a cost, but the
mass-circulation newspaper has certainly suffered, and this
directly as a consequence of television, especially commercial
television, because commercial television lives off the advertising money which would otherwise go to the mass-circulation
newspaper and *not* the quality newspaper. Since 1960, the *Daily
Mirror*, the *Daily Express*, the *Daily Mail* have all lost a substantial proportion of their average daily circulation; the *Daily
Sketch* died in 1970; the exception, the *Sun*, has almost four
times the circulation of the *Herald* which it replaced in 1962, but
has forfeited any pretence of *representing* popular opinion.

Broadcasting, then, has cut the readership of the mass circulation newspaper. More to the point, it has replaced it almost
completely as a source of news and information about current
affairs. Yet there is every indication that BBC news and current
affairs, ITN, and current affairs programmes of ITA companies
all operate within the same 'consensus-band' as the quality
newspapers. The range of opinion available to newspaper

readers, radio listeners and television viewers, all, has narrowed much more than is indicated by the decline in the range and number of national newspapers.

Moreover, this narrowing of range has not necessarily been towards any particular political, social or cultural mean (whatever this might signify in any of those three respects). The limits for broadcasting are roughly those within which the quality press operates.

The conclusion is, then, that although it has been manifest to everybody that political, social, economic and cultural interests, values and opinions have appeared to become more and more disparate, and this disparity more and more organised, the kind of opinions and attitudes and values and, above all, information, conveyed by broadcasting and the press has tended to become more constrained and more internally consistent.

NOTES AND REFERENCES

1. Cf. Aspinall. No fewer than nine of Aspinall's sixteen chapters are filled with his account of the extent to which Government was involved in subsidies and bribery, in discriminatory taxation, and in legislation and court proceedings in its endeavours to suppress or control the dissident press. The titles of the chapters themselves are illuminating: Government Subsidies (England); Government subsidies (Ireland); Indirect Subsidies (Advertisements); Newspapers and Pamphlets Circulated Gratis; Treasury 'Hirelings'; Assistance from the Post Office; Official Intelligence for Friendly Newspapers; The Government 'Instructs' the Press.

2. Robin Day, 'Troubled Reflections of a TV Journalist', *Encounter*, May 1970, p. 88. Mr Day took what might be thought a more reasonable line – and what was in the circumstances assuredly a more accommodating one – in his evidence to the Select Committee on Broadcasting of Proceedings in the House of Commons in 1966, when he said, as his second argument for televising Parliament, 'In particular, television viewers would be able to see parliamentary leaders being questioned and challenged by those elected to do so on the floor of the House and not *merely* [my emphasis] by television journalists in studio interviews'. (*First Report from the Select Committee on Broadcasting, etc., of Proceedings in the House of Commons*, 1966, Minutes, Evidence, p. 62.)

3. John Whale, quoted by Charles Curran in 'Researcher/ Broadcaster Co-operation: Problems and Possibilities', in J. D. Halloran and M. Gurevitch (eds), *Broadcaster/Researcher Co-operation in Mass Communication Research*, Centre for Mass Communication Research, 1971, p. 43.

4. A. W. Benn in F. S. Badley (ed.), *Fourth Symposium on Broadcasting Policy* (mimeo), University of Manchester, 1972, p. 37.

288   *Description, Explanation and Understanding*

BIBLIOGRAPHY

Adam, K., 1972: 'Fifty Years of Fireside Elections', *The Listener* 91
(14 February).
Angell, Norman, 1933: *The Press and the Organization of Society*,
Gordon Fraser.
Aspinall, A., 1949: *Politics and the Press, 1780–1850*, Home and Van
Thal.
Barrett, Marvin (ed.): *The Alfred I. Dupont – Columbia University Survey
of Broadcast Journalism 1969–70*, Appendix A.
—*The Alfred I. Dupont – Columbia University Survey of Broadcast
Journalism 1971–2*, Appendix 4.
Blackstone, 1857: *Commentaries*, ed. R. M. Kerr, Murray, vol. 4.
Blumler, J., 1974: 'The Media and the Election', *New Society* 27
(7 March).
Bryce, James, 1914: *The American Commonwealth*, 3rd edn, Macmillan.
Cole, Margaret (ed.), 1956: *Beatrice Webb's Diaries, 1924–1932*,
Longman.
Crowther, Geoffrey, 1943: *The Economist, 1843–1943*, Oxford University
Press.
Ensor, R. C. K., 1936: *England, 1870–1914*, Oxford University Press.
Epstein, Edward J., 1973: *News from Nowhere*, Random House.
Habermas, J., 1962: *Strukturwandel der Offentlichkeit*, Luchterhand, 2nd
revised edn 1965.
Hirsch, F., and Gordon, D., 1975: *Newspaper Money: Fleet Street and the
Search for the Affluent Reader*, Hutchinson.
Hollis, Patricia, 1974: *Pressure from Without in Early Victorian England*,
Arnold.
Lambert, R. S., 1940: *Ariel and All His Equality – An Impression of the
BBC from Within*, Gollancz. Quoted by Anthony Smith, 1973: *The
Shadow in the Cave*, Allen and Unwin.
Lang, Kurt, and Lang, G. E., 1968: *Politics and Television*, Quadrangle
Books.
Lapsley, G. (ed.), 1936: Editorial Note to F. W. Maitland, *Selected
Essays*, Cambridge University Press.
McQuail, D., 1969: *Towards a Sociology of Mass Communications*, Collier-
Macmillan.
Miliband, R., 1969: *The State in Capitalist Society*, Weidenfeld and
Nicolson.
Mills, C. Wright, 1956: *The Power Elite*, OUP.
Mitchell-Thomson (Postmaster-General) in *Hansard*, 14 July 1926,
vol. 198.
Reith, J. C. W., 1949: *Into the Wind*, Hodder and Stoughton.
Taylor, A. J. P., 1965: *English History, 1914–1945*, Oxford University
Press.
Thompson, E. P., 1975: *Whigs and Hunters*, Allen Lane.
Watson, Steven, 1960: *The Reign of George III, 1760–1830*, Oxford
University Press.

14

Sovereignty, Interests and Bureaucracy in the Modern State

> This paper signalled a resumption of my central interests. I
> should perhaps observe that the initial concentration on
> organisation, and bureaucracy in particular, was soon left
> behind in favour of a much broader approach in which
> social order and power has figured largely, alongside
> organised collective action.

This brief essay has the status of a working paper, by which I
mean that while it is, I hope, reasonably coherent and complete
in itself, it is part of a larger undertaking; until this is finished,
what I say is subject to qualification and amendment. The
whole enterprise has its origins in a sense of dissatisfaction that
has mounted over the years with the account given by social
scientists – sociologists, political scientists and, latterly, economists – of bureaucracy, its structure, the way it works, and the
part it plays in the contemporary social, economic and political
order. However, when I started to look for a better, or at least
more satisfactory, account, I found myself driven to look suc-
cessively at the ways in which the nature and the role of
bureaucracy had changed, at its origins (which seemed to be
contemporary with those of the modern state) and at those
antecedent social and political orders in which bureaucracy
seems either to have existed in so embryonic a form as to be
recognisable only by hindsight, or even not to have existed at
all.

From *The British Journal of Sociology*, vol. 31, no. 4, December 1980, pp. 491–506.

Tentatively, and perhaps temporarily, I have assumed that bureaucracy made its appearance as a necessary corollary to the establishment of absolute sovereignty. Of course, absolute sovereignty is much more insubstantial in terms of the actual historical power and authority exercised by kings and princes – even of Henry VIII, or Philip II, or Louis XIV – than it is of the theoretical model constructed by Renaissance political philosophers like Macchiavelli, or Jean Bodin. Bureaucracy, as a concept and as a working apparatus of government, raises problems of the same weight, though they are of a different kind. Historians, untroubled by the need to ensure that the terms they use fit other times and other conditions than those with which they are presently concerned, have applied the word 'bureaucracy' to the apparatus of servants and functionaries employed by popes, emperors and kings to attend to vaguely defined sectors of fiscal, military, legal and ecclesiastical affairs. So Helen Cam, one of the greatest of medievalists, could speak of the household and financial officers of kings and of the justices who held pleas as the king's representative as a 'system of bureaucratic government';[1] by 'bureaucracy', she goes on to say, is meant the 'power of the royal household'.

By the sixteenth century, however, there was a change. Power and authority shared or divided in varying proportions between emperors and kings, dukes and barons, popes and churchmen for over a thousand years were once again welded into a single entity. The greatest artefact of the Renaissance, the State,[2] was the product of the legal and spiritual unification of power and authority in sovereignty. And it was bureaucracy in something recognisably like its present form by which that sovereignty came to be exercised: it was in the sixteenth century that '"household" methods and instruments were replaced by national bureaucratic methods and instruments'.[3]

To repeat: both these changes have to be so heavily qualified when it comes to the historical account that, although they remain solidly part of received wisdom that we know as 'the history of political thought', they are very much disputed territory for historians, and likely to remain so. (To take England alone, Edward I acted his 'sovereignty' out much more successfully than did Charles I, and Richard II's administration was 'regularised and normalised'[4] to an extent unsurpassed later until the closing years of Henry VIII's reign.) In fact, both the political theories and the political practices of the time are best seen as reflections, or indicators, of the much more comprehensive historical process of the emergence and establishment of new institutional forms in which we can discern the beginnings of the modern state – 'an abstract entity representing neither government nor governed, nor even an alliance of both'.[5]

There is a third element, a process of institutionalisation in parallel with that of sovereignty. The absolutism which became fully fashioned in the Renaissance state took form with a mirror-image, a logically necessary counterpart: natural law. Natural law, from the sixteenth century, ceased to be envisaged and discussed as the worldly and necessarily defective reflection of divine law, but instead as the articulation of the 'inalienable' natural rights of people. The very qualification of 'divine' which was added to the affirmation of absolute sovereignty not only carried the implication that the 'right of kings' was, by itself, disputable; it virtually guaranteed, as the Reformation gathered momentum, that it would be disputed. In so far as absolute sovereignty became a goal or a claim, in so far as '*raison d'état*' was advanced as ground for government action, was something only the sovereign could assert or define, and was identified by him with his own interest, all other members of society had at least one potential interest in common – that of contesting the power and authority of the sovereign.

The conceptual distinction between state and society of which so much has been made over the past two hundred years was a fact of life in the sixteenth century, although it was not a matter of theoretical dispute until the seventeenth. It was then that the idea of a 'society' as something distinct from a 'state', like the post-reformation idea of natural law as something distinct from divine law or positive law, becomes visible as a necessary complement to the conception of absolute sovereignty, as well as rival to it. The Renaissance state marks a watershed in the final detachment, in principle, of sovereignty from the body of the people from which power and authority were drawn, and it is this split which was to be construed later, with the development of constitutionalism and then of capitalist democracy,[6] as a division between state and society – itself reflected in a division within the individual as citizen and as man. The modern state, then, is heir to the confrontation, articulated fully in the sixteenth and seventeenth centuries, between society, with sovereignty immutably attached to the natural law obtaining between all members of society and to their natural rights, and the state, with absolute sovereignty attached to the identity of interests among all members of society and with logical necessity, no less than divine ordinance, requiring that those common interests be expressed and managed by a single ruler.

I would like to insist on the complementarity of the notions of absolute sovereignty and interests; both in theory and in practice, each assumes the existence of the other. The sovereign powers we know nowadays are mostly limited to quite specific domains of time and action, as well as space: the judge in the courtroom, the captain of a ship or an aircraft. Such powers fall well short of being absolute. Within the United Kingdom, only the sovereignty of Parliament is absolute, and then in a sense which falls somewhat short of Jean Bodin's definition, where it is 'unrestrained by law'. In Bryce's words, Parliament 'can make and unmake any and every law, change the form of government or the succession to the crown, interfere with the course of justice, extinguish the most sacred private rights of the citizen'.[7] Yet even so, if there are no limits to the power and authority of Parliament, there are implicit controls or modifying influences. These lie not only in the threat of defeat at the next election which hangs over the governmental majority and over each and every member, but in the ever-present threat represented by combinations of individual and group interests strong enough to resist or obstruct the execution of Parliamentary decisions which they regard as harmful or wrong, and to resist them in ways which are legitimate, or at least defensible, as well as in ways which are illegal. This relationship which exists between sovereignty and a plurality of interests has its parallel in another dimension of the sovereignty which attaches to the modern state: a sovereign state in the modern world is one which is 'recognised' by other equally sovereign states. The sovereignty of the modern state is a partial, or qualified, sovereignty, therefore – and there are several episodes of recent history, in central and south America, south-east Asia, eastern Europe and Africa which demonstrate just how heavily qualified that sovereignty may be: the distinctive quality of the modern state is not only the sovereignty which attaches to it but the mutual and contingent quality of that sovereignty among existing states, and it is contingent at all times and in all places, whether one is thinking of the absolute monarchies of the seventeenth century or the constitutional establishments which succeeded them, whether one is thinking of liberal-democratic states, in which internal diversity of interests is assumed, or of totalitarian regimes, in which internal diversity is suppressed or treated as non-existent.

Sovereignty, whatever its legal and spiritual authority, and however successful its forces have been in eliminating lesser forces, or in reducing them to dependence or insignificance, is always set over and, to some extent against, the people. The people – 'civil society' – is, after the appearance of the modern state, no longer an order incorporating law and the apparatus of government; it is now visible rather as a vast residue from which power and authority have been extracted and distilled into sovereignty. In order to express its power and authority over and against the society it governed in so different a sense from any previous form of government (in that *raison d'état*, like the sovereign, was now paramount, hence the identity of the interest of the one with the other's), sovereignty had to develop a form in which that power and authority could be brought home – *given*, as it were, like law – to the people.

The means by which the new found sovereignty of the Renaissance and modern state could be exercised was through bureaucracy. 'We often speak,' says Trevor-Roper, 'of the Renaissance state. How can we define it? When we come down to facts, we find that it is, at bottom, a great and expanding bureaucracy, a huge system of administrative centralisation, staffed by an ever-growing multitude of "courtiers" or "officers".'[8] Renaissance bureaucracy was a great chain of command (not of duties, the social cement of the feudal system), originating in the sovereign and extending downwards and outwards through ministers and their officers.

Bureaucracy became the logically inevitable instrument of sovereignty because power and authority, in becoming attached to a single ruler had become detached from possessions (especially of land), suffrage (especially of the nobility) and sanction (especially by the Church). Power could thus be allocated, delegated to officials and so dispersed throughout the realm. Dispersing sovereign power through the many chains of command of a bureaucracy multiplies that power. This, just as much a truism as the proposition (on which the exercise of bureaucratic authority seems increasingly to rely) that collective action 'is a means by which individuals can more fully realise their own values',[9] is something we have tended to lose sight of, although it is constantly implied by attacks on bureaucratic power. Power, once consolidated, and as its potential for influence achieves a greater size than a single individual can utilise, 'seeks to broaden its ability to communicate through messengers, agents and subordinates. Thus power takes on a hierarchic, i.e. reflexive, form in order to be able to accomplish a multiplicity of influences simultaneously . . . This extension of power is put through with the aid of such actions as representation, transfer or delegation, which quite innocently suggest that the power which is being exercised remains what it was, while they actually multiply its effectiveness.'[10]

This multiplier effect comes into force when sophistication about the exercise of power and influence reaches the point at which extensions of derived power are usable as resources of personal power. The total power in any social system, therefore, cannot be treated as constant. 'A zero-sum premise of this kind lies at the root of hierarchic fictions of unity, representation, and of many variants of classical political theory, especially of the concepts of strategy, and ideas about the balance of power embodied in them. The zero-sum premise is, however, unreal – or, rather, can only be realised approximately by means of quite specific institutional procedures . . . To apply power to the reinforcement of power amplifies the total power available in a social system, by means of a sort of relay technique. It is possible for a small amount of power to control a great deal of power, and thus to exercise it at will, provided that there is provision for reflexive institutional arrangements. This means that the ability to magnify power is not something confined to the head of a hierarchy.'[11]

As soon as this situation becomes actual and apparent, of course, opportunism intervenes.[12] Officials may decide to serve their own interests – or those of other people than their superiors – and do so by concealing or distorting the information on which their superiors, and other parts of the system, depend, or by making false promises about their future conduct. Bureaucracy ceases to be tributary to sovereignty.

The bureaucracy of the Renaissance state was different in

many ways from what obtains nowadays. It was a much more arbitrary structure, more elastic, more changeable; when ministers fell, their subordinates could all go out of office with them, and although wholesale changes seem to have been rare, the threat was always there – necessarily so, because the creation, maintenance and expansion of Renaissance bureaucracy was founded on patronage. Ministers and officers were not salaried – or, if so, only in a trivial sense. They were paid – for their loyalty, rather than for the work they did – out of the profits to which their office gave them entitlement. These profits were the sums exacted for favours, personal returns which came to them for investments of public money, for contracts, for appointments, for everything, in short, for which their powers 'in the King's name' had been granted. The king himself had recourse to the same means for increasing income beyond customary and designated taxes.

Bureaucracy, once created, seems to be regarded as possessed by some irresistible principle of accumulation or endogenous growth, or else to have grown step by step as accompaniment to the growth of population, of national wealth, of complexity or some other prime mover. What I want to suggest is that bureaucracy has been promoted, expanded and refurbished through the interaction, sequential dominance, or reactive force of three quite different tendencies, or historical processes – and it is to these three moments that the rest of this essay is devoted. All three are connected with the underlying contrariety which I have already mentioned as responsible for the creation of bureaucracy, and which has continued to be responsible for its continuous reproduction: viz., the perpetual and shifting interplay between sovereignty and a plurality of interests.

The first two moments, indeed, could be seen as together making up a single reciprocating, alternating cycle of fluctuations about a secular growth curve – rather like business cycles. They become identifiable in those periods when sovereignty asserts or reasserts itself and, in the second place, in the intervening periods when the numbers and powers of officers outrun the needs of sovereignty. In the seventeenth century, for instance, the promotion of the *commissaires* and the creation of the *intendants* under Louis XIII and Louis XIV was undertaken largely in order to monitor and, in the long run, supplant the bureaucracy of the court nobility. A parallel case is the development of the Prussian *Beamte* under Frederick William and Frederick the Great so as to subvert the intermediate control exercised by the landowners. The archetypal instances in the nineteenth century are the Stern and Hardenberg reforms (and their later extension to the rest of Germany under Bismarck), the creation of the Indian Civil Service and the professionalisation of the Civil Service in Britain, which robbed the aristocracy of the last vestiges of direct political patronage. And for the twentieth century we can point to Russia in the 1920s and France in the post-war decades.

All these moves were made in the interests of asserting the sovereignty of the central government, whatever its complexion. Yet the selfsame moves had as their consequence yet further extensions of the apparatus of power controlled by officials, and the depletion of the sovereign power of monarchs, parliaments and people. It is a natural – or at least understandable – consequence. In Trevor-Roper's words,[13] just as a capitalist society invests in capitalism, a bureaucratic society invests in bureaucracy. In the Renaissance state, the counter reformation state, in eighteenth-century France and Prussia, in post-Bismarck Germany and late Victorian and Edwardian Britain, the most attractive careers open to talent were those offered by government service, promising prestige and power (and, in the long run, the well-upholstered appointments offered by wealthy patrons and, latterly, by the larger commercial and industrial undertakings to successful senior civil servants).

What amounts to a reasoned defence of the second, 'bureaucratising', tendency of this state of affairs is to be found in Hegel. Hegel's conception of the state is deeply ambiguous, representing sometimes the whole social order as a moral community, sometimes standing for the 'political' section of the social order which governs the whole. Again, the state is presented as a product of the Absolute Subject manifesting itself in history, but is also the ultimate resolution of the particular and varied developments achieved by actual historical men – kings, nobility, bourgeois – in pursuit of their own interests, a resolution in which consciously and unconsciously self-interested action becomes conscious and disinterested action directed towards the public good. But the several parts – the family, civil society, sovereign and bureaucracy – although parts of one harmonious and indivisible organism, remain distinct, just as the legislature, the judicial system and the executive are analytically and naturally separate, but part of the whole.

In the whole apparatus of the Hegelian State, the bureaucracy plays the crucially important role. The other parts are present, to act and be acted upon, but even in the case of the sovereign, rationality enters into his will and his acts only in so far as they rest on the bureaucracy, in which the insights and will attached to all the several parts of civil society, the knowledge and skill and rationality which have to enter into decision-making, are embodied. The ruler, in fact, is reduced to something like the figurehead, the man with the rubber stamp, to which Galbraith's corporation president, the successor to the active, corporation-building entrepreneur, is reduced in the face of the real decision-making processes which take place in the Technostructure[14] – the bureaucratic apparatus of the modern corporation. Like the Technostructure, too, it is in the bureaucratic organisation that wisdom and will inhere, not in the persons of individual bureaucrats.

> What the service of the state really requires is that men shall forgo the selfish and capricious satisfaction of their selfish ends; by this very sacrifice, they require the right to find their satisfaction in, but only in, the dutiful discharge of their public functions. In this fact, so far as public business is concerned, there lies the link between universal and particular interests which constitutes both the concept of the state and its inner stability.[15]

As O'Malley comments, 'the aims of the bureaucracy of civil servants . . . as a civil class are said to be identical with the universal aims of the state, its business identical with the business of the state; hence its title as "universal class" (*der allgemeine Stand*).'[16]

This is not very far from the terminology employed three centuries earlier to identify the interests of the ruler with the 'universal' interests of the state and its constituent elements. Hegel, in fact (as Marx, in his critique, constantly asserts) is celebrating the passing of absolute sovereignty from the prince to the bureaucracy.

Absolutism, then, the creator of modern bureaucracy, became its victim. As Paul Frölich has remarked of absolutism in the eighteenth century, 'The concept of absolutism as the personal rule of the monarch who enforces his will is a superficial one. It is bureaucracy which represents absolute authority, the monarch being the symbol at its head.'[17] And it was the eighteenth century, it is worth reminding ourselves, which coined the term itself – bureaucracy, rule by officials, a fourth category to be added to the classic Aristotelian trinity of tyranny, aristocracy and democracy.

I want to emphasise the positive drive which has been persistently maintained by office holders towards the extension and intensification of bureaucracy. Powers tend, inexorably, to become power – i.e. they have to be vested in a person.[18] Thus *Herrschaft*, Weber's term which may be rendered in English as either 'authority', a moral or legal entitlement to direct or to sanction actions by others, or as 'domination', power to enforce obedience, is used, in describing bureaucracy, for the derived right to command attached to a position in a 'chain of command'. 'Chains of command' are represented as some kind of conductor of authority or domination leading from a sovereign power, limited or unlimited, to strings of office holders who have to assume or claim authority for the exercise of whatever powers they have been accorded from above. Such powers are pointless unless the incumbents are ready and able to use them. So that government *through* appointed officials becomes, in practice, government *by* officials. The rationality, skills and experience which are presumed to make officials effective instruments of government can equally make them effective advocates for the preservation and extension of the powers they have.

The process has to be distinguished from that made familiar by Michels.[19] His use of a time-span of little more than a generation blinkered him to the very different ways in which movements and organisation act on each other. There is a closer approximation to the tendency denoted by Eisenstadt's term, 'bureaucratisation': 'the extension of the bureaucracy's sphere of activities and power either in its own interests or those of some of its élite'.[20]

We come now to the third tendency, or – to adopt the Hegelian term which has become fashionable again – moment, which has been at work in the development of bureaucracy. This has to do with the distinction between state and civil society which has become so much part and parcel of political thought – so much so, indeed, as to amount to almost universally received dogma. Of course, the antithesis does reflect something of the realities of political and social action, but there is a false clarity about it which one needs to get behind.

We can start with Kelsen's flat rejection of the distinction which, although itself no more acceptable in the long run, does provide a lead to a rather more satisfactory rendering of the historical processes which have been at work if one adheres to the strategy I have used in this paper of referring back to historical antecedents and origins.[21] The only way in which we can think of such an entity as 'the State' at all, says Kelsen, is by imputing human action to some assumed legal order. The state, conceptually at least, is therefore indistinguishable from the legal order. It follows that all citizens of the State are, at least occasionally or potentially, 'organs' of the State, i.e. when fulfilling a function determined by the legal order, for example when we vote, or serve on a jury, pay income tax, or even when we enter into a contract of employment, or buy a house, or cash a cheque; indeed any legal transaction is as much a matter of 'making' law as a judge's decision. Of course, there is, as he goes on to say, a narrower, more pragmatic concept, according to which 'an individual is an "organ" of the State only if he has a specific legal position' – a judge, an officer of the Inland Revenue, a Member of Parliament, a postman, a housing official, i.e. if he receives payment from the revenues collected by the State in return for the functions he performs in one of these capacities. Their activities are perceived as activities of the State, i.e. imputable to or designating it, and in aggregate, therefore, the bureaucratic apparatus of the State. But this is only a part of the State; it is, he says, 'a figure of speech signifying the system of norms constituting the "Fisc" (the State as a subject of property) and determining the activities of the officials financed thereby'.[22]

For Kelsen, then, there is nothing categorical about the distinction between the individuals who man the bureaucratic apparatus and the totality of citizens; both categories are equally 'organs' of the State in so far as they perform acts which are in accordance with, and presuppose, a legal order. Any distinction between this and some entity we call the State is, he says, an 'animistic superstition', parallel to the idea that 'behind everything there is a soul, a spirit, a god of the thing'.[23]

To dismiss the dualism of state and civil society as yet one
further manifestation of the 'Ghost in the Machine' myth is in
effect to revert to the notion of a single undifferentiated social
and legal order, of the body politic as a single entity which was
in fairly good intellectual currency in the later Middle Ages.
Yet it was during those selfsame centuries that the embryonic
forms of modern bureaucracy were conceived. They lie in the
administrative apparatus of the king's household. This now
had as its main concern not just the management of the king's
property, but it was far from playing any substantial role in
affairs of state, which were not properly its concern but that of
the king and his family, the baronial and ecclesial magnates
and – on occasion – Parliament. Least of all was it there to
'administer services', for there weren't any to speak of. Most of
the extra-mural work in which the royal household was
increasingly engaged consisted in laying claim to his rights and
his dues and in collecting his tax revenues and subsidies. These
tasks, especially the last, had to be accomplished in the face of
avoidances, resistances and challenges so obstinate and persistent that it is their successful accomplishment over a period of
several years which did more than anything to establish the
'greatness' of Edward I and his grandson. For, in the process,
this kind of work fostered – almost incidentally – the development of nationhood (as well as statehood). In Powicke's per-
ceptive words, taxes were 'the expression of a social unity
which they did much to create'.[24]

Practicalities of this kind lie behind the rhetoric of nineteenth
and twentieth century theories of the 'transcendental' (or the
'instrumentalist') state,[25] and of pluralism, corporatism and the
rest. If we are in a period of crisis (and it would be very odd if
we were privileged to live in the one period of history when
there wasn't one), then it is best described as one marked by
the overt intervention by the variety of interests which 'society',
in this context, stands for, into the system of rule, comprehended during previous centuries by sovereignty and bureaucracy,
or 'the State'. This gives the frequently quoted phrase from *The
Holy Family* a new and different connotation from the conventional one: 'Only political superstition believes at the present
time that civil life must be held together by the state, when in
reality the state is upheld by civil life.'[26]

This perception of the current situation is no more than an

extrapolation into the present century of the general thesis advanced by Patricia Hollis and her co-authors in *Pressures from Without;*[27] this was to the effect that during the middle decades of the nineteenth century popular pressure expressed in movements, associations and organisations acted on successive Parliaments so as to expand very considerably the range of affairs regarded, in turn, as of public interest, then as affecting *the* public interest and finally as properly the concern of Parliament – almost all of which ultimately became the objects of systems of production, supply and services provided and administered by 'the state'.

Pressures from without have, of course, maintained themselves during this century. There is a long sequence of administrative systems which have been set up to provide essential services or to remedy deficiencies in existing systems where entrepreneurial activity in the market has demonstrably failed to meet needs. And the call for these provisions, while it was made, eventually, in Parliament and a response found in government action, certainly did not start here.

This is not a history of state intervention, of Government eager to extend its control over the economic life of the nation in order to ensure political stability and promote social welfare. The first call for a national health service came from the medical profession in the 1930s, faced with what seemed the imminent collapse of the voluntary and municipal hospital services, and the growing need for a primary medical care service beyond that which was provided for by the health insurance scheme. It was the miners who called for the nationalisation of mines, thirty years before it happened. The Central Electricity Board was brought into being to fill gaps, and only ten years later, in the 1930s, opened up the prospect of a nationally operated service of electricity generation and distribution with the National Grid. It took fifty years for similar moves to occur in the equally vital water supply services. From the Port of London Authority, created in 1908, to Rolls Royce (1972) Ltd, the State intervened reluctantly or tardily more often than it has militantly or hastily. (It is the subsequent tinkerings that create the opposite impression.) Of course, the 'contract State' in either its American or its British form, is a small part of the story, which is, presumably, the transformation of capitalist society from the stage which is now called mature capitalism (rather oddly, because presumably it refers to the crisis-ridden couple of generations which stretches from the 1870s to the 1930s) to what is presumably 'over-ripe' (late) capitalism. But the point I am trying to make is that there is a dimension in the development of the Corporate State, the Contract State, the Corporatist State, or the Fiscal Crisis State, or simply of late capitalism, which is simple enough, but I think has been left out of most of the different accounts we have. Items get added to the political agenda in ways which are simply not accounted for by any of the treatments of those developments which seek to explain them. The report of the Ditchley conference on developments in public policy in Britain and the United States, which is rather more lucid, much less speculative, more restrained and perhaps more authoritative than any of the other accounts, underlines the seemingly haphazard way in which the political agenda gets made up: 'There are "things that must be done", and organisations are needed to see that they are done. It is often not quite clear why the things in question need doing and there is rarely any explicit point at which a decision is taken to have them done. For example, who decided, when and how, that Britain must have a national opera and ballet of international standard; that the BBC must not have a monopoly of television as it had of radio; and that the BBC's monopoly of local radio should later be broken? Who decided when and how, that the United Kingdom must not allow the Americans to monopolise the technologies of computers and aircraft; that the British shipbuilding industry must be sustained; that it was socially undesirable to end ship-building on the Upper Clyde abruptly?'[28]

The answers to all these questions are, of course, not very difficult to discover, if one is really interested. The point is, as the editors go on to say, that 'there are many fields of activity where we want action' – and just what instruments we choose to get the action done is a matter of expediency.

'Expediency' is not a word one likes to hear in the mouths of politicians or of political scientists, but what is interesting about the passage, and the whole intellectual stance of the Ditchley conference, and a great deal of the discussion about these things which has gone on, is that enquiry is directed to what happens when these things appear on the agenda of government, but not to why they appear on the agenda of government at all. As Kenneth Arrow has pointed out, what governments regard as 'appropriate agenda' does change, sometimes, rather rapidly; nor can it be maintained that the new agenda necessarily correspond to the emergence of new problems in the world or of new techniques for their solution.

The new phase in the development of bureaucracy which has become apparent in country after country is what is best described, I think, as the politicisation of bureaucracy. This is, for our generation, a more pervasive and significant development than its more familiar, Michelsian, converse, the bureaucratisation of politics. But it is just as complex and insidious a process, and one of its outcomes – the reduction of originating and declared purposes to ideological surrogates – is much the same.

Simplifying a good deal, there are three logical (and, less definitely, chronological) stages in this process. The first, inevitably, is the accelerating growth in the sheer complexity of public affairs and governmental business. But this is not merely the straightforward consequence of the assimilation of more and more public interests (society) into the business of government (sovereignty). The so-called 'revolution of rising expectations' now plays as familiar a role in the economic and social policies of nations as it does with individuals, corporations and trade unions. Long-term, intermediate and the more important short-term decisions must have regard to the need to provide for larger resources which can be allocated in the future; it is the promise of returns from decisions to spend in the shape of increased resources for *future* allocation which enables the decision-making system to operate without breaking down through internal dissension. But the fulfilment of such promise also becomes essential for the maintenance of the system. Hence the need for economic growth. The salience of economic growth as a political goal in contemporary capitalist democracies lies in its emergence as a major support of the legitimacy of their political institutions. As the number of relevant 'factors' (interests) which have to be taken into account multiply, so allocative decision-making replaces lexicographic; and more money *has* to be found (or wealth generated) so as to keep discontents, which can make their appearance at all levels of society, within bounds and ward off the dangers which instability brings.[29]

The second stage is the confounding of the principle of superior competence on which the hierarchy of bureaucratic authority rests. One elementary characteristic of that structure is that action at lower levels is governed in both scope and direction by decisions made at higher levels; but such decisions have to be made in the light of information which is gathered, or generated, at lower levels and 'processed' upwards. 'Processing' involves a perpetual translation of information bearing on decisions into a homologous language – usually money – so that it becomes compatible with other information on its way up; also because of the increasing limitation of channel capacity, information has to be compressed, reduced and filtered. So the 'bounded rationality' that Herbert Simon built into his model of economic and organisation man is, in many respects, still more narrowly bounded for people in the upper, decision-making, reaches of bureaucratic hierarchies. Nevertheless, their decisions are made in the light of a greater span of information and of considerations than is available at lower levels, so there is little opportunity for effective criticism of decisions or for appeal against them – a feature which is reinforced by confidentiality rules.

Furthermore, senior people in government, officials and politicians alike, are now confronted with tasks which are more and more abstruse, unfamiliar or entirely new in their experience; worse, they demand, more and more often, technical skills and expert knowledge which belong, more and more exclusively, to the young and the recently qualified. To be an older man used to mean that one was wiser, better qualified, more effective; the hierarchic structure of bureaucracy, with the average age rising with each rank, still accords with this presumption. But in the new situation of technical, political and economic change, the whole structure of authority implicit in this arrangement is becoming invalidated.

Which brings us to the third stage, the alternative means of control over subordinate levels which have had to be found to replace the legitimacy of superior competence. If superior technical information – not just about material technology, but about economic and social affairs themselves – is now to be regarded increasingly as the prerogative of the young, and if the initiative in new ideas and projects has to be left to them, then superiors are forced more and more to rely on other sources of power. The most obvious comes from their right to adjudicate between the advocates of rival proposals and the claims of competing departments and from their role as monitor of performance and as court of appeal. Further compensation for the diminution of the old 'legitimate' authority of superior competence can be found in the enhanced prominence given to the machinery of promotion, training for promotion and career development. This both increases control over the career chances of subordinates and enlarges the preoccupation of individuals with the career system.[30]

And yet further, there is communication control, which is a positive source of power rather than the defensive mechanism which confidentiality rules provide, although these provide the necessary screen. With decisions having to be made and policies formed on the basis of information which is either technically obscure or has been laundered clean of technicalities (and thus of any qualifications and of verifiability) and which has in any case been filtered, reduced and, usually, distorted, and on the basis, too, of information about the 'outside world' conveyed through consultation with opinion-leaders and decision-makers who are similarly placed, the familiar world of politics and government becomes fraught with hazards and threats. Uncertainty actually increases with the widening range of information available at each rising level of the decision-making hierarchy. So communication control becomes both the administrative basis and the overt expression of power. Senior officials can reinforce the administrative divisions inherent in the increasingly specialised nature of the information provided for them and ensure that decision-making processes at lower levels which might be analytical are in fact political, and so have to be referred up to the point at which the people at the top become the 'experts' who alone are able to treat bargaining and political conflicts as if they were analytical.[31]

The agenda before political rulers and the bureaucracy is increasingly dependent on the flow of information and of demands from the individuals and the corporate entities they are designed to administer.[32] The flow has become increasingly subject to distortion, interruption and pollution by the channels through which it has to pass and by the media which carry it. They, rulers and administrators alike, are unable to preserve the distance necessary for independent decision.[33] Individual sectors of society can, as it were, privatise parts of the system of government, so that competition between different social interests is translated into internal conflict within the state apparatus itself. And bureaucracy becomes what it is now: a modality of politics.

NOTES AND REFERENCES

1. Helen Cam, *England before Elizabeth*, Hutchinson (2nd edn), 1960, p. 107.
2. Jacob Burckhardt, *The Civilization of the Renaissance* (1860), trans. S. G. C. Middleton, Phaidon, 1945, part I.
3. G. R. Elton, *The Tudor Revolution in Government*, Cambridge University Press, 1953, p. 415.
4. T. F. Tout, *Chapters on Medieval Administrative History*, Manchester University Press, 1920–37, vol. IV, p. 214.
5. J. H. Shennan, *The Origins of the Modern European State, 1450–1725*, Hutchinson, 1974, p. 9.
6. I have adopted John Dunn's term to specify 'the only democracy we [i.e. those who live in Western industrialised societies] have'. See John Dunn, *Western Political Society in the Face of the Future*, Cambridge University Press, 1979, p. 23.
7. James Bryce, *The American Commonwealth* (1893), revised edn 1918, Macmillan, pp. 36–7.
8. H. R. Trevor-Roper, 'The General Crisis of the Seventeenth Century', *Past and Present*, no. 16, 1959 (reprinted in T. Ashton, *Crisis in Europe 1560–1660*, Routledge and Kegan Paul, 1965, p. 72).
9. Kenneth J. Arrow, *The Limits of Organization*, Norton, 1974, p. 16.
10. N. Luhmann, 'Reflexive Mechanismen', *Soziale Welt*, vol. 17, 1966, p. 7.
11. Ibid., p. 8.
12. Oliver E. Williamson, *Markets and Hierarchies*, Free Press, 1975, p. 26.
13. H. R. Trevor-Roper, 'Religion, Reformation and Social Change', in *Religion, the Reformation and Social Change*, Macmillan, 1967, p. 35.
14. J. K. Galbraith, *The New Industrial State*, Hamish Hamilton, 1967, pp. 60–71, 86–97.
15. G. W. F. Hegel, *Hegel's Philosophy of Right* (1821), trans. T. M. Knox, Oxford University Press, 1952, p. 191.
16. J. O'Malley, 'Introduction', in Karl Marx, *Critique of Hegel's Philosophy of Right*, trans. A. Jolin and J. O'Malley, Cambridge Unversity Press, 1970, p. xiix.
17. P. Frölich, *1789, die grosse Zeitwende: von der Burokratie des Absolutismus zum Parlament der Revolution*, Frankfurt, 1957.
18. The 'over-socialized' concept of man which worried Dennis Wrong ('The Over-Socialized Conception of Man in Modern Society', *A.S.R.* vol. 26, 1961), seems as often as not to be a matter of the 'over-institutionalization of social action'. In their attempts to develop concepts which may be applied comparaively or analytically to a range of empirical situations differing in scope, importance, and history, sociologists and political scientists seem to be driven beyond the abstract to the impersonal. So the power

wielded by officials (often, admittedly, anonymous or remote) becomes powers attached to offices. A paper by T. H. Marshall illustrates this rather appropriately:

> Power, says Dahrendorf, is essentially tied to the personality of the individuals. I find this too restrictive of the generic character of the concept . . . In the case of bureaucratic organisations, which Weber had particularly in mind, the distinction is brought out by the English usage which speaks of the *power* (of a man) and the *powers* (in the plural) of his office. Power is measured along a continuum; powers are located at points in the discontinuity of an articulated structure. If I have understood him rightly, the case studies which Michael Crozier uses to illustrate his theory of bureaucracy have a bearing on this point. The conflicts and manoeuvres he describes seem to be examples of struggles for *power* between individuals or classes of individual rather than disputes about *powers* – or what the Germans call Kompetenzstreit. Though the outcome of such struggles may often lead to an alteration in the formal distribution of power. . .
> (T. H. Marshall, 'Reflections on Power', *Sociology*, vol. 3, 1969, pp. 14–15)

Yet immediately after making this critical distinction between 'power' and 'powers' (and quietly disembowelling Crozier's main argument), he goes on to say (p. 16): 'The power exercised by an office-holder derives not only from the authority vested in his office but also from his personal ability to make use of it'.

19. Michels, *Political Parties* (1911), trans. E. and C. Paul, Free Press, 1962.
20. S. N. Eisenstadt, 'Bureaucracy, Bureaucratization and Debureaucratization', *Administrative Science Quarterly*, vol. 4, 1959, p. 312.
21. For a reasoned account and defence of this strategy, see Helmuth Plessner, 'With Different Eyes', in T. Luckman (ed.), *Phenomenology and Sociology*, Penguin Books, 1978.
22. See Hans Kelsen, *General Theory of Law and Society*, trans. A. Wedberg, Russell and Russell, 1961, pp. 188–94.
23. Kelsen, op. cit., p. 191.
24. Maurice Powicke, *The Thirteenth Century*, Oxford University Press, 1953, p. 523.
25. One familiar example is Walter Ullmann's 'ascending' and 'descending' theories of the source of 'power in the public field'; see W. Ullmann, *Medieval Political Thought*, Penguin Books, 1975.
26. K. Marx and F. Engels, *The Holy Family* (1844), Foreign Language Publishing House, Moscow, 1956, p. 163.
27. P. Hollis (ed.), *Pressures from Without*, Arnold, 1974.
28. D. C. Hague, W. J. M. Mackenzie and A. Darken (eds), *Public Policy and Private Interests*, Macmillan, 1975.
29. This interpretation is compatible with those offered by, say Fred Hirsch and James O'Connor, but is, I think, simpler than Hirsch's, in that it is structural rather than psychologistic, and of wider application than O'Connor's, in that it does not require the inclusion of such special factors as the unholy alliance between monopoly capital and trade unionism. (See Fred Hirsch, *Social Limits to Growth*, Routledge and Kegan Paul, 1977; and James

O'Connor, *The Fiscal Crisis of the State*, St Martin's Press, 1973.)
The process outlined here draws on the longer account given in
Tom Burns, 'The Rationale of the Corporate System', in R. Marris
(ed.), *The Corporate Society*, Macmillan, 1974. (See also K. Krumar,
Prophecy and Progress, Penguin Books, 1978, pp. 272–7.)

30. 'While formal organizational power rests on the competence to
    give official directives, the recognition of which is a condition of
    membership and which can thus be sanctioned by dismissal, the
    actual power in organizations depends far more on influence on
    careers.' N. Luhmann, *Macht*, F. Enke Verlag, 1975, p. 104.

31. The terms and the analytical model used here are taken from J. G.
    March and H. A. Simon, *Organizations*, Wiley, 1958, pp. 129–30.

32. Much of this has been apparent for at least a generation:

    > Power is not concentrated by the structure of government
    > or politics into the hands of a leadership with a capacity to
    > budget it among a diverse set of administrative activities.
    > A picture of the Presidency as a reservoir of authority from
    > which the lower echelons of administration draw life and
    > vigour is an idealised distortion of reality.
    >
    > A similar criticism applies to any like claim for an
    > agency head in his agency. Only in varying degrees can the
    > powers of subordinate officials be explained as resulting
    > from the chain of command. Rarely is such an explanation
    > a satisfactory account of the sources of power. A structure
    > of interests, friendly or hostile, vague and general or com-
    > pact and well-defined, encloses each significant centre of
    > administrative discretion. This structure is an important
    > determinant of the scope of possible action. As a source
    > of power and authority it is a competitor of the formal
    > hierarchy. (Norton E. Long, 'Power and Administration',
    > *Public Administration Review*, vol. 9, 1949, pp. 258–9).

33. Not only does political power flow in from the sides of an organi-
    zation, as it were; it also flows up the organization to the centre
    from the constituent parts. When the staff of the Office of War
    Mobilization and Reconversion advised a hard-pressed agency to
    go out and get itself some popular support so that the President
    could afford to support it, their action reflected the realities of
    power rather than political cynicism (ibid., p. 259).

Publications

[This excludes short stories, essays and articles contributed to *New Writing, Life and Letters Today, Horizont* (Sweden), etc., 1935–40].

BOOKS

1956   *Local Government and Central Control* (for The West Midland Group), Routledge and Kegan Paul.
1961   *The Management of Innovation* (with G. M. Stalker), Tavistock.
1969   *Industrial Man* (ed.), Penguin.
1973   *Sociology of Literature and Drama* (ed., with E. Burns), Penguin.
1977   *The BBC: Public Institution and Private World*, Macmillan.
        Erving Goffman, Routledge.

RESEARCH REPORTS ETC.

1952   *Local Development in Scotland* (with A. K. Cairncross), Scottish Council (Development and Industry).
1958   *Management in the Electronics Industry: A Study of Eight English Companies*, Social Science Research Centre, University of Edinburgh.
1963   *The Child Care Service at Work* (with S. Sinclair), HMSO.

1981   *Rediscovering Organisation: Aspects of Collaboration and Managerialism in Hospital Organisation* (mimeo) Nuffield Provincial Hospitals Trust.

JOURNAL ARTICLES, ETC.

1944   'Calamity Bay', *Penguin New Writing*, no. 19, pp. 9–21.
1945   'Men and Barbed Wire', *The Fortnightly*, new series, no. 940, pp. 272–7.
1947   'Social Development in New Neighbourhoods', *Pilot Papers*, vol. 2, pp. 21–31.
1950   'Village, Town and Suburb', *Cambridge Journal*, vol. 4, pp. 96–105.
1954   'The Directions of Activity and Communication in a Departmental Executive Group', *Human Relations*, vol. 8, pp. 73–97.
1955   'Friends, Enemies and the Polite Fiction', *American Sociological Review*, vol. 18, pp. 654–62.
1956 (a) 'The Reference of Conduct in Small Groups: Cliques and Cabals in Occupational Milieux', *Human Relations*, vol. 8, pp. 147–67.
1956 (b) 'The Social Character of Technology', *Impact*, vol. 7, pp. 147–67.
1956 (c) 'The Cold Class War', *New Statesman and Nation*, April, pp. 331–2.
1957   'Management in Action', *Operational Research Quarterly*, vol. 8, pp. 45–60.
1958 (a) 'The Idea of Structure in Sociology', *Human Relations*, vol. 11, pp. 217–28.
1958 (b) 'The Forms of Conduct', *American Journal of Sociology*, vol. LXIV, pp. 137–228.
1960   'The City as Looking-Glass', *Prospect: RIAS Quarterly*, no. 122, pp. 9–11.
1961 (a) 'R&D and Production: Problems of Conflict and Co-operation', *Institute of Radio Engineers: Transactions on Engineering Management*, vol. 8, pp. 15–23.
1961 (b) 'Social Norms and Social Evolution', in M. Banton (ed.), *Darwinism and the Study of Society*, Tavistock.
1961 (c) 'Micropolitics: Mechanisms of Institutional Change', *Administrative Science Quarterly*, vol. 6, no. 3, pp. 257–81.

1962 (a) 'Des fins et des moyens dans la direction des entre-prises', *Sociologie du Travail*, vol. 3, pp. 209–29.

1962 (b) 'The Sociology of Industry', in A. T. Welford, M. Argyle, D. V. Glass and J. N. Morris (eds), *Society: Problems and Methods of Study*, Routledge and Kegan Paul.

1963 'Industry in a New Age', *New Society*, vol. 1, pp. 17–20.

1964 (a) 'Non-Verbal Communication', *Discovery*, vol. 25, pp. 30–7.

1964 (b) 'What Managers Do', *New Society*, vol. 4, no. 116, pp. 8–9.

1965 'Technology' and 'Social Change', in J. Gould and W. L. Kolb (eds), *Dictionary of the Social Sciences*, Tavistock (for UNESCO).

1966 (a) *Sociological Explanation*, Inaugural Lecture, no. 28, University of Edinburgh.

1966 (b) 'On the Plurality of Social Systems' and 'Report of Discussion, and Commentary on Final Session', in J. R. Lawrence (ed.), *Operational Research and the Social Sciences* (Cambridge International Conference, 1964), Tavistock.

1967 (a) 'The Comparative Study of Organizations', in V. Vroom (ed.), *The Study of Organizations*, University of Pittsburgh Press, pp. 113–70.

1967 (b) Introduction to *Social Theory and Economic Change*, T. Burns and S. B. Saul (eds), Tavistock.

1967 (c) 'Consumer Behaviour: A Sociological View', *European Journal of Sociology*, vol. 7, pp. 313–29.

1967 (d) 'A Meaning in Everyday Life', *New Society*, pp. 760–2.

1968 'Models, Myths and Images', in W. H. Gruber and D. Marquis (eds), *Human Factors in the Transfer of Technology*, M.I.T. Press, pp. 11–23.

1969 (a) 'The Revolt of the Privileged', *Social Science Information*, vol. 7, no. 4, pp. 137–49.

1969 (b) 'Public Service and Private World', in P. Halmos (ed.), in 'The Sociology of Mass Communications', *Sociological Review Monograph*, no. 13, pp. 53–73.

1969 (c) 'Comment on Peter M. Blau's "Objectives of Sociology"', in R. Bierstedt (ed.), *A Design for Sociology: Scope, Objectives and Methods*, Monograph 9, American Academy of Political and Social Science, pp. 72–9.

1969 (d) 'Possible Industrial Futures', *Education and Culture*, Council for Cultural Cooperation of the Council of Europe, pp. 20–4.

1971 'Television and the Public Good', in J. D. Halloran and M. Gurevitch (eds), *Broadcaster/Researcher Cooperation in Mass Communication Research* (Report on an International Seminar, 1970), Centre for Mass Communication Research, University of Leicester.

1972 'Commitment and Career in the BBC', in D. McQuail (ed.), *The Sociology of Mass Communication*, Penguin.

1973 'The Rationale of the Corporate System', in R. Marris (ed.), *The Corporate Society*, Macmillan, pp. 121–77.

1974 'Leisure, Work and the Social Structure', in M. A. Smith, S. R. Parker and C. S. Smith (eds), *Leisure and Society in Britain*, Allen Lane.

1980 'Sovereignty, Interests and Bureaucracy in the Modern State', *British Journal of Sociology*, vol. 31, no. 4, pp. 491–506.

1987 'The BBC and Government Control', *Harvard International Review*, vol. 9, pp. 18–20.